Praise for *Reinventing Marcos*

Dalton makes the nation's story also his personal story...you will feel its truth because it comes from his actual experiences. For young readers and specialists of the Marcos years, Reinventing Marcos will be a fast-paced, refreshing and exciting read. Don't take my word for it, read it yourself!

Prof. Xiao Chua 'Filipino Public Historian'. De La Salle University, Dept. of History.

Sharp, cutting and incisive, it minces no words in portraying the gutter conditions many Filipinos found themselves in under Marcos's brutal one-man rule. It ranks among the outstanding current books on Philippine history... A must read for future citizens who strive for authenticity and freedom in a world trapped by misplaced nostalgia for traditions of self-serving strong-man rule.

Etta P. Rosales, Former Philippine Chair of the Commission on Human Rights

Reinventing Marcos is a useful reference for truth seekers as Marcos supporters continue to engage in historical denialism and other forms of disinformation. The message is clear: A plunderer and murderer can never be called a hero. May we all never forget, horrendous reinvention notwithstanding.

Danilo Araña Arao, Professor of Journalism, University of the Philippines Diliman

The book powerfully exposes how the machinery of Marcosian wealth has weaponized social media to manipulate impressionable minds, using orchestrated disinformation to whitewash the atrocities of the Marcoses, their corruption, extrajudicial killings, and manufactured poverty to mythologize a fictitious "golden age" ...His revelations are riveting, and many Filipinos who wish to revisit that brutal era can gain so much from reading his recollections in this book.

Project Gunita, Filipino academic organization on Martial Law History and Human Rights

Reinventing Marcos © 2025 Keith Dalton

All Rights Reserved. No part of this book may be reproduced in any form or by any electronic or mechanical means including information storage and retrieval systems, without permission in writing from the author. The only exception is by a reviewer, who may quote short excerpts in a review.

This book is a work of non-fiction. This publication is designed to provide accurate and authoritative information in regards to the subject matter covered.

These are the memories of the author, from his perspective, and he has tried to represent events as faithfully as possible.

Printed in Australia

Cover and internal design by Alana Lambert

First printing: November 2024

Second edition: May 2025

Paperback ISBN 978-1-7640209-5-4

eBook ISBN 978-1-7640209-6-1

www.keithdaltonauthor.com

 A catalogue record for this work is available from the National Library of Australia

Distributed by Lightning Source Global, Amazon Publishing and IngramSpark

REINVENTING
MARCOS

FROM DICTATOR TO HERO

KEITH DALTON

Manipulating truth to manufacture lies.

Social media disinformation has mythologised former Philippine president, Ferdinand E. Marcos, whitewashed his dictatorship, and helped his son become the nation's second President Marcos.

Former foreign correspondent, Keith Dalton, remembers the real Marcos before the social media makeover.

PREFACE

Visions that made a book.

At various times, I have been a journalist; a broadcaster; a writer; a foreign correspondent; a speechwriter; a press secretary; a magazine editor; and a corporate communications manager. Now, in my eighth decade, I can add 'author' to the list. It sits there, isolated, the last entry on my 'occupations' list separated by years of retirement.

It's a career highlight I never expected, planned for, or even envisioned. Karma? Maybe. Visions? Definitely. I became an author when I became sick and had visions.

Over the years, on many occasions, for many weeks, I had been hospitalised for numerous ailments, but this time it was different. In September 2021, a routine operation that normally requires an overnight stay in hospital, became a complicated procedure requiring a 22-day hospital stay. For five days, I was a *Nil-by-Mouth* patient with a feeding tube and a drip until the doctors could agree on the best way to keep me alive on the operating table.

I was in a stupor and that's when the visions began. Not dreams. Not hallucinations. Semi-conscious visions, both day and night. Visions with a clarity I never believed possible. Snapshot visions. Visions with no sound. Visions of faces... many, many faces. And visions of places and events I recognised to be in the Philippines where I had lived for a decade. But that was more than 40 years ago! Why visions of the Philippines now? For what reason?

It's true that in my retirement I had followed closely events in the Philippines, particularly in recent years. A systematic social media disinformation campaign had been unleashed. Its aim was to change the country's historical narrative, and the task of social media manipulators was to rehabilitate the Marcos name. But rehabilitate means to 'restore'. How could Marcos be restored to something he never was? So what these social media manipulators did was to imagine a Marcos who met their propaganda needs. They reinvented Marcos.

For years, history deniers have questioned the truthfulness of long accepted historical facts, and unashamedly proffered alternative facts which they believed validated their fantastical reimagining of Marcos and his place in Philippine history. To them, there was no fact that could not be challenged, no event that could not be denied, or positively reinterpreted in this single-focused social media campaign to reinvent Marcos. In their phantasmagorical world, new 'truths' could be invented. Denialism was the stock response to hitherto unquestioned facts. They played on the gullibility of Filipinos who had not lived through the Marcos years.

I was incensed. Angry. Frustrated. This deliberate,

relentless assault on historical orthodoxy seemed unchallengeable. But was it unstoppable? I was one voice, a journalist who once enjoyed front row access to pivotal events in the Philippines which led to the toppling of Marcos and changed the Philippines national identity and future political direction. The events I reported on all those years ago, had returned as visions. What did these visions portend? A subliminal call to action? It dawned on me: my journalist days were behind me, but my author days lay ahead. The significance of the hospital visions was obvious: they were niggling subconscious prods for me to tell of my time as a foreign correspondent in the Philippines, to rebut the lies, the superficial gloss and dross of pro-Marcos propagandists intent on whitewashing the brutality and authoritarianism of the Marcos regime.

I am not religious or spiritual in any way, but these visions were gnawing on my conscience like an omen, a psychological go-ahead to start writing while I still could. My experiences in the Philippines and life under Marcos needed telling. Long ago, I had brushed aside my wife's suggestions that I write about my 'Philippine days'. Back then I thought: who would be interested? Today, it's different. Today, I believe many Filipinos – especially the young – would be interested in my account of events under the Marcos dictatorship.

Most Filipinos have grown up in a post-Marcos counterfactual world where social media disinformation has repeatedly and relentlessly chipped away at history, poisoned impressionable minds, and instilled the lie that Marcos was the Philippines best-ever president who presided over a 'golden' age.

Thankfully, there are doubters to this pro-Marcos propaganda, enquiring minds seeking answers. So maybe these hospital bed visions had a purpose: to prick at my conscience, to tell what I saw and experienced during the Marcos years to countless Filipinos robbed of the truth. My reluctance to write became a need to write. I asked the nurse for a pen and some paper, pulled the hospital bedside table in front of me and began to write in shaky longhand. Characters floated by and incidents flickered to life. The barely readable handwritten notes became the first chapters of this book.

*I hope I have found the words to
speak for those who can't.*

Contents

PREFACE
v   Visions that made a book.

INTRODUCTION
1

PART ONE
Settling down and setting up in Manila.

ONE
19   A journey that almost ended before it began.

TWO
25   Getting to Manila the long way around.

THREE
30   A radio correspondent needs a telephone, right!

FOUR
43   Living 'life' in Manila.

PART TWO
Power won, abused, and lost.

FIVE
59   Power by any means, at any cost, for any reason.

SIX
154   The deposing of a dictator.

PART THREE
Repression and resistance.

SEVEN
195   Memories no eight-year-old girl should have.

EIGHT
206   Sparrows and Nice People Around.

NINE
234   Mendiola mayhem.

TEN
243   Even a small chick can grow into a fighting cock.

ELEVEN
250   Sugar's bitter aftertaste.

TWELVE
268   Workers' rights. What rights?

THIRTEEN
281   Gloria's life in a box.

FOURTEEN
290   Imelda's folly and the concrete tomb.

FIFTEEN
297 To buy a life, you sacrifice three.

SIXTEEN
301 How did that body get there?

SEVENTEEN
307 I'm watching you.

EIGHTEEN
313 An apology to Butch Cassidy.

EPILOGUE
319

REFLECTIONS
322

Meandering to Manila
331 An Excerpt

About the Author
336

INTRODUCTION

Ferdinand E. Marcos has not been 'rehabilitated' as his supporters claim. He never was a good and inspired leader, and it is historical revisionism to try to make him so. The true Marcos is defined by history as a ruthless autocrat who damaged and brutalised the Philippines. That is how Marcos must be remembered. That is the real Marcos with his social media mask torn off.

Social media miscreants have perniciously rewritten recent Philippine history and fabricated a fictitious Marcos. They are fantasists, crusading propagandists who have weaponised the Internet in the hope that the revisionist history they concoct, and the image makeover they give Marcos, will swing public opinion of the former dictator from vilification to veneration.

These glorifiers of an imaginary Marcos are not delusional. Far from it. They are calculating, self-serving, deceivers – disciples of disinformation – who practice selective historical amnesia. Theirs is a world of myths, made-up facts, and outright lies. In this lopsided fantasy world, unpalatable facts about Marcos are ignored or smothered under an avalanche of positive accounts. Lies squeeze out truths and very quickly history becomes the victim.

It is this duplicity that must be challenged. As a foreign correspondent, I was an eyewitness to history, not the re-imagined version peddled by pro-Marcos history deniers. Lies cannot be allowed to transmute into facts. That's the reason for this book.

The Beginning

Long before I began to write this book, probably a year earlier, I used 'Notes' on my mobile phone to jot down something that had kept me awake in the pre-dawn hours, something I didn't want to forget before I fell back into a fitful sleep.

> *Ferdinand E. Marcos was a rash on the Philippine body politic that festered and infected the nation until it was gone. But a new Marcos rash, Ferdinand 'Bongbong' Marcos Jr., has appeared, right on top of the old. The new President Marcos ignores history and claims his father's 21-year rule was a 'golden' age. I disagree. I was there. I was a foreign correspondent and saw what happened. I write about it here.*

The 'Note' – the imagined cover blurb of a book I had not yet written – was there in the morning, the tell-tale musings of a troubled mind. Obviously, the words had been mulling in my mind for months, probably years, as

I watched in far off Philippines the emergence of a man, the son of a dictator, seeking absolution of his discredited father in a bid to become the Philippines second President Marcos.

Lies fester. And if they go unchallenged, they multiply. And the more they are repeated over time, lies gain credibility among those who *want* to believe them, and they become 'truths' among those who *need* to believe them, for they are the ones who spread the lie that under Marcos the Philippines was a place of peace and progress. And when asked for proof they point to the 'new' truth that they themselves have helped create from a lie. It's a circle of deceit.

My early morning phone entry on 'Notes' was a subconscious memory jog to do something, to challenge the lies, to provide a first-hand account of what I saw. I was a foreign correspondent in the Philippines for half of Marcos's 21 years in power. I witnessed a 'bloody' age not a 'golden' age.

Type 'Marcos Philippines' into Google's search engine and Ferdinand E. Marcos, the Filipino dictator who was toppled in a People Power revolution in 1986 and died in exile three years later, is listed first. Second on the list is his son, Ferdinand 'Bongbong' Marcos Jr. He, too, became president of the Philippines in 2022.

The father's outranking of his son – decades after his death – is a poignant reflection of the staggering impact Ferdinand E. Marcos had on the nation and on the Filipino people; a power so consuming and so deeply rooted that the repercussions still ripple through the nation's heart today.

Once, Ferdinand Marcos held the highest office in the land. Now his son does. All his life, Marcos Jr. has lounged smug in his father's shadow. He has relentlessly leveraged Marcos's political notoriety to advance his career, and when he campaigned for president, he evoked his father's name as if it gave him some birthright to power. His campaign rhetoric of selective recollections was peppered with embellishments and false claims about his father's presidency. The fabricated heroic past became even more alluring, or troubling, depending on your point of view, because 'Bongbong's' looks, his mannerisms, even the way he walked and talked evoked memories of his father.

Marcos Jr.'s rise to power was mesmerizing for many young Filipinos caught up in the exciting hoopla of a media manufactured political celebrity who had the highest public profile and the heaviest political baggage. They had not lived through the Marcos years. What they knew of the former president who led their country for 21 years, they had learned from social media. For older Filipinos, however, it was different. They had first-hand experience of the Marcos regime. They had bitter, often traumatic memories of Ferdinand Marcos Sr. For them, to hear the dictator's son proudly claim he had inherited his father's legacy, filled them with anger and sorrow. How was it possible?

The election of 'Bongbong' Marcos, 36 years after his father was deposed, was a victory for the power of social media to challenge facts, reinterpret history, to distort reality. The election confirmed social media's insidious power to control the message and to frame the national debate. The Filipino people elected 'Bongbong' Marcos Jr., but it was social media's manipulation of the message that persuaded them to vote for the son of a dictator. The result was undeniable: Marcos Jr. won the election, but social media won the campaign. I thought Marcos had been consigned to history. But who was writing the history books? 'Bongbong' Marcos spoke of a man I did not know.

Ferdinand Marcos, the dictator whose ruthlessness I had chronicled for a decade, who was driven from the Philippines by exuberant People Power, and who had died in exile, was now being reinvented and reimagined by social media as a titan, a progressive, a doer of good deeds whose legacy was a stable and progressive Philippines. A social media cavalcade of misinformation, sanitised stories, and revised facts had twisted reality. It was revisionist history peddled by 'Bongbong' Marcos and his followers. As a young man, 'Bongbong' had witnessed his father's voracious misdeeds, he had even joined him in exile. But now the centrepiece of Marcos Jr.'s grab for power – for his turn to be president – was a highly calibrated disinformation campaign to venerate and exonerate his father; to upturn history. And he won. The historical narrative was upended. In the eyes of many young Filipinos, 'Marcosian' history has become the nation's true history. To these Marcos devotees, my on-the-scene stories were falsehoods, and my memories were imaginings. For almost four decades these memories had languished at the back of my mind, but now there was an urgency for them to be told, to counter the untruths.

My memory of the Marcos years mirrors the experiences of so many others. These stories must be told to a disbelieving younger generation captured by social media's distortions and lies: a counterfactual world of duplicity and malevolence. Under Marcos, I saw the country's wilful decimation, the trampling of human rights, the hubris driven and voracious pillaging of the economy, not the nirvana his modern-day supporters claim.

Those Filipinos who lived through the Marcos years know what they experienced, saw, and felt. They know the truth, and the reality, and no social media avalanche of lies by history deniers and political charlatans can change that.

History needs the verification of no one. It cannot be altered to suit anyone's needs. History is an assemblage of facts that defines a nation, that can never be denied, falsified, or qualified by outrageous lies or deeds, because truth underpins facts. History should never be cynically manipulated nor whitewashed for devious and crude political ends. But it has been. I once thought that history was inviolable. But no. A false historical narrative has gained a foothold in the Philippines through social media, and it can't go unchallenged.

Social media is riddled with contorted half-truths and calculated lies. It is deception – deliberate, coordinated, and systematic deception – when incontrovertible historical facts are disregarded and ignored by social media manipulators. They relentlessly use lies and half-truths to cleanse the Marcos name, champion his reputation, sanitise his authoritarian rule, and fabricate a blemish-free account of his despotic rule.

Marcos left a caustic legacy. But his son drew sickening inspiration from Marcos's lie-strewn life. To him, his father was the hero, the benefactor, not the dictator. The past was good, not bad. History had to be reinterpreted, revised, rewritten to make it so. And the way to do it was through social media. Filipinos are among the world's top Internet users (eight hours and 52 minutes per day) according to Meltwater, an international online media monitoring company. Those aged 16 to 24 spend three hours and 34 minutes each day on social media, more than an hour longer than the world average. Facebook is the most popular social media app, and YouTube is the most used platform. The Internet is where most Filipinos get their news.

Well before 'Bongbong' became president, apologists and propagandists were able to reconstruct and reinterpret his father's reputation by telling different 'truths' about a benign and successful Marcos. Blitzed by social media's barrage of lies, most young Filipinos, according to the polls, believe what they read, hear, and see.

Combatting the lies with truth is vital. Truth must be told to preserve the Philippines rightful place in history. That's the purpose of this book. It is not a book about politics in the Philippines today. Rather, it is about politics in the Philippines more than four decades ago which give context and relevance to contemporary Philippine politics. To know the past is to understand the present. The chapters of this book cover a brutal period in Philippine history subsumed by an insatiable powermonger – Ferdinand Marcos – who manipulated the system, brutalised the nation, and created an all-powerful political culture that laid the groundwork for his son's ascendancy.

For many years, when Marcos was at the height of his

power, his overwhelming dominance of the Philippines fascinated me and ultimately determined my future. From afar, and as a budding foreign correspondent, Marcos filled my head. It was his presence – a ruthless dictator in a country of democratic traditions – that kindled my interest in the Philippines. And it's where I chose to try my luck as a 25-year-old journalist in search of a story. I found plenty. I arrived in Manila in 1977 with a backpack, a typewriter, and a burning ambition to be a foreign correspondent. What I stumbled into was a jarring, exhilarating era of political volatility which upturned the fabric of Philippine society and realigned the nation's political trajectory. I achieved my childhood goal, became a radio and newspaper correspondent, and 10 years later, with my Filipina wife, left the Philippines with several suitcases, an upgraded typewriter, and plenty of memories.

I had reported on a decade of turmoil, tumult, and change; witnessed an autocracy supplant democracy, and then watched as the suppression grew and worsened until a fractious military revolt garnered the mass support needed to dislodge the tyrant and send him into exile. The Philippines was the fulfilment of a journalistic ambition to become a foreign correspondent, which was nurtured in my childhood and achieved in my early adulthood.

There are some things I call 'big picture moments' and others I refer to as 'little picture memories'. They jostle for place in my memories queue. Undoubtedly, the People Power revolution was a 'big picture moment'. I had been in the Philippines long enough to absorb the importance of that moment; I could only image how Filipinos felt. They were not just witnessing history, they were making history, for they knew what they did over those four days could determine the nation's future. Right there, right then, their decisions and their actions put them in command of history.

My 'little picture memories' are some of the clearest, the most heart rendering, and the most inspiring. Noble people populate my memory, people on the boundaries of big events; disempowered people fighting for justice and for a better life; poor people confronting misery, and hunger; and downtrodden people denied respect and robbed of their human rights. I met inspiring people and resilient people, but shattered and distraught people too. Their experiences deserve to be heard, must be heard, if others are to escape a similar fate. That these things happened at all is reason enough for these stories to be told in the hope that they never happen again. I am not a historian, and this is not a history book. Nor is it an autobiography or a diary; the chronological narrative is missing. It's a book of recollections, some I'd rather forget but can't, and people I'll never forget and won't.

Events make the pages of history. Personal stories rarely do. In this book, I have tried to strike a balance. Even though they are not as consequential as the overthrowing of a dictator, the myriad 'victim' and 'witness' stories of injustice, violence, harassment, and intimidation rattled my impartiality and changed me, from an observer to a recorder of events. Mine was a world of typewriters and telephones, well before the Internet, mobile phones, and laptop computers. It was both a journey of discovery and a mission of maturity; from cub reporter to foreign correspondent; from childhood dreams to adult reality.

On my first day in the Philippines, I stepped off the plane into a one-man dictatorship. And when that man was overthrown and died in exile, I believed the name Marcos died too and could never be redeemed. Today, the deeply sad reality is that the name Marcos must be qualified – Ferdinand Marcos Sr. or Ferdinand Marcos Jr.? The son has proudly inherited the legacy of the father.

The Marcos years saw the ruination of the nation's institutions, trampled in Marcos's inexorable march to power. For a decade I watched the entrenchment of a dictatorship, and when Marcos boarded a U.S. helicopter and fled the country never to return, I witnessed the end of the Marcos epoch. At least, I thought I did.

It is this decade – 1977 to 1987 – that I write about. This is the period I lived through. These are the events I witnessed first-hand. The repercussions of yesterday's events can be felt today, particularly when it comes to the Philippines presidency. But I cannot claim the validation of hindsight, nor the wisdom of foresight. In the following pages, I write about the things I knew then, not coloured by the things I know now. Back then, for instance, I was convinced the politically astute and ambitious Imee Marcos was being groomed to succeed her father, rather than the unsavvy political dilettante, 'Bongbong' Marcos.

Had I stayed and remained a foreign correspondent in the Philippines no doubt my opinions would have changed and evolved. But I left in 1987, emotionally saddled by sadness, melancholia, anger, and frustration. When I looked around, I felt despair, not inspiration. Rebellious military malcontents threatened to dislodge the newly installed Aquino Government. In the streets, popular protests had got rid of Marcos, but People Power proved no match against the entrenched party-political machinery of vested interests and oligarchs.

Unable to control or direct the exuberance and novelty of People Power, the Philippines traditional power brokers instead championed a swift return to the ways of old. Power was restored to the powerful with a new constitution. Once again, the people's hopes for change were dashed. And the old-style American-inspired presidential political system – despite its acknowledged faults – reasserted itself without any real consideration of the alternative: a parliamentary form of government.

Among the rich and powerful, I sensed a hankering for the familiarity of the past. Even with Marcos gone, the ambivalence of Filipinos to democracy remained. I found it perverse. Filipinos hold an uncontested belief in the righteousness of the direct election of the president by the people. But beneath this avowed commitment is the widely held pragmatic view that sometimes in national turmoil or crisis the need for a 'strongman' president is justifiable and necessary; someone to take quick decisive action to restore law and order, to bring things under control. Marcos was a 'strongman'. But the wrong one. And the wrong kind.

Ningas kugon is a phrase used to describe a well-acknowledged trait of Filipinos who erupt with sudden enthusiasm and excitement about something new or untried. And then, just as quickly, this commitment wanes and burns itself out like a 'spot fire'. Without direction, commitment, and leadership, the spirit of *ningas kugon* did not live on beyond Manila's revolution of the streets. With

Marcos gone, the worst was over, and things returned to normal. The 'spot fire' went out.

The People Power revolution, born from oppression, ignited by anger, motivated by popular will, toppled an autocracy. Marcos fled. On the surface, things changed, but beneath the surface, there was a disturbing sameness – familiar faces, unresolved disputes, unkept promises, and unfulfilled hopes.

The four-day revolution was years in the making, but in the years following its significance and long-term impact declined, especially among the young who had no first-hand knowledge of the events their parents had lived through.

To the Marcoses, the history they chose to believe was the disjointed history that suited them, that vindicated Marcos – the tenth president of the republic – and smoothed the way for the ascendency of Marcos's son – the seventeenth president of the republic – who took up residence in the same palace his father abandoned to a riotous Manila 36 years earlier. It was achieved with the connivance of social media which mythologised and propagandised the Marcos name.

Over the years, things changed but the past returned.

Anger drove me to write this book. I was driven by the need – inconceivable in pre-social media times – to correct perniciously contrived Philippine 'history' promulgated by the vanquished for political purpose. 'Bongbong' Marcos rode to power on a wave of historical revisionism that angered me deeply. I was there. I know what happened. I saw it happen. I needed to write it down. These Marcos devotees were tampering with history, contemporary history so recent that I had lived through it, witnessed it. My story – decades old but still relevant – needed telling at a time when truth was under attack in the very country in which I spent 10 years of my life. I was an eyewitness to a corrupt and brutal regime and because of that, I felt obligated to tell current and future generations of Filipinos the truth. By honouring truth, history is preserved.

For more than three decades, my memories of the Philippines and Asia went undisturbed. I had returned to Australia, a foreign correspondent with an unusable thermal typewriter that was soon discarded; cassette recordings that eventually oxidised and had to be thrown out; boxes of radio news scripts written on thermal paper so faded that they were dumped; and a tape recorder that, to this day, remains somewhere in some cupboard.

Any thoughts of writing about those 'Asia years' seemed fanciful, downright boastful. Besides, I had no diary, only a few scatty notes. But memories linger. Memories don't have 'use by' dates. The calendar doesn't determine when memories fade or lose relevance. Mine didn't. And haven't. They sprang to life on hearing 'Bongbong' Marcos invoke positive images of his father in his presidential election campaign speeches. Every time he extolled his father's record, I felt incensed. And each time my infuriation rekindled dormant memories. That's when I began to write.

My recollections vault was my source, and the clarity astounded me. Recollections tumbled randomly to front of mind; people and incidents presumably forgotten but obviously never erased sprang forth to remind me of the decade I spent in the Philippines. Other incidents in Southeast Asia crowded my mind and jostled for attention too. These were intertwined memories of other Southeast Asian countries I travelled through on my way to the Philippines where I weathered my journalistic blooding as a foreign correspondent.

The events I witnessed and the people I met in these countries rounded out my reporter's on-the-ground tuition and convinced me that the story I wanted to tell was about becoming a foreign correspondent. What I have written is not a handbook on how a person becomes a foreign correspondent. Rather, it is how I became a foreign correspondent. Me. How I did it. Like the novice I was, I learned as I went, with no mentors to learn from, no rules to follow. I had the necessities: a typewriter, a telephone, a bit of daring, and lots of curiosity.

When I left Australia, alone, on my first international flight – bound for Malaysia – I didn't have a return ticket. That was a commitment I couldn't and wouldn't make. To do so would have confined my travels to a schedule and put a mental dampener on my itinerary-free travel plans. In any case, it all seemed inconsequential hours later when, over Indonesia, it appeared we were about to crash into the Timor Sea.

PART ONE

SETTLING DOWN AND SETTING UP IN
MANILA.

PART ONE

ONE

A JOURNEY THAT ALMOST ENDED
BEFORE IT BEGAN.

In my backpack was a small Corona typewriter, the lightweight metal type that seem to grow heavier by the hour, and I hadn't even left Australia. I recall, in the departure lounge at Melbourne airport, doing a mental check of my luggage that was so small I was about to take it onboard and stow it in the overhead luggage compartment.

The manual metal typewriter had pride of place – right on the top of everything else. It squashed the restricted number of clothes I had brought. Cushioned beneath was a cassette tape recorder and a small microphone. The backpack's two side pockets were equally important. In the right pocket – the tools-of-trade pocket – was a small transistor radio, an equally small shortwave radio, a packet of typewriter ribbons, spare batteries, blank cassette tapes in a plastic bag, and pens, lots of pens.

The left pocket had two dictionaries, one the size of a cigarette pack, and the other I found in some obscure Melbourne book shop which was the size – I kid you not – of a box of matches. It was a novelty dictionary, too small, and eminently losable, which I did within weeks. I also had packed a paperback book. I can't remember if it was a novel or a guidebook to Asia. In any case, I didn't get to read much of anything in the weeks and months ahead.

I carried in my pocket a thin leather-bound book of blank pages, lined and ready to go. It was not a diary. It was there for me to record all the profound thoughts I was going to have, the insights, the revelations, the memories, and all the personal encounters that I was bound to experience and needed to record. There were a few of those 'captured moments' in the early days, but afterwards I realised I had recorded almost nothing but names of people. Just names. Months later, as it turned out, I could not remember why I wanted to remember them. Often, when reviewing the entries in the book, I found indecipherable scribbled notes, intended to be memory jogs, which meant that most of my memories were left un-jogged.

What was not in the backpack, of course, was a laptop computer and I didn't have a mobile phone in my pocket either, or any of today's indispensable, portable, electronic gadgets. They still had not been invented. I was travelling light for a purpose. I was about to embark on a journey to Asia – a childhood dream – and, hopefully, become a foreign correspondent – another childhood dream. In the years between childhood and adulthood, the dream had become a burning ambition.

In my luggage I had a big map of Asia – so new it

folded like a concertina – but I deliberately kept it blank. I didn't want to mark the map with a pre-departure 'ideal' route drawn in wriggly lines with a black marker pen, or circle 'must-go' places even before I had been there. I wanted the elation of discovery and the joy of spontaneity when I travelled, not pre-booked accommodation and an inflexible itinerary. My plan was simple and basic: fly to Asia, then decide what to do.

In fact, it was a cheap airfare to Kuala Lumpur, Malaysia, that determined where I would begin my Asia journey and transition from curious traveller to seasoned foreign correspondent. However, I was in for a shock. Even before I landed in Asia, I thought my trip had ended, before it began.

It was a jolt and then another jolt that heralded my entry into Indonesian airspace. We were experiencing engine trouble, the captain explained. We will dump some fuel and land in Singapore. Those onboard, mostly students, would be billeted overnight and Cathay Pacific would resume its flight to Kuala Lumpur the next day.

On the tarmac the following morning, a half-filled transit bus transported the passengers who had accepted the airline's offer to stay the night in Singapore. There were about 20 of us trundling across the tarmac, heading towards the Cathay Pacific airline until, without warning, the bus skirted around the aircraft and there, waiting for us, was a Fokker Friendship which, even to untrained eyes, looked like it had seen better days. It was a four-decades old twin prop aircraft and obviously Cathay Pacific believed it was good enough for one last hop to Kuala Lumpur, especially if there were only students onboard.

Sit where you like, we were told, after clambering up the gangway. I was still a little awed by the wonders of first-time travel and so predictably I plonked myself down in a window seat. My plonk must have been too heavy because instantly the entire internal window frame fell heavily on my head. Startled, I remained calm but a little anxious. I looked around, but there was no one with whom I could share the moment. No one had seen it happen. My thoughts were in high drive. What's going on? How old is this plane? How safe is it? What do I do with this window frame? I put it on the seat next to me, fully intending to give it to the flight attendant, wherever she was.

Moments later, a few rows down, a young student extended her arm into the aisle. 'Does anyone want this?' she asked, dangling half a seat belt, roughly frayed at one end, and with the buckle hanging limp at the other end. I remember my rather smug reply. 'No,' I said, 'but I'll swap your half a seat belt for my window frame.' I thought it was a good response. Others did too. They had heard the exchange. Some spilled out into the aisle, wanting to find out more, to share the banter. After all, it was pretty funny: an airline falling apart before our eyes.

Then, instantly, everything turned quiet when a passenger gasped: 'Oh my God, look at that!' All of us looked to where she was looking. There was no mistaking what we saw. The door to the cockpit was held open by wire stretched between the handle of the cabin door and some unseen fixing point in the captain's cockpit. Standing at the entrance, just metres from the seated pilot, was a flight attendant reading aloud from some book.

'Is it a 'learn to fly' manual?' someone asked. 'Did you notice 'L' plates on the front of the plane?' By now there were about six of us in the aisle, nervously chatting. From somewhere, a second flight attendant emerged and asked us to return to our seats. But that didn't stop the half-humorous, half-worried banter between us. Witticisms flew, but silence quickly descended the moment the plane shuddered into motion and began to taxi for take-off. The city of Singapore gradually fell from view, and I slowly relaxed as the plane levelled off at cruising height. I remember thinking, what else could go wrong?

'We're on fire,' screamed a passenger a few seats away. 'Look,' he pointed out the passenger window. In the commotion, other panicked passengers jumped up to see black smoke billowing from the left engine. Fear instantly killed the tittle-tattle we had been enjoying. From the front of the plane, one of the flight attendants rushed down the aisle, peered through the passenger window, and immediately pulled down the shade, blocking the view of billowing clouds of dense black smoke. Perhaps, she thought, it was better we did not see the danger we were in. But, from other windows, flames could be seen. She turned and hurried back to the cockpit. I doubt she made it before the plane suddenly lurched to the left, moments after the left engine spluttered and stopped.

With just one engine, the mid-fifties designed Fokker Friendship could easily make it back to Singapore, the pilot assured us in a voice of practiced calm. We sat in our seats in a permanent, uncomfortable 30-degree angle, solemn, silent, lost in our thoughts, as the plane flew in circles over the Singapore Strait dumping aviation fuel.

Finally, we landed without further incident at Singapore's Changi Airport. We were offered a free flight to Kuala Lumpur the next day.

I took the bus.

Postscript.

My mode of travel in Asia was by land or sea. Airplanes were too fast, too direct, too convenient, and too predictable. For me, getting to my chosen destination was the challenge and the very essence of travel. It was the uncertainty of how to get there and how long it would take, and the unpredictability of what I would see along the way, and the people I would meet, that I liked. I would end up in the Philippines, that much I knew. How and when, I didn't know. 'What's over the border?' was my travel creed, and it was curiosity rather than careful planning that led me through Singapore, Malaysia, Thailand, Burma, Indonesia, and Borneo before I reached the Philippines. And there I stayed.

TWO

GETTING TO MANILA THE LONG WAY AROUND.

Creased, frayed, a little torn, dirty, and smudged, my tattered map of Southeast Asia showed the rigors of 18 months use.

With a thin-tipped black marker pen, I methodically and regularly traced my bus routes throughout the region in an unbroken wriggly line that criss-crossed countries. Inter-island shipping routes I had taken were marked by an unbroken black line, port-to-port. And to record unavoidable short-hop air travel, I drew a broken line, city-to-city. My map showed few broken lines; airlines were to be avoided wherever possible. To others, I'm sure this map was unremarkable. But to me, this extensive maze of lines, here, there, and everywhere, was a proud reminder of where I had been and an indelible memento of more than 18-months travel through six countries before reaching the Philippines.

It was travel on the cheap, to countries I had never been, to historical places, recommended places, no-go places, off-the-beaten-track places, and places where you take a gamble and hope for the best. For a year and a half, everywhere I went I was on my own. Not once did I travel with anyone; I chose not to. Mostly, I rode local buses, not tourist buses; chose local hotels, not tourist hotels; kept away from tourist haunts and bars; and when I did meet fellow travellers, they were similar to me: self-reliant, self-discovery types. There were times I would like to have said 'Gee, look at that!' to an imaginary companion, but most of the time exclamations under my breath were good enough.

I had arrived in Southeast Asia after a harrowing flight from Australia, knowing no one, without an itinerary, and not sure where to begin. I knew my destination – the Philippines – but didn't know how and when I would get there. In the end, it was an impulse-driven route through half a dozen countries – mostly on buses, trains, trucks, sometimes on inter-island ferries and cargo ships, occasionally on second-rate planes – that brought me to my destination. And when I got to the Philippines, I ended up staying more than a decade.

A harbinger of what lay before me on my must-do journey to Asia, came at the very beginning. Within a week of my arrival, I witnessed my first killing on the remote Thai-Malay border – beset with a long-term and active communist insurgency – when Malaysian soldiers ordered a suspected communist rebel off the bus and shot him in a scuffle. It was a foretaste of the violence, the injustice, and the powerlessness suffered by the poor, that I witnessed as I travelled from country to country. They were the emblematic and enduring images that I brought to the Philippines, and which stayed with me long after I left.

Along the way, there were moments of exuberance. None could beat the reward, after a four-day canoe journey deep into the Borneo jungle, of coming face-to-face with half-naked tribesmen who once had been headhunters, and whose children had never seen a white man. In various places, in different countries, I coped with malaria, dysentery, kidney stones, and gout, all of which tested my stamina, but never my resolve.

On my ever-present typewriter I wrote occasional magazine features on illegal logging in Indonesia and racial tensions in Malaysia (mailed from a local post office) which made the inside back page of Asia's most prestigious weekly, the *Far Eastern Economic Review*. But mostly, I observed, and each day brought discoveries and revelations.

Many times, in remote villages, I was the attraction – a rarely seen Westerner – who intrigued and excited chatty children who crowded around and followed me the moment I got off the local bus. To them, I was a novelty – someone who had disrupted the routine of village life – but every time it happened, I felt embarrassed that my arrival had caused a short-lived ruckus. I wanted to slink into the community, unnoticed. Of course it never happened.

Beyond the big cities, in many towns and villages, the best place to find a bed was in the one-star or no-star hotels that clustered near the bus depots. And the communications centre was the Post Office. It was there you could pick up your mail and make an international phone call.

If you planned ahead and knew where you would be in a few weeks or a month, the best thing to do was to tell your family or friends to address their letters to you via the Post Office of that particular town or city. The letter would sit in the Post Office's Poste Restante box until you retrieved it. Similarly, a phone call from remote areas required a Post Office visit, and lots of patience. The number of phone booths inside a Post Office depended on the size of the city or the town. Each booth, with a glass door, had a wall mounted telephone receiver, a seat, or a stool. Once you provided the phone booth attendant the telephone number you wished to ring, the attendant would phone the out-of-town exchange. Then, as soon as an international line was available – sometimes within minutes, sometimes in an hour or so – the exchange would alert the phone booth attendant. Your name would be called and you would be told which booth was available for your call. The lines were notoriously noisy, prone to drop out, and expensive.

Aerogrammes were another way to keep in touch. They were ultra-thin, ultra-light, and cheap. They were a single piece of light blue paper with glued edges which could be licked then folded to form an envelope. They were so thin that the typed text or the written words could be seen from the outside. The limited writing space – one side of a small sheet of paper – encouraged brevity, and the bonus was the cost of the aerogramme paid for postage. It cost little to send an aerogramme to any country in the world.

Of all the things I stowed in my backpack, my shortwave

radio was equally as important as my portable typewriter. Radio signals from thousands of kilometres away could puncture the most impenetrable rainforests. They could also be captured inside the shabbiest and most remote hotel room if you strung a piece of thin wire (always carried in my luggage) from the central ceiling light, across the room to the top of a cupboard, and then wound the wire around the radio's extendable antenna. True to its name, the radio wave signals of the BBC and Radio Australia routinely came in loud and clear at first but eventually faded and voices were replaced by indecipherable static. The radio waves came in like a tide and then went out with the same regularity. I listened to Radio Australia regularly, at night, to catch up on the news. Others did too, particularly in Indonesia. Radio Australia's Bahasa Indonesia service had dedicated listeners who trusted Australia's reporting of Indonesian news more than local news broadcasts.

Often, in the most remote regions I discovered the most avid Radio Australia listeners who could name their favourite Melbourne-based Indonesian language broadcasters. When I told them these broadcasters were former work colleagues, I was treated as a minor celebrity. News from the outside world was fleeting and random, with the airways mostly filled with radio and television reports in languages I didn't understand, and with newspapers rarely written in English. I relied on the news bulletins of international broadcasters, mostly at night when the reception was better.

THREE

A RADIO CORRESPONDENT NEEDS A TELEPHONE, RIGHT!

Wide-eyed and curious, I spent my first few weeks in the Philippines reconnoitring: from Ilocos, the home province of President Marcos, in the north; to Mindanao, the heartland of the intractable Islamist secessionist movement, in the south; and throughout the central Visayas region, where communist rebels were active.

It was a kaleidoscope of first impressions: unchanged, centuries-old rice terraces, flat farming land and carabaos; Spanish architecture and churches in the north; Islam inspired buildings and mosques in the south. There were bamboo thatched huts in remote villages, timber and brick homes in the towns, and occasional clusters of wealthy homes with a mansion here and there.

In the busy heart of every city and town, talking was near-impossible above the chaotic din of jeepneys, buses, motorcycles, trucks, and cars. Every vehicle jostled for dominance of the roads, only reluctantly giving way to pedestrians and bicycles. For me, it was uncontrolled, confused, noisy, mayhem. But for those in the streets, dodging the traffic, haggling with street vendors, shopping, and minding kids, it was normal.

Long ago, I had decided to try my luck as a foreign correspondent in the Philippines, but now that I was here in Manila, I realised it wouldn't be easy. I was alone in a city with a population half the size of Australia. I knew no one, I was on my own, unsure how to get started, uncertain about what to do. There was no 'enter here' door to knock on, and no 'welcome' mat. It wasn't as if I was replacing a journalist in a news bureau where my desk was waiting and accommodation fixed, with colleagues ready to tell me the dos and don'ts, and where local Filipino contacts were ready and willing to share their advice and tips, and their insider knowledge about the political leaders worth knowing.

They were things I had to learn, on my own. No mentor was waiting to guide me. I had enthusiasm, without experience. In fact, I had left Australia completely ignorant of what to expect with none of the logistical backup and the psychological support of a media company with deep roots in the country and able to provide guidance, give answers, and offer solutions. There were no academic dissertations on how to become a foreign correspondent that I knew of.

Impatience had forced me to leave home. Australian newspapers and the Australian Broadcasting Commission (ABC) tended to give foreign postings as a reward to deserving, long-term, middle-aged employees, almost always men. I couldn't wait that long. And, of course, there was no guarantee that I would ever be posted overseas, and the choice of country would not be mine to make. Instead, I took the short cut, packed my backpack, and left the country. Few people knew of my intention, except my family and a handful of colleagues at Radio Australia, one of whom requested I keep in touch and pitch to him any future stories I may come across.

That was it! A vague promise of future work with Radio Australia which, under the circumstances, was better than nothing. Instead of the security of a tenured foreign correspondent, employed by a media company, I chose to be a freelance foreign correspondent, a 'stringer', with no certainty of success and no guaranteed income.

Even for company assigned foreign correspondents there were no formal pre-departure briefings on what to expect and what to do, just some pub advice from colleagues with past experiences. It was only many years later that seminars on safety procedures, bullet-proof flak jackets, and trauma counselling became commonplace. As a freelance foreign correspondent, I was entirely on my own – a jeans and T-shirt news gatherer – learning on the job. At violent street demonstrations and in the battlefield, I didn't have a flak jacket with 'Press' emblazoned on the front, and no one else did either.

For the first 18 months roaming through Southeast Asia, I lived on my savings, and the income of occasional newspaper and magazine feature articles. Now, the wandering was over. I was in Manila and within six months I had married a Filipina, Bet, and we had found a house – little better than a converted garage – in an average working-class suburb. It wasn't a company house, or a subsidized rent apartment in an upmarket area of the city, I was the only foreigner in the neighbourhood; an oddity in the jeepneys, and a curiosity when I walked the teeming streets.

As a print journalist, I had arrived in the Philippines with a typewriter, but I was also a radio journalist without a telephone. The head office of the Philippine Long Distance Telephone Company is an imposing building, crowded with security guards and scores of people, some standing or sitting on the entrance steps, others mingling in the building's crowded corridors.

Like me, they were there to enquire about a telephone – to apply for one, or to enquire about a connection date. After more than an hour, and two fruitless enquiries in adjoining offices, I made an impassioned appeal about being a journalist in desperate need of a telephone. It seemed to work because, soon after, I was escorted down the corridor to see the 'man in charge'. He listened and he appeared sympathetic when I told him how important a telephone was for a journalist. Finally, unexpectedly, he rose from his chair and from the very corner of his desk seized one of the biggest books I had ever seen. He needed both hands to lift what was a leather-bound, gilt-edged tome, reminiscent of a giant hymn book. He placed it in front of him and resumed his seat. A large chicken feather was the bookmark. It stuck out near the end of the book and that's where the 'man in charge' needed two hands to carefully open the magnum opus.

'Name and address, and sign here,' he pointed. Mine was the last signature. 'How long will it take to get a telephone?' I asked. 'About 15 years,' he responded, expressionless. Inwardly shocked, outwardly calm, I casually asked if there was some way I could speed it up. As I spoke, I withdrew my wallet and held it unopened in my lap. The implication was obvious, but the response was not. Without a word, he looked not at me but at my wallet, and with his outstretched hand he beckoned for it to be handed over. He took out several hundred pesos – a large amount – and handed it back. 'How long?' I repeated. 'A week or two,' was the response. It was the most blatant bribe I had ever given. Instantly, I felt so sorry for the thousands of names ahead of mine. I left and the phone was connected within a week.

A telephone was one thing, a quiet recording space was another. In the lively compound where Bet and I lived, neighbourhood kids played, roosters crowed, dogs barked, car motors revved, and planes flew overhead. They seemed to take turns to interrupt every time I tried to record a news report on my cassette tape recorder.

The answer was to convert a pokey bedroom wardrobe into a crude soundproof booth. Using thumbtacks, I covered the inside walls with sound deadening egg cartons; strung an electric extension cord from the ceiling light, fed it through a hole in the top of the wardrobe, and attached a light bulb to the dangling socket. Then I placed a wooden stool in the centre of the wardrobe on which to sit. It was tiny, cramped, and hot. Stifling hot. The wardrobe-cum-studio was like a sauna. Often, I had to sit in my underpants to record news stories. Perspiration trickled down my body and formed little sweat pools beneath the stool.

Several years later, in another house, in a better and quieter location, my office was a converted bedroom with a big desk and plenty of shelves. I was proud of this house. It had three phones. One was a pre-existing landline which was totally useless. It was a shared line, shared with someone nearby, a neighbour I think, whom I never got to meet. It was annoying. Every time I picked up the receiver, I heard loud and endless women's chatter. Sometimes, in the early days when I was settling in, I would interrupt and ask if they could please hang up and let me make a call. There was instant shocked silence, but it worked, for they hung up every time. I'm sure it was the shock of hearing an English-speaking person at the other end of the line. My wish for a private dedicated phone line was not only answered, I got two. The phones miraculously appeared due to the persuasive request of Bet's father, a retired commander of the Philippine Constabulary, MetroCom, and a man with considerable clout.

I found the best way to do my job was to have a quiet recording room, a dial telephone whose mouthpiece could be screwed off, and lots of patience. To this day, I still believe the most beautiful sound in the world is the soft hum of a dial tone. It's a joy to hear. Usually, on picking up the receiver, I would hear the beep-beep-beep of a busy line; the ear-piercing screech of a faulty line; or worst of all, nothing. Complete silence. A dead line. They were the most frustrating days of all.

My portable cassette tape recorder had an 'in' socket into which I plugged a cable for the microphone, which was held at speaking height by a mini tripod. Sometimes, to dull the sounds of the neighbourhood, I worked with a blanket over my head, a flashlight in one hand, and the script in the other hand. To send the recording overseas, I first had to make an international telephone call, but it was never easy. I would rush home from a press conference or some event, bash out a story on the typewriter, pick up the phone to call overseas, and then the inevitable happened: total silence (a dead phone); constant beeping (a busy line); or a piercing screech (a damaged line). So often it happened. So, so often. The choice was to wait – seething – and sometimes the line would come back after a few minutes, or 10 minutes, or 15 minutes, or… who knows when. I couldn't wait. Sometimes, I would rush next door to see if their line worked. Then, if all else failed, I would drive to the office of United Press International (UPI), 20 minutes away (where the phones always seemed to work) and make what was now an emergency call to meet a deadline.

On those days when the phone did work, there was a procedure to follow. I had to unscrew the mouthpiece of the telephone and use an audio cable that had two alligator clips at one end and a 'male' pin at the other end. The alligator clips I attached to the two exposed wires of the mouthpiece, and the 'male' pin of the cable I plugged into the tape recorder's 'out' socket. Then, if I pressed the 'play' button my voice was amplified. It was cumbersome and annoying because every time I needed to speak to the overseas recording studio, I had to remove the alligator clips and hold the dangling mouthpiece to my mouth, like a mini microphone. Sometimes, for no apparent reason, the telephone line was good enough to simply speak loudly down the phone without having to go through the rigmarole of unscrewing the phone's mouthpiece. They were the good days; few and far between.

As I had hoped, Radio Australia proved to be my salvation in those first trying months. One story after another was broadcast over the station's shortwave service which reached an international audience. Then, one day BBC World Service rang. 'We've heard you on Radio Australia,' some producer said. 'Are you able to work for us?' From that moment, for at least half a year, I was caught up in a slow recruitment cascade. My BBC World Service broadcasts were heard by the CBC (Canadian Broadcasting Corporation) who asked that I become their stringer. Then the CBC broadcasts triggered calls from America's ABC (American Broadcasting Company), NPR (National Public Radio), and MBS (Mutual Broadcasting System). Other radio stations contacted me – Deutsche Welle, Radio Netherlands, Radio New Zealand, and Radio Television Hong Kong. The ABC (Australian Broadcasting Commission) followed, after hearing my reports on Radio Australia.

Sometimes, a noisy and crackly telephone connection was not always a bad thing. I had to speak loudly, but slowly, and enunciate carefully and succinctly. I'm convinced it improved my diction. It was not my intention, but I was told my accent sounded 'mid-Atlantic' and apparently that made it acceptable to the American networks. A producer at America's ABC network confessed he couldn't understand the Australian accent. He approved my audition with one proviso: could I pronounce the name of the Philippine President, Mar-khous? No. I couldn't. 'That would be a mispronunciation,' I said. The producer was adamant. 'That's how we pronounce his name in the US,' he advised me. Again, I refused. He said he would call back the next day, and he did. He had been overruled. 'You can pronounce it your way,' he said, in a tone that sounded like he was doing me a favour. Oh, how I wish I had said at the time 'It's the way the man himself and 55 million Filipinos pronounce it.' But I didn't. I let it pass.

I regularly contributed news stories and feature articles to *The Times*, *The Australian*, *The Sydney Morning Herald*, and occasionally *The Washington Post*. Whereas radio stations had insatiable 24-hours-a-day deadlines, newspapers required copy once a day. Without computers, I dictated stories down the phone to remarkably fast stenographers in London and Sydney.

In the 10 years I worked in the Philippines, no radio station or newspaper paid me a retainer; offered me an expense account; compensated me for any work; or covered any travel costs. Just once I received a gift: two BBC stickers. The arrangement was: you do the story, and we will pay you, but only if it's used.

Self-reliance was the key to survival. I was on my own. It was a hard daily grind – which I knew it would be – with no paid sick leave or annual leave. With my restricted work visa, I had to leave the Philippines every six months and obtain a new visa on my return. Several times I flew to neighbouring Hong Kong, remained in the airport, and caught the next plane back to Manila.

To meet the numerous deadlines of multiple media outlets in different parts of the world, I modified my work patterns. Snatched siestas were the only way I could meet the needs of 10 radio stations and three newspapers in different time zones. I worked a 24-hour clock, meaning I was available to file stories no matter what the time. On busy news days I grabbed sleep whenever I could. My mastery of the catnap was essential. Sitting at my desk, straight backed, fully relaxed, my mind in neutral, I could sleep for however long I chose, usually for 10 minutes, sometimes a little longer. My ritual before bed was to remove my day watch and replace it with my night watch with bright luminous hands so I could check the time during the night.

The style and the demands of the BBC World Service and the ABC (Australia) – the two radio networks that most often broadcast my reports – were quite different. Often, the BBC would conduct live interviews with me, reaching an estimated audience of more than 30 million listeners, but not the ABC. I don't remember ever being interviewed live by the ABC.

The network's attitude to freelance foreign correspondents differed in other ways, too. I was unaware for several years that before the BBC broadcast a story it had to be verified by two or three separate sources unless it came from a BBC reporter or a vetted BBC 'local' reporter. On one occasion, during the People Power revolution when my interpretation of a news story differed from other journalists – I questioned the real motives of the anti-Marcos Reform the Armed Forces (RAM) troops – the BBC showed its faith in my judgement and broadcast my report. The ABC did not.

By far, the most annoying treatment I regularly encountered was when the ABC or the BBC judged the seriousness of a news event – riots, floods, elections, hurricanes – as requiring the despatch to Manila of a 'fireman' (one of their own journalists). I was excluded from reporting on the event the moment the 'fireman' arrived. I didn't object to 'firemen' per se – that was the station's undisputed prerogative – but I did resent the disrespectful way it was done. On no occasion did the ABC give me advance notice that a 'fireman' had been sent. I only found out when I heard the ABC 'fireman' reporting from Manila, or when I rang to offer a story and was told they didn't need it because their 'fireman' was already in Manila. Not once did a visiting ABC journalist seek my opinion of the events that had brought them to Manila. It was a practice I got used to, but one I could never understand.

In contrast, the BBC routinely advised me of the imminent arrival of their Southeast Asia correspondent who invariably phoned me on arrival, often sought my opinion, and on several occasions asked for some assistance. Ironically, it was not BBC Radio, but BBC Television with whom I struck the most rewarding alliance of my career. BBC Television's intention was to make a personalised 50-minute documentary on the Philippines under Marcos, and my suggestion was sought about the best possible program narrator and host. Instantly, I nominated Jose Diokno, a former senator who was arrested without a warrant at the onset of martial law and held in a military stockade for almost two years without charges and without trial. Upon his release, he established the Free Legal Assistance Group (FLAG) and in the following years emerged as the country's preeminent human rights lawyer. He was the most principled, eloquent, and impressive man I met in all my years as a foreign correspondent.

The 1983 documentary, *To Sing Our Own Song*, was a searing exposé on the Marcos dictatorship. I advised the film crew and accompanied them to several locations. Filmed covertly, it exposed the regime's excesses and the abuses and included interviews with trade unionists, slum dwellers, a gun-toting rebel priest, and two child survivors: a girl, whose mother was killed in a civilian massacre, and a boy, whose father was beheaded. (Both of their stories I recount elsewhere.)

In the Philippines, the documentary – which was never broadcast locally – won immediate acclaim among anti-Marcos activists who obtained bootleg copies. Word of mouth ensured its 'underground' distribution nationwide. Marcos vehemently and angrily denounced the documentary and lodged a formal complaint to the British Government via its embassy, an act that added to the film's allure and public prominence and brought the documentary to the attention of new and eager viewers.

POSTSCRIPT.

My work as a freelance foreign correspondent had no rule book. I did my job on my own, with my own resources, without a colleague, an assistant, a driver, or the reassuring backup of a manned office, and with none of today's newsgathering tools – a mobile phone, a laptop, or Internet access to the world. I relied on tipoffs – regular and anonymous – and a network of local contacts, far and wide, left-leaning priests and nuns, government 'insiders', unionists, and academics. I shunned expatriate hangouts, lived among and socialised with Filipinos, limited my dealings with most foreign journalists and diplomats, and kept away from dubious influence peddlers and politicians with obvious agendas and questionable motives. Getting the story mattered. Getting it right mattered most.

FOUR

Living 'life' in Manila.

Something's wrong when, in your loungeroom, annoying gunfire forces you to turn up the TV volume because you can't hear the program. Or when your elderly maid returns from her early morning jog and tells you there's another dead body in the back laneway and all you say is call the police.

Something's wrong, when 200 metres from your front door, on Manila's prestigious Roxas Boulevard, entire families live inside huge abandoned concrete water pipes. And something's very, very wrong when poor mothers hire out, by the hour, their newborn babies to street beggars who know they will make more money weaving in and out of stationary traffic if they carry infants in their arms. Even more money if the baby is crying.

So many people live by scavenging for food in the garbage of others. To walk from the comfort of my home into the squalidness just beyond my doorstep took five minutes. The poverty I saw was a sobering reality check, emblematic of society's stark injustices. A few hundred metres from my door I saw the ever-present reality of generational poverty, where people eke out a living from almost nothing.

A leaky water hydrant is not a nuisance, it's a necessity for some people. With it, they can drink, bathe, and cook. Not just children, even some adults lather-up and modestly bathe here on the footpath each morning. The power poles are a spiderweb of illegal intertwined cables scattering in all directions to provide siphoned power to many homes, most of which are built from the cheapest type of brick and building materials. Other dwellings are no more than tottering, ramshackle shanties.

For many people, the grimy, littered footpath is an outdoor extension of their homes, where meals are prepared and eaten, children play, and dogs sniff and prowl. The footpath is an obstacle course, the daytime workspace for self-taught repairmen of electrical appliances and goods. Often, your path is blocked and you are forced onto the road and then back onto the footpath to avoid the broken-down electrical appliances lined up on the footpath, awaiting repair.

Horseless carts, that men strain to pull, take up valuable roadside parking spaces. The biggest cart, with wooden spoke carriage wheels is packed high with household goods, plastic buckets and stools, collapsible tables, chairs, rugs, and rolls of dress material. Another cart is full of cheap plastic children's toys. And on the footpath are small made-for-purpose push carts selling roasted nuts and 'dirty' (homemade) ice cream.

Several times in this street I saw a totally naked, emaciated, bedraggled, middle-aged woman with long, filthy, matted hair, her body streaked with mud and faeces, flailing her arms around, remonstrating to no one in particular, but to everyone in general, and muttering incoherently. It's telling, and worrying, that such a sight didn't seem to surprise anyone. Apparently, she was a local who lived in a laneway nearby. Some of the children stopped and looked at this stark-naked neighbour as she passed by, but in seconds it was back to play.

This was my closest neighbourhood. But a high wall and a gate separated us from them. We lived in jarringly contrasting alien worlds. This was 1980s Manila for my wife, Bet, and for me. Our rented house was in a middle-class suburb almost exclusively occupied by middle-class Filipinos, virtually in the heart of the city. It was, what they called, a gated community.

There was a high concrete wall around the perimeter and there were only two access points, one west, one east, and both were sealed off by steel gates that were manned by guards armed with baseball bats. Open during the day, the gates were closed at dusk. Our village was nothing special. Elsewhere in the city there were many bigger and better exclusive villages where upper middle-class Filipinos chose to live a cloistered existence of security and comfort where they could enjoy a good life, untroubled by the world outside. Compared to others, our village was a second rank, possibly even a third-rank compound.

Shortly after the end of the Second World War, the most prestigious, most luxurious compounds sprung up around the financial district of Makati, about four kilometres away. These were exclusive compounds for the richest and the most famous citizens, for the multi-millionaires and the billionaires, the business tycoons, the industrialists, the politicians, and the celebrities.

These super-rich gated villages were the Shangri-La objects of envy among many up-and-coming Filipinos who aspired to live there. For so many others, they were the despised symbols of iniquity and inequality. These islands of affluence, surrounded by a sea of squatter shacks and shanties, had big steel gates on tracks that rolled open and shut, some with barbed wire on top, and there were boom barriers, luxury sentry boxes with sliding glass windows, security cameras, and intercoms. All to keep the riffraff out.

The guards could ring households inside the compound to alert them that guests had arrived or seek the homeowner's permission to give entry to visitors from 'outside'. There was a 24-hour rotating security detail on the gate, and round-the-clock security patrols inside the village. Some of the snappily dressed uniformed guards even wore military-style embroidered caps. They were armed, some with rifles, some with pistols, and they saluted when you drove in or drove out. It was reminiscent of a military base and, I suspect, that was the intention.

People could enter the luxury villages on foot, but I only ever saw village maids – Manila's best-dressed servants – do that, and only after showing their IDs. The vans of repairmen, delivery vehicles, and lawnmower men were thoroughly checked. In this world of conspicuous indulgence and luxury, Forbes Park was the trendsetter, the premier estate, the 'Beverley Hills of Manila'.

Hidden away from public view behind high walls and heavily guarded gates, Forbes Park was a galling, contemptable display of elite isolationism, of outright indifference to the plight of others, to the millions of Filipinos in the 'real world', where clean drinking water, if available, was shared; electricity was illegally tapped; sanitation was an open cesspit; healthcare was unaffordable; and all forms of a decent life were fanciful dreams, beyond reach.

Forbes Park was the first luxury, exclusive, private estate built in the late 1940s. Others followed, at least half-a-dozen, all of them measured on a sliding scale of affluence. My first visit there was a jaw-dropper. There were mansions with carports the size of a small home, tennis courts, swimming pools, manicured gardens, a golf course, a country club, a polo club, several churches, a supermarket, a bowling alley, gyms, a cinema, speciality shops, cafes, and restaurants.

It was an incongruous Western-style urban wonderland of efficiency and beauty, an oasis, a fantasy transplant from somewhere else, reminiscent of the world's most exclusive residential havens. Even Forbes Park's garbage was special. Unlike everywhere else in Manila, the garbage was regularly collected, the streets mechanically and manually swept, the water was high pressure, and the electricity supply was not plagued by blackouts.

In this bubble, residents could – and did – live without venturing outside its walls. People could live in air-conditioned homes, ride in chauffeur-driven air-conditioned cars to their air-conditioned offices and return home to a meal prepared by their cook, served by their live-in house maid, and afterwards the nanny would prepare the children for bed. At sunrise, they could survey the work done by the gardener, assign a job to the handyman, leave some laundry with the laundry maid, and call for the chauffeur.

In comparison, our village was tiny, with regular houses, not sprawling mansions, garbage that was collected when the council found the time, and we had 'brown outs' when the electricity was shut off for less than two hours, and 'black outs' when it lasted beyond two hours. The water supply was so irregular, the owner of the property installed a deep-water pump that instantly died when the power was shut off.

Only bona fide street sellers were allowed past the gate: the mango man with a large basket of fresh mangoes; the bicycle-riding door-to-door kitchen knife sharpener, whose pedal power turned the sharpening stone; and occasionally the bell-ringing ice-cream seller who pushed a two-wheel brightly painted cart. Dressed in identical, military-style uniforms and armed with baseball bats, the security guards on both village gates were intimidating. They stopped anyone they didn't recognise from getting inside. It was a safe neighbourhood, but every time I ventured out into greater Manila I remained alert, wary of possible danger in unfamiliar places.

Only once was I robbed. It was on a late afternoon Manila bus so overflowing with passengers crammed shoulder to shoulder that for the most meagre comfort I had to raise both arms and hold on to the metal bar of the seat in front. It lessened the body crush caused by two male passengers on either side of me, but it left my body exposed. The moment I alighted in Ayala Avenue, the main boulevard in the business district of Makati, the right pocket of my jeans, where I kept a small wallet, flopped open, empty. Without feeling it, without even suspecting something was wrong, my fellow passenger had obviously used a razor blade to slash down, across, and up my right pocket, to skilfully remove my wallet. I was shocked but also amazed that he could do such a thing in public, inside a crowded rocking bus. Had I noticed and protested he could have slashed me.

On another occasion, I was knifed in the neck, a shallow stab, by one of two men who tackled me and tried to grab my watch in a midday robbery attempt on one of Manila's busiest streets. We scuffled on the crowded footpath. One man held me in a headlock and stabbed me in the neck, while the other robber attempted to pull my watch from my wrist. But the latch stuck and they ran off empty handed. These were isolated incidents – just two in 10 years – and unrepresentative of a city where most people just got on with their lives.

For many, 'life' in Manila was a relentless, demoralising, energy-sapping, submission to helplessness, where a tossed-aside half-eaten Big Mac was a thing of joy, washed down with the dregs of a discarded soft drink can. Street begging was common. So, too, was snatch-and-grab thievery by light-footed 'street urchins'. But hope prevailed. People scrounged an existence through novel money-making means: a rookie footpath hairdresser; a self-taught tailor or a manicurist whose 'shop' was their tiny street-facing bedroom; a trinket seller of hand threaded beads; a collector of newspapers, bottles, and cans; a shoeshine man; a bicycle-riding knife-sharpener; a food vendor of homemade soup; or the footpath washer woman on her haunches over a sudsy basin of clothes doing other people's laundry. They made sure they survived.

Soon after I arrived in the country and got to experience Philippine hospitality, one thing caught me by surprise: I realised that maids existed at all levels of society, not just the rich. The middle class, even the lower class, relied on maids for all sorts of domestic help. Often, among the poor it was the poorer relatives – usually from the provinces – who did maid-type duties in exchange for bed and lodgings. Even families on moderate incomes somehow could afford a maid, or two. Mostly, these maids were young girls with little education and often they were expected to be a combination of cook, cleaner, and babysitter. Many became much valued, long-term, on-site additions to the family. But there were others who were overworked and underpaid, sometimes underfed. Occasional news articles reported maids being forced to work seven days a week and to sleep on the floor under the stairs. But those reports were rare.

Manila is a big city with a big population and a sprawling metropolis. A jeepney ride across the city to Bet's parents' home in a moderately sized working-class residential subdivision, took at least an hour. Like most housing estates, infrastructure lagged development. The only thing reliable about the tap water was it tended to dribble through the pipes beginning about 3 a.m. and ended with a few pathetic drops sometime before sunrise. The water collected overnight was generally the only water available all day. So it was vital to fill at least two giant plastic barrels each day, and that meant someone had to get up in the middle of the night, push one barrel out of the way when it was full, and replace it with the empty barrel.

The toilet was flushed with a bucket of water after every second or third use. There was great excitement when, on rare occasions, a steady flow of water emerged from the taps. So rare, in fact, I was never there to witness it. The electricity supply was exasperating. It was worse than the water supply. Unlike the dribbling overnight water supply, there was nothing predictable about the electricity supply. It would cut off and come back on without explanation or warning. Candles were a necessity and half-cooked meals a reality. Over time, the rich invested in car batteries and diesel-powered generators.

As both Bet and I worked full-time, it was expected that we hire a maid. In fact, we hired two – Stella, in her early 20s and Auring, in her late 60s – for different tasks, and for reasons that suited them both. Auring was a well-regarded, older woman more suited to cooking and lighter duties, whereas Stella was a highly charged young woman, keen to combine her housecleaner responsibilities with her college studies. The two got on well.

At the rear of the house, they shared a small bungalow with bedrooms at either end, and a kitchen, toilet, and a bathroom in between. They stayed with us for years, and they too became de facto family. Between them, they divvied up the chores. We paid for Stella's college course and encouraged Auring to take much needed siestas. After several years, Stella graduated, but Auring became sick and had to be hospitalized.

The Philippine General Hospital was close by. I had never been inside, but I knew its reputation for overcrowding and its rudimentary conveyor-belt handling of patients, almost all of them poor. There was no room for Auring, so she was consigned to a hospital gurney in the main corridor where eventually a doctor assessed her condition, writing occasionally on a clip board. It wasn't a diagnosis, but a list of medications the doctor scribbled down and handed to me. He said I had to buy the medicines at a pharmacy across the road and gave me the list. He didn't say it, but he implied that Auring would only be treated if I bought the medicines he prescribed. Was this pay-before-service a requirement for everyone? I wondered. Would she have remained unattended if I was not present? Or did it only apply to me because he assumed I was a rich Westerner? I never found out. I bought the medicines, and Auring was discharged a few days later.

Before our current house, Bet and I lived for a year or so in another not-so-nice house next door. This house's pantry was so infested with termites that if you stood still and listened you could hear the termites chewing through the timber beams. Another time, a monsoon sent knee-high water coursing through the house.

Our first home, in another suburb, was little better than a converted two storey garage at the end of a narrow laneway. It was part of a family compound dominated in the centre of the grounds by a huge tree. Our strongest memory – a bad one – was of being woken at 3 a.m. by an indistinct noise and to find we had been burgled. Robbers had removed a single wooden window louver which had provided enough wriggle room for a child to be lowered through and onto the lounge room floor inside. From there, the child unlocked the front door. They were quick. They stole my tape recorder, a microphone, some cassette tapes, a shortwave radio, and Bet's watch. All items that could easily be sold. Irate that we had been victims of such a brazen robbery, and mindful of the police's woeful record of crime-solving, Bet called for help from an unlikely source – her father.

He may have retired as Central Sector Commander of MetroCom, the special crime fighting unit of the Philippine Constabulary, but Colonel Leodegario Victorino, Bet's father, was remembered and respected. His call to his old command triggered a quick response. An hour or so after the robbery, and still before dawn, plainclothes officers arrived, assessed the scene, spoke to us, took notes, and left.

Less than two hours later, they returned with two casually dressed men in handcuffs and with all the stolen goods, except for Bet's watch, which was never found. The officers proudly recounted their successful dragnet of the neighbourhood, the apprehension of the suspects, and their confession to the crime. As they spoke, the policemen brazenly bullied the two suspects, shackled and standing before us, shoving them, and threatening them with sudden raised fists and feigned blows to their heads. Then followed real blows to their chests that brought instant grimaces and howls of pain. It was obvious to me that these men had been beaten on their upper bodies, unseen beneath their T-shirts, and would probably suffer more brutality when in police custody. They were bent over in pain. Silent, but snivelling.

It was then that I criticised the obvious brutality done to these men. All the stolen goods had been recovered, I said, so I would not press charges against them. It was a shock to the officers. They had returned with the suspects and the stolen goods, and apparently, they expected praise, maybe even a reward. Instead, I criticised their tactics and, to them, I showed ingratitude.

The men were taken away in a prison van – I later heard one of them died in a prison brawl – and I was asked to accompany the officers to their station to sign a 'incident' report. As it was being typed, they asked pointed questions about Marcos, Cardinal Sin, the Archbishop of Manila, and the military. They were inconsequential, harmless questions, asked in a light-hearted casual manner, but immediately I realised their significance.

They had listened to the cassette in the stolen tape recorder which was my report of an interview with the outspoken leader of the Catholic church in the Philippines who had spoken disparagingly of Marcos. As best I could, I laughed off their enquiries with as few words as possible. 'So, you're a journalist,' I remember one of them saying. 'It's a dangerous job.'

I wondered. Was that a veiled threat, or an observation? Nothing came of it, but my uneasiness remained.

PART TWO

POWER WON, ABUSED, AND LOST.

FIVE

Power by any means, at any cost, for any reason.

I had never seen a dictator up close before.

With my just released media pass hanging from a chain around my neck, I easily passed the police body frisk at Manila's imposing Convention Center and took my seat among the local government officials.

As usual, Marcos was running late. The conference was about to begin; the dimming of the lights signalled Marcos had arrived. Heads swivelled to watch the closed doors at the back of the hall just as a voice boomed over the public address system. 'Ladies and gentlemen, please stand for the president of the Republic of the Philippines, President Ferdinand E. Marcos,' the voice commanded with great solemnity; a trumpet fanfare recording filled the room.

Everyone stood and everyone turned. A spotlight instantly illuminated the two large doors which magically swung open, seemingly by themselves, to reveal Marcos, standing alone in the centre of the doorway. Theatrically, he paused for a few seconds. On cue, the dimmed lights suddenly blazed bright. It was time. With royal-like pageantry, Marcos triumphantly strode into the hall with the trumpet fanfare recording playing on rotation. Everything that day was new to me, but obviously routine for everyone else.

Two earnest-looking bodyguards scurried ahead of Marcos, two stood guard in front of the now closed doors, and other bodyguards hurriedly took up positions at regular intervals at the back of the hall. The enthusiastic applause did not cease until Marcos mounted the stage and with a dismissive wave of his hand signalled for them to stop. The audience of regional governors and mayors – who probably owed their positions to Marcos – did just that and then waited, in silence, until Marcos readied himself for the next galling display of ceremonial excess.

From the side of the stage, a woman attendant came forward and carefully placed a garland of white jasmine flowers over his head with the care and reverence of a religious ritual. To me, an outsider, it was a moment of cringeworthy servility. Here was Marcos being treated with godlike veneration to the approval of a fixated audience. More gobsmacking was Marcos's response. He showed an air of entitlement and chin-thrusting arrogance in equal measure. To the woman, he said nothing. Instead, he turned his back and took his seat.

Marcos – the 'master' – gave an eye-opening display of bravura that day and the local government officials

– his 'subjects' – showed demeaning acquiescence to their benefactor with rapturous applause. Marcos had appointed or 'anointed' many of them and they showed their gratitude. It happened that day and it happened often in the years to come. These were the acolytes and the sycophants, the flatterers and the lickspittles who gravitated to Marcos. They were uncritical defenders of Marcos, supporters of his self-given powers, enamoured by his authoritarian streak. Many of them, if not most, were beholden to Marcos for their own mayoralty or governorship and that made them indebted to Marcos. His was the inspirational example of how to win, hold, and wield power, and many of these devout Marcos admirers in the audience were known to employ Marcos-like practices when back in their home provinces. Their power was derived from him, from his example. They were Marcos's pillars of support. They knew it and so did he. They needed each other to survive and prosper.

Marcos ruled with absolute, menacing power over the people and over the generals. Everywhere he went, Marcos was accompanied by a bevy of armed bodyguards and trailed by 'yes' men and toady characters. He had a king-like omnipotent aura and everyday people jumped to attention in his presence, ogled, oohed, and aahed excitedly, and cleared a path for his royal passage.

I arrived in the Philippines in 1977. Martial law had been in place for five years and Marcos was at the peak of his power. I saw him make his imperious entrance to the convention center hall that day and I was there, years later, to witness his inglorious helicopter flight into exile – a broken, diminished man.

A Monopoly of Power

In the 21 years Marcos was in power (1965-1986) he issued 4,675 Decrees, Letters of Instruction, Executive Orders, and Administrative Orders that covered every facet of life, work, freedom, and justice in the Philippines. It was one-man rule. A dictatorship. Marcos methodically hijacked democracy to perpetuate himself in power and called his creation 'constitutional authoritarianism'. Others called it 'constitutional manipulation'. Marcos became the most powerful and polarising figure in modern Philippine history through calculated legislative tinkering, whereby everything was cloaked in the garb of pseudo legality.

Elected in 1965, Marcos was the first president to win re-election in a campaign described at the time to be the costliest and dirtiest ever held. He had served two four-year terms and was constitutionally barred from seeking a third. Unwilling to release his grip on power, Marcos came up with a plan.

Fifteen months before he was due to leave office, Marcos proclaimed martial law and effectively, through ruthless legal and political manoeuvring, entrenched himself in power for the next 14 years. Power, complete domineering power had been the undeniable goal of Marcos throughout his political career.

He believed that his presidential incumbency depended on manipulating the country's Constitutional Convention to secure the legality and legitimacy he so earnestly craved. In 1971, the 320-member Convention had begun work on a replacement to the 1935 Constitution. Marcos favoured a parliamentary-style constitution that would, theoretically, allow him to run for a parliamentary seat as the party leader, win election, and then the prime ministership, thereby retaining office indefinitely.

The moment he declared martial law in 1972, Marcos hobbled all Convention proceedings. Among thousands of people immediately arrested were 11 of the most vocal anti-Marcos Constitutional Convention delegates. Other delegates went into hiding. Marcos used martial law as a weapon to silence his critics and within two months a new draft of the constitution was written and passed by the remaining delegates, most of whom were pro-Marcos.

Marcos now needed popular approval for the proposed new constitution and once again he flouted the rules. Instead of the mandated national plebiscite, he issued a presidential decree and ordered that an untried system of Citizens' Assemblies conduct the vote in every one of the nation's 35,000 barangays (barrios). It would be an election decided not by ballots but by the raising of hands. Marcos purposely railroaded events to produce a predetermined result. With martial law's sweeping draconian laws curtailing basic freedoms – speech, media, and assembly – the use of Citizens' Assemblies was denounced as a charade by opposition and legal figures who questioned its legality and validity. Voting was not secret inside booths, but it was outdoors in full public view and those who voted 'no' were immediately identified by raising their hands. The voting was not supervised by the Commission on Elections. Non-registered voters could be included too. The voting age was dropped from 18 to 15. There were no rules for the tabulating or counting of votes. In many polling centres, armed soldiers and policeman were reported to be stationed close by, arousing fears of intimidation. News reports quoted local officials as saying they were given 'quotas' to meet, and some locations reported the Assemblies were never held.

It was a voting system never before undertaken, with untried procedures, and untested supervision. It was a massive logistical exercise involving millions of voters in 35,000 barangays in a nation comprising more than 7,000 islands. Yet, remarkably, 48 hours after the national 'show of hands', Marcos issued a presidential proclamation that claimed that more than 90 per cent of eligible voters (15 million) had voted in favour of the 1973 Constitution.

Conducted under the oppressive restrictions of martial law, the holding of the Citizens' Assemblies was condemned as a mockery and the results dismissed as rigged. More significantly, it was the first of many electoral exercises overseen by Marcos in the following years; every one of them notable for widespread cheating, intimidation, and violence.

According to Marcos, the Citizens' Assemblies 'show of hands' was a vote of support for martial law 'which shall continue in accordance with the needs of the time and the desire of the Filipino people'. The vote also approved: a moratorium on elections for the next seven years; and the indefinite suspension of the convening of the Interim National Assembly. Another four Citizens' Assemblies – 1973, 1975, 1976 and 1978 – gave Marcos carte blanche powers and consolidated his one-man rule.

Human rights and legal groups filed a petition with the Supreme Court challenging the legitimacy of the Citizens' Assemblies, but the result was upheld by the

Marcos-appointed Supreme Court whose record for the entire Marcos presidency was condemned by many legal luminaries as one of acquiescence and subservience.

By its vote, in the very early days of martial law, the Supreme Court enabled the emasculation of democracy in the Philippines. It effectively endorsed the subsequent dictatorial powers Marcos used to govern the nation until he was forced from office in February 1986.

Just as Marcos wanted, this constitutional juggling allowed him to use the transitory provisions of the 1973 Constitution to rule by presidential decree from 1972 until 1978, at which time a parliamentary system of government with a National Assembly would replace the presidential system. Marcos exercised all the powers of president under the old system, and all the powers of the prime minister under the new system. Even after martial law was lifted in 1981, Marcos retained all his decree making powers with the enthusiastic support of the country's rubber stamp parliament.

ONE-MAN RULE IN A NATION OF MANY

In the early years of martial law, Marcos flexed his political muscle with a ruthless determination, exploiting all the powers he now possessed and all the military might he now enjoyed.

Amnesty International estimates that in the martial law years more than 3,200 people were killed, 70,000 jailed, 35,000 tortured, and more than 1,000 'disappeared'. The Armed Forces – the backbone of the Marcos regime

– grew at dizzying speed. Before martial law, the Armed Forces numbered about 60,000 men. Ten years later, it is estimated the Armed Forces exceeded a quarter of a million men, with possibly another 100,000 paramilitary troops – the Civilian Home Defence Forces (CHDF) – armed and trained by the military.

Civilian control of the nation's police force was stripped away in 1975 when Marcos created the Integrated National Police and brought it under the control of the paramilitary Philippine Constabulary which – with the Army, Air Force, and Navy – comprised the Armed Forces of the Philippines. The Philippine Constabulary, with expanded police, intelligence, and combat duties had primary responsibility for internal security and for fighting communist insurgents and Islamic secessionists.

In 1975 – three years into martial law – Amnesty reported 'widespread and systematic torture by the security forces'. In 1986 – five years *after* martial law was lifted – it was worse. Amnesty reported the number of 'disappearances' and extrajudicial executions had 'increased dramatically'. The victims included politicians, lawyers, priests, church workers, journalists, and students, all accused of engaging in or supporting 'subversive activities'.

Marcos, a former lawyer, used civil and criminal law as a weapon to silence criticism and to imprison his critics. He controlled the courts. He alone, without anybody or any court's consent or approval, could appoint all the Supreme Court Justices and all other judges, at all levels, throughout the nation. Marcos also had the power to appoint every provincial governor, city mayor, and municipal mayor.

Arbitrary arrest and indefinite detention were sanctioned under martial law. In addition, military courts were given exclusive jurisdiction over cases involving civilians. In June 1977, five years after martial law was imposed, Marcos admitted that more than 4,700 civilians were held in military stockades. Amnesty International found that military prosecutors, in most cases, 'failed to pursue cases of alleged human rights abuse' no matter how serious the offense.

Marcos had a warped set of priorities, a massive ego, and an unshakeable self-belief that equated national security with his own security. And so he spent big on the armed forces, but for other things, such as education, health, and welfare, he spent little. Prior to martial law, 37 per cent of the national budget was spent on education – school construction, teachers, desks, and books. After martial law was imposed, the education budget was slashed to nine per cent, and the bulk of the money transferred to the military. From 1972 to 1975, the defence budget grew from 13 per cent to 22 per cent.

Marcos's martial law powers were extraordinary and so too was his neglect of the nation's health needs. Key health indicators were deplorable. Under Marcos they plateaued, or they declined. As evidenced by the 1982 Ministry of Health Annual Report, power was Marcos's priority, the state of the nation's health was not. Marcos determined the nation's priorities, and he was the one who set the goals. And what did Marcos have to show 10 years after he imposed martial law?

Infant mortality was 60.55 per 1,000 live births; 17.2 per cent of children under seven years of age were moderately or severely underweight; acute malnutrition affected 9.5 per cent of children; tuberculosis, diarrhoeal and malnutrition diseases were among the 10 leading causes of death; 35.46 per cent of Filipinos did not have safe drinking water; only 53 per cent of households had sanitary toilet facilities; and more than half of all Filipinos lived in rural areas where communicable diseases (which were preventable and curable) accounted for 43 per cent of all deaths. This was the state of the nation's health in 1982 and Marcos had been in power for 17 years.

Power Without Limits

The Philippines was Marcos's fiefdom which he meticulously, systematically, corruptly, and brutally controlled. He ruled with an iron grip; embezzled an estimated US$10 billion; looted the treasury; oversaw the re-writing of the constitution to suit his political ends; stacked government agencies with political and military cronies; politicised the bureaucracy; suppressed trade unions; muzzled the media; controlled the Supreme Court; promoted provincial mates to top military posts; and oversaw a system of crony capitalism that generated wealth and created monopolies for his family and friends.

Years later, as Marcos was ailing, an opposition leader snidely quipped how cluttered Marcos's headstone would be – Dictator. Autocrat. Despot. Demagogue. Plutocrat. Kleptocrat.

From his earliest days, Marcos was a divisive, ruthless, ambitious politician. Elected president in 1965 following a bitterly fought campaign against Diosdado Macapagal, he won a second term in 1969 against Sergio Osmeña in an election denounced at the time for its unprecedented violence, vote buying, and electoral manipulation.

The history books record a relatively successful first term in office for Marcos – infrastructure development, industrialisation, and increased rice production – but his second term is particularly noteworthy for rampant infrastructure over-spending, leading to a balance of payments crisis, and a steep devaluation of the peso.

The spending on high visibility, immediate impact, prestige projects was a precursor of the many monuments to excess built during his authoritarian rule. The massive spending was also a harbinger of things to come – a mismanaged economy drowning in debt. The repercussions were inevitable. The economic downturn, coupled with growing militarisation and suppression, spawned unemployment, and social unrest. It also triggered political agitation and student demonstrations on an unprecedented scale.

More than 20 bombings occurred in the year preceding martial law. The government blamed the 'communists', although some critics suspected government complicity. They believed the government wanted an excuse to eliminate opponents and then claim immunity under martial law's catchall dogma: 'Excusable violence for the national good'.

The most serious incident occurred in August 1971 when two grenades were hurled by unknown assailants onto the crowded stage of an opposition rally in Manila, killing nine people and injuring 95 others. As always, and without producing evidence, Marcos blamed 'the communists', suspended the writ of habeas corpus, and launched a military crackdown on left-wing opponents of his regime. At the time, opposition leaders dismissed out of hand government claims the bombing was the work of 'communists' and instead said it was a government engineered plot – a practice run for martial law.

The nation's increasingly serious economic and social troubles were blamed for a sharp rise in urban left-wing radicalisation. Growing street protests and civil disobedience campaigns provoked repeated threats from Marcos that he would have to take drastic action. The opposition retorted that Marcos was wilfully exaggerating the communist 'threat' and they accused him of deliberately fomenting a state of unrest and a climate of fear as an excuse to justify the imposition of martial law.

Then, without warning, in an unscheduled nationwide television address from his office shortly after 7 p.m. on 23 September, Marcos announced he was imposing martial law, with immediate effect. His claim that it was necessary to save the country from a communist-Muslim insurgency, was widely disputed by a large cross-section of incredulous Filipinos, including academics, students, and Marcos's political opponents, many of whom were swept-up in synchronised military raids. A month later, Brigadier General Fidel Ramos, chief of the Philippine Constabulary and vice chief of staff of the Armed Forces, told the *New York Times* he estimated there were only 1,000 'guerrilla troops' and possibly 10,000 communist supporters in the Philippines. The communists were not a problem, and they were not an imminent threat, the newspaper editorialized. Martial law was not imposed to quell a rebellion or insurrection 'but rather to perpetuate the personal power of the president and his collaborators and to increase the power of the military to control Philippine society', the International Commission of Jurists wrote after a 1977 mission to the Philippines.

Initially, among many Filipinos, especially business leaders and the wealthy elite, there was hesitant support for martial law. There was hope it would restore 'law and order' nationwide, settle economic volatility, and resolve national security issues. There was latent support for a 'strongman' to restore control within a short timeframe and without excessive force, but when it became clear that Marcos's martial law powers were capricious, open-ended, and arbitrary, whatever popular approval there was quickly dropped away.

The martial law decree, Proclamation No. 108, was backdated two days – to 21 September – which allowed the military 48 hours to coordinate after dark, pre-emptive raids to round-up senators, including leading Marcos critic Benigno Aquino, media proprietors, and more than 100 prominent opponents.

They were all in military cells several hours before Marcos made his nationwide address. One martial law pretext was an alleged assassination attempt the previous night on Defence Minister Juan Ponce Enrile. He claimed communist rebels invaded a gated village near his home and machine-gunned his car. Fourteen years later, Enrile admitted it was staged. The car was empty and the 'attackers' who had sprayed his car with gunfire were soldiers.

With his draconian powers, Marcos shut down congress; suspended the constitution, the writ of habeas corpus, and other civil rights; imposed a nationwide curfew; banned political parties; took control of the media, the courts, and the military; and arrested and jailed his political opponents, journalists, and publishers.

At least 30,000 arrests occurred in the first few weeks of martial law. By November 1975 – three years later – Amnesty International reported the number of political prisoners had risen to 50,000. In the years that followed, Marcos accumulated autocratic powers enabling him to systematically pillage the nation's coffers, and to ruthlessly trample on Filipinos' human and civil rights.

He was a despot who controlled the military through expansion and patronage; the parliament, through political coercion and intimidation; the media, by suppression and ownership transfers to a coterie of relatives and friends; and the economy, by blatant cronyism and elaborate financial schemes and shadowy corporate manipulation.

Martial law was a power grab, and Marcos used the nine years of martial law (1972-1981) to reign politically unhampered and economically unvetted. His economic plunder of the Philippine economy was brazenly rapacious. Cloaked by quasi legality, Marcos corruptly used his untrammelled power to enrich his extended family and friends, and to create monopolies for his shadowy business partners. In a 1984 report by the University of the Philippines School of Economics, 10 professors listed 688 presidential decrees and 283 letters of instruction in which Marcos directly intervened in the economy to the ultimate benefit of business friends and family members.

Presidential kickbacks were the invisible ink in government contracts. Corporate embezzlement was endemic and there was systemic siphoning of funds from international financial institutions. The money tap flowed freely, especially for Imelda Marcos, who unashamedly enjoyed a sumptuous lifestyle of indecent excess and flagrantly flaunted her wealth to an impoverished nation. A joke at the time had Imelda Marcos in a helicopter flying above Manila with a foreign dignitary. 'I'm in the mining industry,' she boasted, pointing below, 'that's mine, that's mine, that's also mine, and mine.'

The hallmarks of the martial law years – political harassment and intimidation, military thuggery, and corporate corruption – were made easier by Marcos's self-gifted power to write his own laws by issuing decrees that went straight onto the statute books. Business cronies were awarded government commissions and projects. In many cases, family friends, business associates, and political allies were given strategic appointments in the government and in the private business sector.

To gain advantage for himself and his allies, Marcos issued presidential decrees to set-up companies in leading sectors – sugar, coconut, tobacco, banana, and logging – for cronies and relatives, and then issued other decrees that provided his business allies with government contracts, exclusive import and export rights, tax exemptions, and cheap loans.

If that wasn't enough, government largess enabled these Marcos-indebted industries to gain the upper hand through fiscal, legal, and regulatory measures. Competing companies stood no chance against selective enforcement of government regulations. Singled out for special attention, these rival companies told a common story: taxes and customs duties were raised; regulations were selectively applied; loans were suddenly withdrawn or denied; health and safety regulations were scrupulously enforced; and negative stock market rumours were perniciously circulated.

Marcos's grasping business tentacles ensnarled other sectors. Marcos 'cronies' dominated or controlled electricity, telecommunications, shipping, airlines, beer, tobacco, textiles, hotels, casinos, and media companies. Massive and unchecked deforestation occurred during the Marcos years. The logging industry was spectacularly exploited by Marcos's relatives, and business, and political allies. They were granted hundreds of logging licences and frequently relied on paramilitary troops to forcibly drive indigenous groups and farming communities from their lands.

Marcos ruthlessly stripped the 'old oligarchs' of Philippine society of their political and economic power and assiduously replaced them with his personally chosen 'new oligarchs'. Marcos placed more importance on political cronyism than on business acumen, and so he built an economy heavily skewed to loyal business and political associates who benefited disproportionally from government contracts, favourable tax policies, and specifically crafted corporate legislation.

Looking After Number Two

A centrepiece of Marcos's martial law declaration was

his commitment to create a 'New Society', to revamp the nation's social and political values. Throughout his entire political career, Marcos used his presidential powers – before, during, and after martial law – to appoint his wife to a series of specially created positions, each one more powerful than the last, until her cabinet rank and portfolio budget exceeded most others, and her political clout was second only to his.

Marcos promoted his wife to unassailable power simply by writing two decrees. The first decree, in 1975, created Metro Manila, which combined four cities and 13 municipalities. It was the country's biggest administrative jurisdiction of more than six million people. Marcos appointed his wife governor. There was no selection committee. No discussion. No prior announcement. Marcos had carte blanche power to do whatever he wished. Three years later, Marcos wrote another decree. Again, he created a special ministry just for her – the Ministry of Human Settlements. This cabinet position gave her ill-defined and unprecedented nationwide control over resources such as finance, housing, education, hospitals, and public works. Imelda Marcos occupied both positions concurrently. She also was the chair or the director of an estimated 14 government and private agencies, including the National Food Authority, the National Electrification Commission, the National Housing Corporation, the National Pollution Control Commission, the National Home Mortgage Corporation, and the Rural Waterworks Development Corporation.

Interchangeably dubbed the de facto vice president, or the de facto foreign minister, Imelda Marcos was a member of her husband's rubber stamp parliament (1978-84) and undertook numerous overseas diplomatic trips as a roving ambassador, formalising relations with China, the USSR, and several East European countries. Imelda Marcos was her husband's chief accomplice in running the country. The 'power couple' created the Marcos dynasty through unparalleled nepotism, boundless conceit, and limitless power.

Imelda Marcos's calculated rise to power began six months after Ferdinand Marcos won the presidency in 1965. In June the following year (six years before martial law), Marcos issued an executive order creating the Cultural Center of the Philippines (CCP) on 88-hectares of reclaimed land on Manila Bay. The plan was to create a cultural hub to showcase to the world the modernity and the sophistication of the Philippines through iconic events and 'brutalist' architectural structures. The seven-member board of trustees, all appointed by Marcos, dutifully elected Imelda Marcos the CCP chairman.

Over the years, I watched the frenzied construction – to meet Imelda Marcos's impossible deadlines – of monumental buildings of stupefying grandeur in a country of deplorable deprivation and poverty.

Some of these monuments to megalomania included: the Folk Arts Theater, built in a dizzying three months to hold the Miss Universe Pageant; the multi-million-dollar Coconut Palace built to accommodate Pope John Paul II but who refused to stay there because it was too opulent; the rushed construction of the Manila Film Center whose roof collapsed killing scores of workers; and the construction of an International Convention Center in 23 months to host the 1976 IMF World Bank meeting. This prestigious meeting of the world's financial leaders required the forced removal of thousands of people from Manila's Tondo squatter area (for appearances sake) and the speedy building of 14 international hotels, many of them by construction companies owned by Marcos's friends and relatives who received about US$275 million in government funding.

While this was happening, Marcos – in one of his most bizarre, self-indulgent acts – evicted more than 200 families from Calauit Island, 285 kms from Manila, in order to create a private zoo of more than 100 African animals – giraffes, zebras, waterbucks, gazelles, bushbucks, and other animals.

The animals, from Kenya, were packed in wooden crates and shipped from Nairobi on a specially commissioned cargo vessel that took three weeks to travel the 9,700 kms to the remote 36 square kilometre island. The private zoo was off-limits to the public and soon it became known as 'Bongbong' Marcos's 'Safari Park' after the president's son reportedly flew there by helicopter on several occasions to hunt wild boar.

Marcos's despotic actions and grandiose plans were matched only by Imelda Marcos's blinkered obsession with constructing large ostentatious buildings. According to her, this was evidence of the Philippines modernisation and its transformation under her husband's rule. To Filipinos, however, these buildings were exorbitant monuments to Marcos's hubris and to his wife's 'edifice complex'. Instead of concentrating on 'traditional' civic infrastructure, Marcos squandered billions of dollars of foreign loans on inappropriate, overpriced, glitzy 'show off' buildings that plummeted the Philippines into record debt.

In 1965, when Marcos took office, the Philippines foreign debt was US$600 million. It skyrocketed to US$26 billion in 1986, the year Marcos was deposed. Over that period, World Bank figures show the Philippines GDP per capita dropped from sixth place to sixteenth place in Asia, earning it the reputation as the 'Sick Man of Asia'.

The Philippines recorded in 1983-85 its biggest decline of income per person in its history. It took 21 years (2003) before the country returned to its 1982 'personal income' level. In comparison, other Asian economies – South Korea, Thailand, Indonesia, and Malaysia – had income rises two to four times greater than the Philippines. Poverty jumped from about 40 per cent of the population to almost 60 per cent during Marcos's long administration.

TRAMPLING ON WORKERS' RIGHTS

With martial law, worker rights were severely curtailed, trade unions outlawed and strikes banned. When martial law was lifted after nine years, unemployment exceeded 10 per cent and under-employment was 33 per cent. Marcos saw organised labour, with its latent political muscle and its ability to mobilize against him, as an obvious and ever-present threat to his power base, and like everything else in Marcos's world, that meant union power had to be controlled.

Under Marcos, trade unionism was actively and often

violently suppressed, with activists harassed, jailed, and scores killed. Over the years, hundreds of strikers and trade unionists were detained without a warrant, jailed without charges, and held indefinitely. Union offices were regularly raided and ransacked by soldiers or police.

Even with the lifting of martial law, the nationwide ban on strikes was only partially lifted; severe constraints remained. Marcos could order the arrest of anyone, anytime, without charge, and his actions and powers could not be challenged. He gave himself unlimited powers; he could act on his own, without any judicial or legislative authority. He alone could declare a strike – even the threat of a strike – illegal. If Marcos believed the 'national interest' was at stake, he could forbid it and no one could challenge his decision. Furthermore, the affected business or industry concerned need not be an 'essential service', in fact most of them were not. Union picket lines and lockouts were regularly broken up by police or hired thugs. In 1983, the International Labour Organisation reported that Marcos had personally exempted 350 companies from paying even the minimum wage.

Marcos promised a structural transformation of the economy. Instead, it stagnated under rampant corruption, indebtedness, and heavy-handed government interference. The income gap between the rich and the poor widened, and the nation's economic and social inequalities grew glaringly stark.

Disillusionment spurred empowerment. Protest rallies became more commonplace; student activism moved from the campuses to the streets; union membership expanded, and their demands grew bolder; and perhaps most significantly, membership of the communist New People's Army expanded dramatically.

Marcos's vow to fight communism had helped him win office in 1965, and his (widely disputed) warning of a communist conspiracy to seize power had underpinned his martial law declaration. Yet, paradoxically, the New People's Army (NPA) did not even exist when Marcos was first elected in 1965. It formed four years after he took office and grew to its maximum strength during his 21 years in power – from several hundred guerrilla fighters in the early 1970s, to about 25,000 in the late 1980s. The revival of communism had everything to do with Marcos. The longer he stayed in power, the stronger the Communist Party and the NPA became. Repression bred resistance. And the worse life became under Marcos, the stronger the communist's resolve to intensify their liberation war.

From its original base in northern Luzon, the NPA expanded throughout the nation. It armed and mobilised a growing band of supporters in the countryside, rural towns, and major cities. The NPA oversaw a campaign of ambushes and attacks on military patrols and outposts, and the selective assassination of government officials.

Marcos's Growing Military Machine

With martial law powers, Marcos moved with predictable speed to build up a key pillar of power – the Armed Forces. In just three years, the Armed Forces of the Philippines more than quadrupled to over 250,000 personnel in 1975.

Basic pay rose 150 per cent. The military budget increased by 500 per cent in the same period.

As commander in chief, Marcos then did what he had done so many times as president: a favour for a favour, a quid pro quo. The military chiefs got what they so desperately wanted – money, equipment, power, and prestige. In return, Marcos demanded their loyalty, which was generally forthcoming because their careers depended on it. As commander in chief, Marcos had the final say on promotions, demotions, and extensions in the Armed Forces.

With an eye to long-term political control, Marcos needed a reservoir of obedient civil administrators, and he found a ready untapped pool among high-ranking military commanders. Senior officers – many long past retirement – were appointed mayors, governors, diplomats, and heads of public utilities – electricity, railways, airlines, sewerage, and water. Serving officers were assigned to the Board of Transportation, the Land Transport Commission, the Philippine Coconut Authority, and the Sugar Commission. Many quickly amassed inexplicable wealth.

Under Marcos, it was not merit that underpinned military promotions or postings, it was the birthplace of senior officers – preferably Marcos's home province – that was paramount. An overwhelming majority of generals in the Philippine Constabulary and the Manila-based Metropolitan Command were from Marcos's home province, Ilocos Norte.

Perceived to be the second most powerful man in the Philippines after Marcos was General Fabian Ver, the chief of the Armed Forces. Known as Marcos's most loyal henchman, Ver was born in the same town as Marcos. They were cousins and childhood playmates. Once Marcos's personal bodyguard and driver in the 1960s, when Marcos was Senate president, Ver remained a captain for 11 years before Marcos shepherded him through the ranks, until finally promoting him to the top military post in the nation.

He was, concurrently, chief of staff of the Armed Forces, head of the Presidential Security Command, and head of the all-powerful and feared National Intelligence and Security Authority. Ver did for his sons, what Marcos did for him. Under Ver, the Presidential Security Command was boosted to an estimated 1,200 men and Ver's eldest son, Col. Irwin Ver was made the Command's chief of staff. Ver's second son, Lt. Col. Rexor Ver, oversaw the military unit that protected the Marcos children. And Ver's third son, Maj. Wyrlo Ver was commander of the armoured unit on the grounds of the presidential palace.

Ver was the ultimate 'yes' man who kept a low public profile, 'the man in the shadows' who rarely held a news conference. He was immensely powerful, and feared, because he was part of Marcos's inner circle of advisers; probably the most loyal and most obsequious because he owed everything to Marcos. Ver was so slavishly loyal to Marcos, he lived on the grounds of the presidential palace, not in his official residence at the Armed Forces general headquarters. A joke, enjoyed by a jaded public, had Marcos, in a test of loyalty, order Ver to jump from a window in the presidential palace. 'Yes sir,' Ver replied. 'What floor?'

Marcos's obsession with provincial fealty and slavish

personal loyalty was glaringly apparent to the public, and annoyingly frustrating and destabilising to the military hierarchy whose promotion path was routinely stymied if they didn't come from Marcos's home region.

Ver was not only the cousin and province mate of Marcos, Ver was also a cousin of the nation's second highest military commander, Fidel Ramos, chief of the Philippine Constabulary, who also was born in Pangasinan province, south of Marcos's birthplace. Although the defence minister, Juan Ponce Enrile was not related to either Marcos, Ver or Ramos, he did have the good fortune to be born in Cagayan, a province that shared a common border with Marcos's home province. Marcos, Ver, Ramos, and Enrile all spoke the Philippine dialect Ilocano.

Once ensconced in power, Marcos embarked on the most significant armaments rebuilding and personnel reshuffling in the nation's military history. Instead of performance, competence, and seniority, Marcos promoted politically connected officers, or military proteges of provincial allies. He surrounded himself with a protective network of officers he believed he could trust because of their implicit provincial loyalties and obedience to a fellow Ilocano. They owed their promotion to Marcos, and Marcos demanded their loyalty.

Marcos inherited a mostly professional and apolitical military structure, and then proceeded to transform it, to politicise it. Within the civilian administration, Marcos created a new military layer of public administrators – generals who supplanted civilians, and who enjoyed immense power and prestige in what had been civilian posts. In doing so, Marcos polarized and alienated most Filipinos.

Marcos broke possibly the most fundamental tenet of the Armed Forces. Instead of meritocracy, battle successes, and aptitude being the criteria for promotion, Marcos made loyalty to him the key benchmark for promotion through the ranks. As commander in chief, Marcos could sack and promote whoever he chose. And he did. Officers became beholden to Marcos; whatever he wanted he got, and they did what he commanded.

In the eyes of many Filipinos, the Armed Forces had become shamefully subservient to Marcos's one-man rule. Its integrity plummeted. So, too, did the Armed Forces professionalism. More experienced senior officers were overlooked and there was growing resentment in senior ranks that less qualified, less battle-hardened commanders were leading them into battle. Morale declined and with it, battlefield performance. In some encounters with the New People's Army, even the state-run newsagency reported the communists often had the upper hand.

Suppression, Arrests, Torture and Killings

During the Marcos regime, tens of thousands of people were arrested and tortured. Thousands were killed or 'disappeared'. Military power went unchecked, and harassment and abuse were commonplace. A pattern – predictable and inevitable – emerged. Wherever the military was most heavily concentrated, there were abuses. 'Political killings' got worse, not better after the lifting of martial law. Over seven years, 1973 to 1980 (encompassing most of the martial law period) there were 532 'political killings' according to the respected human rights group, Task Force Detainees (organised by the Association of Major Religious Superiors of the Roman Catholic Church). But in just two years, following the lifting of martial law, 595 'political killings' were recorded – 63 more killings than in the preceding seven-year period.

Every successive year under Marcos, the violence and the abuses got worse, culminating in 1983. In the first nine months of that year – more than two years *after* martial law was lifted – Task Force Detainees (TFD) reported that in Mindanao alone, the armed forces were responsible for 191 individual killings, the deaths of 126 people in group massacres, and 74 'disappearances'. The report, cited by the International Commission of Jurists (ICJ), said that in 1983 more than 2,000 people had been arrested nationwide ('considerably more than in 1981') and reported an increase in 'salvagings' (extrajudicial killings).

The ICJ explained the term:

'Salvaging' is a term used in the Philippines to refer to summary execution or extrajudicial, surreptitious, killing of individuals by the armed forces. The person 'salvaged' disappears after being picked up by the military or security forces and is found dead some days later. There is often evidence of torture.

For every year I was in Philippines, people were salvaged. Many, many people. 'Salvage' would have to be the world's most obscene misnomer. It's not a cynical term, nor a snide expression. It's a disgusting military term; a term that applies only to the military, and a term they use openly. So common is the word 'salvaging', it has become a standard, readily understood, newspaper headline. The word's meaning has been upended and bastardised. It no longer means 'recovered'. Instead, it means to kill somebody. It's done, almost exclusively, and always covertly, by specialist military 'hit squads', often at secret locations, and frequently follows acts of torture. It's equivalent to the appallingly sanitized euphemism 'extrajudicial' killing.

Task Force Detainees reported 644 cases of torture in 1983, a 'great increase' over the previous year, indicating an 'alarming trend', worse than even during martial law. The International Commission of Jurists (ICJ) also condemned the use of military 'safehouses', another deplorable military euphemism which means a secret torture and detention hideout, often inside a military camp, and not, as many would assume, a location of refuge and safety. To their great discredit, the Philippine military cynically and intentionally mangled the true meaning of both words with calculated, contemptible indifference.

In a further rebuke, the ICJ found that in those 'rare' military trials – when a soldier is charged with a serious crime against a civilian – proscribed procedures are 'routinely ignored with impunity' or dismissed. And if the case does go to trial, the ICJ found the public is excluded; and if convicted, the soldier's sentence is 'often incommensurate with the gravity of the offense'.

The ICJ and TFD both reported that most civilian cases against the military were never investigated because the victims were threatened or feared retribution. If a case was heard by a military court, in most instances the accused soldier was exonerated after the complaint was withdrawn, or witnesses disappeared, or changed their testimony, mostly under duress. In the countryside, NPA justice was seen to be swift and final, unlike military justice which was no justice at all. Frustration turned to anger, and anger turned to revenge and consequently membership of the Communist Party grew, and recruits to the New People's Army multiplied.

The Rise of Paramilitary Armies

For generations, political dynasties have enjoyed immense power through a vice-like stranglehold on local politics. Many of these landlords were warlords too, maintaining private armies to quell unrest among urban and rural workers who were increasingly critical of maladministration, corruption, and abuse. In the countryside, anti-government sympathies bubbled up and became a recruitment pool for the communists.

The Communist Party was making inroads, geographically and psychologically. Their calls for agrarian reforms and better wages and conditions were gaining adherents, and rebel fighters of the New People's Army were infiltrating more regions. Marcos's answer to the communists' advances was to form, in 1970, civilian militias, Barangay Self-Defence Units. Then, in 1977, he radically transformed this structure into a paramilitary force, the Civilian Home Defence Force (CHDF) which quickly earned a reputation for ruthlessness, criminality, and vigilantism. Even so, for all the Marcos years, the CHDF remained immune from government criticism or any presidential rebuke.

Most rural farmworkers and urban townsfolk regarded the CHDF – numbering between 70,000 and 100,000 nationwide – as among the worst violators of human rights during the Marcos regime. Formed ostensibly to support the military in counter-insurgency operations, primarily in village defence protection, they were ill-chosen, badly trained, poorly equipped, and ill-disciplined.

Most CHDF recruits were selected by local civilian and military leaders; equipped and trained by the military; and deployed and utilized through a complex arrangement involving the regional governor, city and municipal mayors, the military, and local police. It was a confusing mix of separate, often contradictory agendas, motivations, and allegiances. The prospect of a monthly wage, a uniform and a gun appealed to the unemployed (and there were many of them), and to low-income earners, the criminally minded, farmers, security guards, and others. The CHDF was a ragtag army that often was assigned to local political 'kingpins' (landowners) for their personal deployment. Sometimes, they acted as 'bullyboys' (bouncers or bodyguards) or 'errand boys' (civilian-military go-betweens).

Worst of all, they were a motley group of marauders who gained a reputation for stealing from poor farms, demanding food and drink at gunpoint, abusing and harassing farm workers, and occasionally burning huts, raping women, and killing innocent people. As for confronting and doing battle with the NPA, the CHDF forces were better known for avoiding or retreating from battles, abandoning their equipment, or discarding their weapons to aid their escape.

Many times, communist cadres told me that their biggest source of weapons was the CHDF – either weapons discarded in battle or sold covertly. CHDF soldiers were serial human rights abusers whose actions drove more recruits to the NPA than any other single factor. On several occasions, battle-hardened military officers apologised to me (off the record) for the behaviour of some CHDF troops. Despite this, the CHDF was an integral component of Marcos's military machine and remained so for his entire presidency.

Gagging the Media

At the onset of martial law, Marcos had made his intentions very clear – he not only wanted to control the levers of power, but also the instruments of communication. To control the media was to control the message, and Marcos didn't hesitate; the very instant he imposed martial law he targeted the media. Hours before his early evening television address declaring martial law, Marcos authorised the pre-dawn military round up of newspaper proprietors and prominent journalists; they were held without charge in military cells. Marcos made media control his top priority. His very first martial law directive – Letter of Instruction No.1 – allowed him to 'take over and control...all privately owned newspapers, magazines, radio, and television facilities and all other media communications'.

In all, Marcos issued 11 presidential decrees curtailing or restricting media freedoms. He used martial law to stifle the combative press that had hounded him in his early congressional career. He condemned the 'gutter press' for its 'false, vile, foul, and scurrilous' reporting and threatened a crackdown.

It's almost certain that in the months, possibly years before he declared martial law, Marcos planned a counter strategy to ensure favourable media coverage in the pre- and post-martial law periods. Marcos needed someone to guarantee him positive media coverage. And that someone was one of Marcos's oldest and most loyal friends, Roberto Benedicto. If he owned a newspaper, Benedicto could counteract the bad news with the good.

Most media pundits agreed that to launch a newspaper in normal times was difficult; in hostile times, with martial law speculation rife, it was downright foolhardy. That was not the view of Benedicto; he could not be deterred from launching a newspaper to help his friend in the presidential palace. With remarkable timing – four months before Marcos declared martial law – the *Philippine Daily Express* was born. It was Benedicto's national broadsheet; it was well-resourced and boasted a stable of writers with a pro-Marcos bent. With his friend at the newspaper's helm, Marcos would later show his gratitude to Benedicto, first with an ambassadorship and then with a corporate power base in the sugar industry.

The *Philippine Daily Express* was on the scene just in the nick of time. It began publishing in May 1972 and had settled into a comfortable existence when, in September, just four months after its launch, Marcos declared martial law. A media blackout followed. At least 16 national newspapers, seven television networks, and hundreds of radio stations were swept up in a coordinated military net of suppression and silenced. For seventy-two hours, the printing presses remained silent, and radio and television broadcasts ceased.

Finally, Marcos allowed one newspaper to resume publication – the *Philippine Daily Express*. It was no surprise. From its first edition, four months earlier, the Benedicto-owned newspaper showed itself to be a loyal Marcos mouthpiece. During the three-day media blackout thousands of people had been jailed, the military had taken control of the streets, and civil liberties had been curtailed, but the front page of the *Philippine Daily Express* sympathised with 'FM' (Ferdinand Marcos) and appealed to its readers to stay calm. '*FM declares martial law*' was the banner headline, and a series of reassuring sub-headlines covered the front page: '*But civilian gov't still functions; no military take over*'. Another said: '*To save the republic and form a new society*'. And another: '*Nation is calm; business, life goes on normally*.'

Later that year, Benedicto was rewarded with an ambassadorship to Japan, and several years after that, Marcos used his decree-making powers to make Benedicto the monopolistic 'sugar baron' of the Philippines. With its chief editor, Enrique Romualdez (a relative of Imelda Marcos), the *Philippine Daily Express* remained praiseworthy of Marcos for his entire leadership and only ended publication the year after Marcos was deposed.

During martial law, journalists were routinely arrested, detained, and sometimes tortured and killed. Scores of city and regional newspapers and magazines were banned, and television and radio stations in Manila and nationwide were closed. Newspaper proprietorship was transferred to Marcos supporters, including Imelda Marcos's brother (three newspapers), a personal aide of the president (four newspapers), and one of his closest business friends (one newspaper, one magazine and two television stations). Filipinos contemptuously called the pro-Marcos newspapers the 'bootlicking press' or the 'tuta' (lapdog) press.

Over the following years, the Philippines once famed media of defiance became the media of compliance. Friends and relatives of Marcos took control of media companies, editorial control was tightly regulated, and government directives meekly observed. Invariably, government press releases were published unaltered, and government announcements went unchallenged. Most disturbingly, a pattern emerged. Journalists who stepped out of line were threatened with dismissal, physically threatened, arrested, questioned, jailed, or coercively silenced by vexatious libel suits. All-encompassing censorship rules silenced the mildest criticism, and journalists practiced self-censorship to keep their jobs. Fear overshadowed everything.

Many journalists were killed in pursuit of stories. UNESCO reported in 1989 that 27 journalists were killed during Marcos's rule. In a 1985 open letter to Marcos, the National Press Club denounced the killing of 22 journalists between 1979 to 1985 and demanded answers. It got none.

With his stranglehold over the media, Marcos became

a practiced manipulator of television appearances. They were so regular, almost daily, year after year, that they served as a constant visual reminder – a reaffirmation of his omnipresence – at least to younger Filipinos who knew no president other than Marcos. It was axiomatic: Marcos was the president; the president was Marcos.

Gradually, in the 1980s, encouraged by a faltering economy and an increasingly assertive opposition, small independent newspapers emerged to challenge the stifling orthodoxy of government-controlled media channels and the compliant timidity of the 'crony' press. The handful of 'alternative' tabloids increased during the 1980s and they enjoyed greater public credibility than the established pro-Marcos media. Marcos disparagingly called these publications the 'Mosquito Press', implying that they had an annoying sting but no bite, and surprisingly he allowed them to operate, mostly un-swatted. It was a sop to his critics, and his rhetoric worked – at least superficially – for the government was able to point to the 'Mosquito Press' as an example of press freedom in the Philippines.

The so-called 'Xerox Press' was another outlet for dissent. It was a furtive, clandestine, exercise in press freedom that was nothing more than a randomly produced collection of foreign newspaper and magazine clippings, photocopied, stapled, and passed hand-to-hand among news hungry Filipinos. It was an underground news network for those desperate to know. Throughout the late '70s and early '80s, magazines, including the *Far Eastern Economic Review*, *Time*, and *Newsweek*, were regularly banned because of articles critical of the Marcos government, his family, or his business ties.

On one occasion, I was granted rare approval to attend a press conference in the presidential palace. I was to sit at the back and observe. Several times I was told my presence was a privilege, and no, I could not ask questions. Notable for its deferential, inoffensive questions, this was a press conference over which Marcos had masterful control.

I recall cringingly courteous, seemingly pre-arranged questions that elicited from Marcos the predictable, rehearsed, rote answers. Often, instead of answers, Marcos would ignore the question, seize the moment, and launch into a totally unrelated 'character assassination' of his opponents or critics. Other times, he would ramble in an uninterruptable diatribe against someone or some project. Rather than a press conference, it was an orchestrated charade of sanitized questions and prepared answers, exemplified by the blatant effrontery of a presidential press officer who distributed the supposed transcript of one question before Marcos had even finished speaking.

At home, after the two-hour press conference, I flicked through my notes. There were one or two stories there, I concluded. But I had no sound. I had been refused permission to bring my tape recorder. That night, as usual, Marcos led the television news bulletin, but it was not the story I would have chosen. Of all the stories they could have selected from the press conference, the government TV channel picked something I considered innocuous. Uncannily, it was the exact same 'top story' pick of the other television and radio news bulletins. Then, the following day, and every day thereafter, for the rest of the week, every television station and newspaper (by some miraculous coincidence) chose the exact same story to lead their news bulletins, and every time the first sentence began: 'President Marcos said today…'

It was clumsy, obvious déjà vu television. And it was done badly. It was a deliberate, calculated strategy of media manipulation, beginning with a weekly press conference by the president that was methodically divided into daily news bites, and then made available to the media. The intent was to have Marcos lead every night's television and radio news bulletin, and to grab every newspaper headline the next day.

No matter what else was happening in the world, or in the Philippines, nothing was as important as the daily doings, thoughts, and opinions of the 'father of the nation'. Yet, it was so transparent. And there was one blindly obvious logistical problem. The president's once-a-week press conference inside the palace usually lasted an hour or two which meant there was only a limited amount of film footage available. Very boring, and very obvious repetition was the result. Every day, the topic would change, but television viewers would see the same location shots, the same close-ups of journalists, the same presidential demeanour, the identical shirt, the same room fixtures, the pen that never moved, and the half-filled glass of water that never emptied.

It was a synchronised 'big brother' delivery of a curated press conference and the palace insiders were so contemptuous of their viewers' intelligence that they naively believed their duplicity would go unnoticed and unchallenged. Marcos made himself and his government the centre of the news, day after day, not just because he was able to, but because he had to. His health was rapidly declining, and he needed to keep it secret to retain his carefully crafted public image as the nation's incomparable and indispensable leader.

One weekly press conference, parcelled into selected daily news snippets, guaranteed the favourable news coverage he wanted, and the invaluable out-of-sight free time he needed for rest and medical attention. Widespread rumours, at the time, had Marcos suffering from the kidney disease lupus erythematosus – an autoimmune incurable disease that also affects joints, skin, the brain and lungs, and whose symptoms can include fatigue, skin rashes, fevers, pain, and swelling of the joints.

The Iron Butterfly Called Imelda

For most of the Marcos years, the obsequiously skewed pro-government media portrayed the self-styled 'royal couple' as selfless benefactors – Ferdinand Marcos was a war hero, a charismatic, intelligent, machismo figure who was demurely and ably supported by Imelda Marcos, a compassionate, sympathetic, noble, and eminently capable former beauty queen.

Beyond the adulation of her courtiers and the fawning media, Imelda Marcos was known as the 'Iron Butterfly' because of her insensitive flaunting of her fashion sense while methodically adopting a steely political strategy of self-aggrandizement. Meeting her on several occasions over the years, I noticed she grew increasingly plump-faced, her gaze appeared transfixed somewhere over my shoulder, never at me, and it was almost always frozen in a snooty, head-tilting imperiousness. Once, I had morning tea with Imelda Marcos.

She sat, queen-like, in the middle of a three-seat exquisitely upholstered antique divan with sculptured gilded mouldings. I sat opposite on a single chair of similar ostentatiousness. Between us, on a marble table, was a majestically large antique teapot, presumably French, surrounded by a matching set of bone China cups and plates, one with tiny biscuits which remained uneaten. Likewise, the tea went untouched. A heavy air of uneasiness descended the moment we met.

In keeping with her regal countenance, Imelda Marcos – dressed entirely in white and with every strand of hair captured in a stiffly sculptured coiffured bun – sat straight-backed and unmoving on the very edge of the divan for the entire interview. She wore expensive, haute couture clothes (she once boasted she never wore the same dress twice) and flaunted an aura of shameless self-glorification that accentuated her insensitive indifference to the poverty beyond the palace gates.

'The people love me,' she insisted, and she denied her lifestyle and manner showed a callous disregard of the poor. With the insufferable logic of a despot, she told me that her actions were nobly altruistic. 'I need to be beautiful for the people because that's what they expect. My people look up to me. I need to show beauty and compassion in the face of ugliness and despair.' Her words were so insufferably odious, I have never forgotten them. Likewise, her feigned concern for the poor was galling, as was her affected indignation that anyone would doubt her honesty or sincerity. It was delusional, almost piteous.

What rankled most was her unashamed 'Marie Antoinette' persona on her occasional visits to poor communities. Among her retinue would be her personal parasol holder and an unobtrusive assistant who clutched a glitzy purse of money and doled out pesos to eager well-wishers. With an air of regal condescension, Imelda Marcos would venture uneasily into the excited crowd. It was a royal procession of startling contrasts. Madonna-like, perfectly coiffured, exquisitely dressed, bedazzled in jewellery, Imelda Marcos would smile demurely at those who kissed her hand in gratitude. This was the worshipful homage that Imelda Marcos relished and had come to expect. It made for great television.

As a couple, the Marcoses were condemned as the conjugal dictatorship, particularly by their middle- and upper-class critics. From early in their marriage (some called it a power partnership) they set out to create an image, and to foster a narrative, of deserved political dominance.

Keeping it in the Family

In a country known for its political dynasties, Marcos moved purposefully to continue his own. His father, Mariano Marcos, had been a congressman from the northern province of Ilocos Norte and that's where Marcos began his own political career when he was elected to his father's old seat in 1949. Ilocos Norte was Marcos's bailiwick, his home base over which he enjoyed life-long political dominance and which he bestowed to his children through shrewd, calculated political manoeuvrings.

Martial law had been in force for six years when Marcos created his own political party, Kilusang Bagong Lipunan (New Society Movement) of which his only son, Ferdinand Jr. 'Bongbong' was a member. At the age of 23, 'Bongbong' ran, unopposed, for the position of vice governor of Ilocos Norte. His pre-ordained election was never in doubt, and three years later, he was elected governor, a post he held until he joined his father in exile in Hawaii in 1986.

Marcos's eldest daughter, Imee, had a similar cushioned ride into politics. Marcos simply wrote a presidential decree in 1975 creating the Kabataang Barangay (Youth Council) and appointed 20-year-old Imee, chairman. Its members, aged from 15 to 18, would be selected from every one of the country's tens of thousands of barangays (barrios) and they would be instructed in the guiding philosophies of Marcos's New Society. Mostly discredited for its overtly political pro-government activities, the Kabataang Barangay was largely moribund by the time it was disbanded soon after Marcos fled the country.

Marcos, however, had bigger plans for his daughter. In 1984, when Imee was 29, and a member of her father's governing party, her political fortunes were boosted when she was elected to the Marcos-dominated national parliament as a representative from her father's home province. She remained a member of parliament until the People Power revolution when, like her brother, 'Bongbong', she joined Marcos in exile in Hawaii.

Of all the Marcos children, Imee was the one most

often seen in public, often on stage in the background during some presidential appearance, other times standing shoulder-to-shoulder with her father at some function, and most often addressing members of her youth organisation, Kabataang Barangay. Marcos had created the organisation just for her. It was her stepping stone to a political career.

In contrast, 'Bongbong' kept a low profile. Rarely in the limelight, he spent his education years abroad and even after winning the vice governorship of his father's home province at the age of 23, he spent great slabs of his life outside the country. Unlike his sister's early political baptism through the Kabataang Barangay, Marcos Jr. chose a more conventional career path: wheeling and dealing in provincial politics.

I once requested an interview with Imee Marcos, who was articulate and personable, but I never felt the need to interview 'Bongbong', given his frequent absences and low public profile. He appeared in awe of his father, meek, servile, and self-effacing and his academic achievements – or lack of – were the brunt of public speculation, often ridicule. Oxford University denied his claim to have been awarded a BA in Philosophy, Politics, and Economics. He enrolled in 1975 but did not complete his studies. Instead, Oxford awarded him a 'special' diploma in social studies in 1978. His academic underachievement was counterbalanced by his shrewd political nous and a penchant for power, having served a 21-year apprenticeship under his father's tutelage in the presidential palace. Even so, he remained – mostly out of sight and out of mind – behind the scenes.

Only years later, on the gruelling last day of his father's

presidency before he fled the country, did 'Bongbong' show his hitherto hidden side. He appeared, in army fatigues alongside his father, mother, and sisters on the presidential palace balcony at his father's fatuous inauguration ceremony. In hindsight, that moment captured the emergence of a new assertive 'Bongbong', with probable dreams of succession.

The third Marcos child, Irene, was known as 'the quiet one' for her lifelong avoidance of publicity and her apparent disdain for holding any public office. The rise of the Marcos dynasty came to a temporary halt when Marcos fled into exile in the USA, but Marcos had ensured the family name would continue after his death.

For 41 of the past 53 years (1971-2024) a Marcos family member has been a governor of Ilocos Norte: Marcos's sister (Elizabeth Marcos Keon 1971-83), Marcos's son ('Bongbong' Marcos 1983-86 and 1998-2007), Marcos's nephew (Michael Keon Marcos 2007-2010), Marcos's daughter (Imee Marcos-Manotoc 2010-2019), and Marcos's grandson and son of Imee (Mathew Manotoc 2019-present).

Governors appointed by Marcos had to please the president rather than satisfy the people's needs. In the royal court atmosphere of the presidential palace, governors – fawning and deferential – had to hustle for an audience with Marcos in the hope that they could convince him to issue a presidential decree favourable to their province, and almost invariably beneficial to them.

Family Dynasties and Political Patronage

Political, economic, and social elites dominate Philippine

politics and monopolise power in every province. With their status, power, and political clout, the aim of these political dynasties – numbering several hundred – is to win for the family patriarch the prestige of public office as mayor or governor, if not for them then for their children, and if not their children, then for trustworthy cohorts who, on election, become the political pawns of their benefactors. Reaching all corners of the Philippines, these 'old money' fiefdoms acquire, preserve, and entrench power, generation after generation.

Political dynasties existed long before Marcos took control. However, everything changed the moment Marcos was able to wield his unchallengeable decree-making powers. Instantly, everything he wanted was possible. Nothing was beyond his arbitrary, idiosyncratic, self-serving decisions. He could settle political scores by favouring one powerful family over another and expect their loyalty in return. At any stage, Marcos could snatch away power and bestow power. He could purge those dynasties he couldn't control and replace them with those he could. Often, these power elites were relatives, business, political, or military allies, or close friends, whose loyalty Marcos could rely upon.

Since Spanish colonisation, political dynasties have held a stranglehold of power in the Philippines; multiple members of the same family have routinely, often concurrently, held a range of political offices, and business and cultural posts as well; their power and influence are overwhelming. From one administration to another, the survival of these political dynasties depends on their malleability to harness their power, influence events, and to deliver results.

After Marcos fled the country, many of the old dynasties emerged from their self-imposed political hibernation – where they had bided their time and kept a low public profile – and insolently returned to dominance. There is a sense of entitlement among the country's rich and powerful families, imbued with the belief that they hold an incontestable birthright to positions of power and it is their responsibility to continue their family's political pedigree.

I equate the Philippines political system to a merry-go-round. It is not for ordinary Filipinos, just the rich and powerful. Only they can line up. And only they can get onboard the political merry-go-round. Generation after generation, these inheritors of power – from family dynasties and powerful business empires – enter politics to win and exercise power. They act as self-anointed overlords who believe their heredity power and historical wealth gives them an almost inalienable right to public office. Once they climb aboard the political merry-go-round they rarely get off. Power is boundless and intoxicating and public office brings lucrative rewards. Notoriety and money buy these power brokers a seat on the political merry-go-round. Once onboard, they acquire even more power, wield even greater influence, and revel in even more wealth. In time, these political power brokers get stuck to their merry-go-round seats, get giddy with power, and hold on tight. So tight that the more deserving, better qualified, and more capable people are prevented from getting on. And so the Philippines political merry-go-round goes around, and around, and around with the same people holding tight to their seats and getting more and more giddy with power. Finally, one family member gets off and gives up his seat to another family member or a relative. It's a blatant, arrogant, political 'baton change' which enables the ruling elites to share power among sons, daughters, and relatives. They give up seats on the political merry-go-round so that each can take a turn. Power is all-important, not qualifications, experience, or competency. Consequently, almost inevitably, corruption flourishes and ineptitude prevails. It's a practice so routine and so entrenched in Philippine politics that it is regarded as 'normal politics' – barely questioned and almost never challenged. It's a perplexing, self-perpetuating phenomenon: the same family names re-occur, year after year, decade after decade, occupying offices at all levels of government and in public administration.

For most politicians, party politics in the Philippines is little more than a charade: a cynical, calculated exercise in political entrenchment. It's power they covet, and when they have power, they abuse it. When an election draws close, the rich and powerful routinely congregate under a party's political umbrella. But there is no deep-set philosophical or ideological dogma that unites them, no commitment to the common good of everyday Filipinos. On the contrary, they are there for themselves with no regard to the collective aspirations of the party. In their minds, the party is there for them to use. It's their launching pad to power and they show no constraint in using the party's well-proven political apparatus to win public office. Once in power, they practice what most Filipino have come to expect of them: influence peddling, patronage, and personality politics.

For any elected official – national, provincial, regional, or council – or any head of a government ministry or a private entity, it seems that their first priority on assuming office is to find jobs for their kin, which extends far beyond their immediate family, often corralling cousins, second cousins, distant relatives, and friends. It is normal, they say. Everyone does it. And, by consensus, that makes it right and acceptable. To 'share the spoils of office' is an ingrained concept of familial responsibility so commonly practiced that it is blithely accepted, even among the poor, as an unchangeable and implicit way of life. 'It's always been like that,' people often say, not in angry frustration but with weary resignation.

Many times, I've spoken to governors who have introduced me to their sons (mostly it's sons) saying: 'This is my son. He'll replace me when I retire.' It is spoken not as a hope, but as a fact, and with the staggering arrogance of someone who can't see the impropriety of a system so corrupt that political inheritance is regarded as normal and acceptable.

For generations, legislators have been able to point to grandparents, parents, brothers and sisters, uncles and aunts, cousins, nieces, and nephews, who have been politicians before them. Politics in the Philippines is a transferable vocation; a rich person's inbred inheritance akin to an endowment that is passed from one generation to the next and, invariably, it penetrates the business world where families and relatives benefit from special favours and backroom deals.

In some provinces, these political dynasties monopolisation of power at all levels and for so many generations, is so entrenched and impenetrable that many, if not most Filipinos, see elections as irrelevant, and their votes as inconsequential, a tradeable commodity available to the highest bidder. Their political impotence is the consequential product of a class-ridden society and a deeply flawed electoral system.

These king makers are rule makers. They are the patrons of some, and the enemies of others. Money gives them power over the powerless. They know 'payola' (bribes) can buy votes, silence, or support. Whatever they want. This is ground-level Philippine politics at its most basic and base. Ordinary Filipinos – millions of them – have long accepted the reality of Philippine politics as an unfair, unchangeable, embedded system. And they know that they exist at the bottom of Philippine society, in poverty, and without any real input into the political process. Politics is reserved for the rich; it's their playground, not to be shared with the poor.

Long-term incumbency leads to skewed political priorities; personal ambition always prevails over the common good, and almost always vested interests trump public interests. To these politicians-for-life, personal fortune comes before public welfare, and 'public service' means little more than a quick paint job on crumbling infrastructure. Invariably, in the Philippines, it's the high-impact, vote-winning projects that these political dynasties champion. These projects may generate good public relations, and help re-elect governors and mayors, but they come at the expense of those more urgent, more impactful, more beneficial, and more long-lasting projects.

I recall passing through many small towns with

impressive, costly, well-maintained monuments to national or local heroes, or freshly painted government offices or medical centres that are named in honour of the latest gubernatorial member of a patriarchal dynasty, often dating back more than a century. And, just metres away, in the town's pot-holed streets, are open fetid gutters and neglected buildings and houses where the water supply is intermittent and the electricity supply is unreliable.

In 1970, only 22 per cent of the population (mostly urban) had electricity, 86 per cent of rural Filipinos had none. Marcos promised to electrify the entire nation by 1987, but only 55 per cent of the nation had been connected by the time he fled the Philippines in 1986.

When, in 1980, the Agency for International Development (AID) released its report on Rural Electrification in the Philippines, Marcos had been in power for 15 years. He controlled the nation's purse strings and he and his wife had spent billions of dollars on extravagant structures in Manila. But in the countryside, in millions of households, families could not even afford electricity.

'Most of the Filipino rural poor are unable to make productive use of electricity,' AID reported. 'Either they cannot afford electricity at all or can only afford the minimal use of a light bulb or two.' It was too expensive for a house to be connected and wired. And, too costly to buy cooking appliances, so they used wood. A refrigerator cost too much, so they used ice. Quoting 1975 figures from the National Economic Development Administration, AID estimated that 40 per cent of the Filipino rural poor were 'not able to afford power under current rate levels and tariff structures'.

Despite the hollow bluster of 'better times' and the shallow promises of 'new projects', in many rural areas the fields were tilled by barefoot farmers with wooden hand ploughs pulled by carabaos; the produce was taken to market by horse-drawn carts; water was hauled, bucket after bucket, from wells; clothes were hand-washed in rivers; and at night, houses were illuminated by kerosene lamps. Long before Marcos fled the country, it was apparent to most Filipinos that his New Society looked very much like the old one.

Insufferable Arrogance

Systematically and comprehensively throughout his two decades in power, Marcos contrived to position himself and his wife as the benefactors of the nation as if imbued with a divine providence to rule. And, whenever a public project was announced, the cloying media drew veiled parallels between the Marcoses and benevolent parents bestowing gifts to the nation out of the goodness of their hearts. Often, national public works projects were announced or unveiled – the date sometimes brought forward, sometimes delayed – to coincide with the birthday of the president or Imelda Marcos. Frequently, depending on whether Marcos or his wife was inaugurating or unveiling a project (a bridge or a building for instance) the taxpayer funded structure was described by the media as a birthday gift from him to her, or from her to him.

They acted like self-absorbed, self-righteous demigods. Their birthdays became public holidays.

Marcos's birthday, 11 September, was proclaimed 'Barangay Day', in recognition of the nation's smallest administrative hubs. Imelda Marcos's birthday, 2 July, was proclaimed 'Working Women's Day'. And the date martial law took effect, 21 September, was proclaimed 'National Thanksgiving Day'.

In the presidential palace hung a widely lambasted adulatory painting of Marcos and his wife, portrayed as Adam and Eve-like characters. Titled *Malakas and Maganda* ('strong' and 'beautiful'), the commissioned painting is a modern depiction of an ancient myth about the birth of the nation. It shows a muscular, bare chested, dagger-holding Marcos emerging from a bamboo jungle, and a half naked, long-haired, coy-looking Imelda modestly clutching a flowing white veil to her chest.

They are portrayed as the ideal couple. He is the hypermasculine hero type, strong and handsome, and she is demure, alluring, and beautiful. They are the parents of the nation. It's a propaganda painting of crude intent, designed to equate the Marcoses with the myth of nationhood. On the presidential palace walls there were other paintings of deeply questionable taste. Several remained on Imelda Marcos's bedroom wall when I ventured inside the ransacked presidential palace the day after she and her husband fled into exile.

Mostly, they were amateurish Renaissance-inspired paintings that depicted Marcos in a heroic straight-backed Napoleonic-type pose. Imelda Marcos was invariably portrayed as a cherubic, angelic young woman of mystical beauty. Together, in the opulence and extravagance of the palace, the Marcoses enjoyed a lifestyle of unabashed ostentatiousness and displayed the mannerisms of pretend aristocrats with a taste for the profligate and the frivolous. Some in Manila's opposition, contemptuously referred to the 'King' and 'Queen' occupants of the presidential palace. In a game of their own making, some diplomats would guess the political allegiance of each cabinet minister, whether they were the political acolyte of Ferdinand or of Imelda, or the beneficiary of their patronage. Each cabinet minister was cynically identified as one of 'his' or one of 'hers'.

The media was muzzled. The coverage was sycophantic. Simpering accounts were broadcast nationwide of every utterance, appearance, or opinion of the 'first couple'. And so it was not surprising that in 1975, Marcos had a five pesos coin bearing his profile minted to commemorate martial law's imposition three years earlier. Then in 1978, a 30-meter-high concrete bust of Marcos was unveiled on a hill in his home province. It was a cringingly crude copy of the busts of four U.S. presidents carved into the side of Mount Rushmore in South Dakota. It was a display of excruciating bad taste, a very public flaunting of Marcos's sickening egoism.

Education was a key plank in Marcos's long-term New Society agenda. Martial law gave him the opportunity and the means to reconfigure and refocus the nation's education system; to make schools the agents of social change, and the messengers of Marcos's New Society. The duty of all schools, colleges and universities was to 'undertake an intensive education campaign, utilizing all possible means, such as classroom lessons, homeroom conferences, community and PTA assemblies, and all school publications to promote a better understanding of the social and economic goals of the New Society'.

Curriculums were overhauled, textbooks revised and reprinted, and special attention given to the development, writing, and the printing of supplementary educational materials, most with a pro-Marcos slant. Except for mathematics and science, all subjects featured themes of nation-building, civics, and citizenship obligations and duties in the New Society. On the opening page of every textbook was an introductory message from Marcos, with his signature beneath. The Philippines humanities textbooks extolled, often in oblique and subtle ways, the values and the virtues of the New Society. One famous Grade 4 Communication Arts textbook (1980) featured Imelda Marcos as the 'model Filipina' and the 'mother of the nation'.

While photos of the president were hung in schoolrooms and in government buildings, Imelda Marcos preferred murals painted in the foyers of many municipal offices and on school playground walls. Most of the murals portrayed a celestial image of an angelic, youthful, Imelda Marcos floating angel-like in a heavenly cloud of adoring underlings. Imelda's ethereal image, stoic and compassionate, dominated the mural. Her image was far bigger than the surrounding portraits of half a dozen men and women positioned beneath her like servile minions, gazing adoringly at the First Lady, as she insisted on being called. I have never forgotten that image: Imelda Marcos, the mother of the nation, hovering over her utterly dependent and mesmerised people like a protective guardian angel.

Sometimes, photos of the two Marcoses were carefully hung side-by-side and equidistant from each other, to infer equal status. Her picture was identical to his, same lighting, same pose, identical frames. Here was the power duo on display for all to see.

A Fake War Hero

Marcos always had a penchant for power and a ruthlessness to succeed. He learned early and quickly about the power of media, particularly how to manipulate it to his advantage, which he did for his entire political life. He was a 47-year-old senator, a year away from the presidency, when he shrewdly commissioned an American author to write his biography, *For Every Tear a Victory*. The following year, a sympathetic biographical movie about Marcos was released. Called *Man of Destiny*, it was produced by 777 Film Productions, Marcos's lucky number, which led to speculation it was fully financed by Marcos.

It's believed the book and the film helped Marcos win the presidential election in 1965, despite being denounced for inaccuracies, historical distortions, and falsehoods, particularly the book, which coloured public perceptions of Marcos for years. In cringing prose, the author described Marcos as 'one of the most extraordinary men alive, a man likely to become president of the Philippine Republic' and a man who 'has been Number One all his life at everything he has laid his hand to'. Not just that, Marcos 'has miraculously survived near-death eight times, including the Bataan Death March and torture by the Japanese secret police (and) before he was twenty-five, he won more medals for bravery than anyone in his country's history'. Marcos claimed to have been awarded 32 medals, a figure disputed by US military authorities, historians, and academics.

Marcos's war record was a sensitive matter for him, and a controversial issue for others. In December 1982, a weekly opposition newspaper, *We Forum*, questioned Marcos's war record and queried whether his medals, or some of them were fraudulent. Immediately, Marcos ordered the arrest of the newspaper's editor and 14 staff on charges of subversion and rebellion. The Supreme Court later ruled that their arrest and trial were illegal on technical grounds.

Four years later, the controversy exploded into a worldwide scandal with headline-grabbing stories declaring Marcos a 'fake war hero'. The story originated from documents found in the US National Archives which accorded the revelations instant authenticity and legitimacy. It was an unexpected treasure trove. The 600 boxes and more than a million pages of US Army files had been 'lost' for more than a quarter of a century which made the files, including Filipino guerilla documents, even more alluring and newsworthy. The documents covered an exhaustive three-year US Army investigation (1945-1948) into Marcos's wartime record and his alleged command of the Maharlika guerrilla unit.

During the Second World War the Philippines was still an American colony, and the Philippine Army was under U.S. command. In 1945, at the end of the Second World War, Marcos petitioned the US Army to recognise him and the Maharlika unit, which he claimed to have led, and reward them with veterans' benefits and back pay for wartime service. But the US Army investigation rejected the reparations claim as a 'malicious criminal act'. It found Marcos's claim to have led the guerrilla resistance unit 'fraudulent' and 'absurd'. More than that, it said Maharlika was a fictious creation and 'no such unit ever existed'. Scepticism surrounding Maharlika was due in part to conflicting claims about its size: 8,300 in 1944, to 1,830 in 1945, and finally 9,200 in 1964.

For six months, American academic Alfred McCoy, who was then Associate Professor of History at Australia's University of NSW, pored over the 'forgotten' US Army intelligence evidence that debunked Marcos's claim to be a war hero. Many of Marcos's claims of wartime gallantry and battlefield successes were found to be unverifiable, lacking documentation, or independent eyewitness accounts. Other Marcos claims – that he and three other fighters attacked a battalion of Japanese soldiers, and that Marcos singlehandedly blew up a Japanese ammunition dump killing 26 – could not be verified by US Army investigators. Also, his sudden promotion to lieutenant colonel was questioned, coming as it did four months after the war's end.

Marcos's disputed war record ignited another concurrent controversy: whether or not he really was the most highly decorated Filipino soldier of the Second World War. His claim to have won two Silver Star medals, the Distinguished Service Cross, the Medal of Honor, and the Purple Heart medal cannot be corroborated by US military records. Relentlessly, long after the Second World

War, Marcos used his legislative influence to bolster his war record. As a senior congressman in 1958 he was awarded the Philippine Medal of Valour, the country's highest military decoration, for his exploits in Bataan 16 years earlier. Then in 1963, Marcos was awarded 10 more medals for his actions in the Second World War which ended in 1945.

Exaggeration and bombast were traits that rippled through Marcos's entire political career. His fantasy of wartime heroism was a concocted series of lies calculated to project himself as a war hero, a battle-tested national saviour, and the nation's protector. At one of the first Marcos rallies I attended, Marcos was introduced as 'the Philippines Audie Murphy', referring to the most highly decorated American soldier of the Second World War.

Murphy became a movie star and played himself in *To Hell and Back*, an autobiographical film (1955) about his war exploits. Fifteen years later, and five years into Marcos's presidency, the film *Maharlika* was released about the supposed guerrilla heroics of Marcos, who was proclaimed to be 'the most decorated war hero of the Philippines'. Not content with that boast, some pro-Marcos media commented that Marcos was the better soldier. His 32 medals beat Murphy's 27.

Marcos was a man with a vision of himself, and of his place in Philippine history. He was the ultranationalist, the war hero, the scholar, the politician, the author. Marcos encouraged his ever-dutiful sycophants to project him as the noble father of the nation and, when he declared martial law, its saviour as well.

From the outset, Marcos made his intentions clear: he

wanted to chronicle his rise to power by taking control of the narrative, and books would be the method. He seems to have harboured some grandiose 'Churchillian' plan to become the nation's chronicler and write about his policies and his actions. He hoped, I presume, that his analysis and interpretation of events, and his justification of his actions, would be grist to Philippines history books.

In 1971, in an audacious act – not uncommon among history's dictators – he 'authored' a book, *Today's Revolution: Democracy* which was a blueprint to martial law's imposition one year later. Other books followed – almost yearly for a time – during his two decades in office.

Mostly, they were book-length political essays of his rule, and even a two-volume history of the Philippines. Thirteen books in all, and not one of them is believed to have been written by Marcos.

Instead, they were written by self-confessed ghost writers and a team of historians from the University of the Philippines. Marcos basked in unearned and undeserved praise. His braggadocio was outrageous and unconstrained. Marcos studiously cultivated the image of an intellectual, but I suspect even his most loyal supporters would wonder how he could have found the time to write 13 books, when the records show that he issued 1,974 Presidential decrees; 1,589 Letters of Instruction; 1,112 Executive Orders; 2,498 Proclamations; 831 Memorandum Orders; 1,263 Memorandum Circulars; and 162 Letters of Implementation.

On one day alone, 11 June 1978, Marcos signed 160 decrees. Eight months earlier, he issued a decree naming a municipality in the southern Philippines province of

Zamboanga del Sur 'Imelda' in honour of his wife. In Imelda's home province of Leyte, and Marcos's home province of Ilocos Norte, numerous public structures and places bore their names.

The Emergence of Aquino

Marcos was a busy, overwhelmingly powerful man, whose power was absolute, and who tolerated no critics or criticism. In 1978, Marcos called an April election for an Interim National Assembly. It was a constitutional political ploy to introduce a parliamentary system of government which was no more than a rubber stamp parliament that ultimately would see him remain president, as well as become the country's prime minister. It was political chicanery by Marcos and the main opposition parties – citing political restrictions and a muzzled press – refused to take part, although jailed former senator and fierce Marcos opponent, Benigno Aquino, did agree to participate, and assembled a 21-man opposition party, Laban (fight).

For six years, until 1978, political parties had been banned and the underground political groups were wracked with faction squabbling and splintered by individuals jockeying for power. Now they had to organise openly, and as a united front. For Aquino, it was a challenge he couldn't resist. Six years earlier, on the very day martial law was declared, Marcos had ordered Aquino's arrest on trumped up charges. Aquino had been in military detention ever since and out of the public's eye. Now, in the strange hurly burly world of Philippine politics, Aquino was allowed to 'campaign' from his prison cell. Even more perplexing, he was granted a 90-minute television interview, inside his cell, conducted by a government-sanctioned interviewer.

If Marcos had hoped to dispel Aquino's aura and popular attraction, he failed. On the contrary, Aquino performed well. Among older Filipinos, the jail interview was proof that despite his incarceration, Aquino was still a formidable politician who could challenge Marcos in a fair election. More importantly, the interview elevated Aquino's public profile to an entirely new group of young people who, up until then, knew little about the incarcerated firebrand.

He, and Laban didn't win of course. But the 1978 election galvanized the nation in a shattering, entirely novel way. It released the supressed, unspoken anger of the Filipino people, fed up with the daily drip-fed propaganda diet of the Marcos regime: the 'glories' of the New Society; the superhuman president who knew all and demanded obedience; and the First Lady whose vanity was only exceeded by her vacuousness.

Days before the election, a flurry of phone calls, door-to-door house calls, and hastily photocopied handbills, made sure people would join a unique Filipino-style protest – a noise barrage. The plan was simple. Everyone, grandma included, could join. Kids too. At 8 p.m. on election eve – an election they knew was rigged and therefore unwinnable – Filipinos showed their defiance by making as much noise as possible. It was a raucous night I will never forget; a loud, boisterous cacophony that could be heard across Manila, probably in the presidential palace, and possibly at the jail where Aquino was held. Everything that could make a noise was fair game.

Besides the chants, squeals, yells, and hollering, pots and pans were banged, TVs and stereos were turned up to full volume, honking cars roamed the streets, the metal shutters of shop fronts were rattled, fences and garbage cans were beaten by timber planks or baseball bats, garbage lids were thumped on roads and walls, trumpets and drums were played, firecrackers ignited, and I heard the unmistakable sound of gun shots fired into the air. Somewhere, tyres were burned, and acrid smoke filled the air.

It was a protest triumph. People filled the streets in a joyous, unrestrained carnival of protest. It was a shear, uncorked, explosion of sound, never done before, and something that gave heart to the previously silenced opponents of Marcos. Instead of one hour, it continued well into the night. It started early; people couldn't wait to unleash the long-suppressed frustration and anger that they had bottled up for years. Before Marcos, there were things they could do, see, and read; but not now. This night was their chance to defiantly yell and make deafening noise, to show their disapproval of Marcos and his regime. The enthusiasm of the Noise Barrage would linger, and be remembered, and be replicated eight years later with the People Power revolution that toppled Marcos.

In May 1980, almost two years after his unsuccessful election bid, Aquino suffered a heart attack and was allowed to leave his jail cell in the Philippines for medical treatment in the United States. He left behind a deflated opposition, a country in deep economic crisis, and a president scheming to keep his stranglehold on power once he lifted martial law, which he did on 17 January 1981.

Martial Law in Everything but Name

Marcos had prepared the legal groundwork. A new constitution, ratified by Marcos-created Citizens' Assemblies in 1973, ensured his powers were untouched and undiminished; the status quo remained; the formal rescinding of martial law was nothing more than hollow symbolism. The United Democratic Opposition applauded the end of two 'visible and repulsive symbols' of martial law – military tribunals and army detention centres – but noted that nothing else had changed. Martial law may have been lifted, but there was no free press, no free speech, no peaceful assembly, no independent legislative body, and no rule of law.

Marcos made sure that every presidential decree and every presidential order he had issued for every one of those nine martial law years remained the law of the land, and the new constitution allowed him to issue future decrees whenever he wished. Marcos also had the right to suspend the writ of *habeas corpus* for 'crimes related to subversion, insurrection, rebellion, and also conspiracy to commit such crimes'.

If that wasn't enough, he went one step further. On the day before he formally announced the lifting of martial law, Marcos issued a presidential decree providing immunity for any civilian or military official who implemented such orders. The decree stated that all martial law decrees and orders should be 'institutionalized and made permanent and lasting'.

What no one knew at the time was that Marcos secretly signed possibly the most repugnant, repressive, anti-democratic decree of his career on the very day before he lifted martial law. Presidential Decree No. 1834 was a safety net of outrageous punitive punishments specifically designed to quell any public dissent, and to silence all opponents by imposing the harshest possible penalties. 'Death' was the maximum penalty for anyone found guilty of using anti-government speeches, proclamations, writings, emblems, even banners to incite 'rebellion' or 'insurrection'. Anyone who organised an 'illegal assembly' also risked a death sentence if found guilty.

Under Marcos's draconian catch-all definition, an 'illegal assembly' was 'any meeting which is held for propaganda purposes against the government or any of its constituted authorities in order to destabilize the government or undermine its authority by eroding the faith and loyalty of the citizenry'. Faith and loyalty? A person's life and liberty rested on such nebulous terms! An organiser of an 'illegal assembly' risked death, and a participant could be jailed for six years. A person could also be sentenced to death if they prevented a national government, regional or municipal authority from 'freely exercising its functions' or if they committed an act of 'hate or revenge' on a public employee or their property.

The presidential decree was ludicrously all-embracing and included a chilling provision aimed specifically at the media. It would be an act of rebellion – punishable by death – if any person in control or managing any print, broadcast, or television services, used or allowed these facilities to mount a 'sustained propaganda campaign' which could 'undermine or destroy' the people's faith and loyalty in the government. Faith? Loyalty? The decree was a punitive, outrageous denial of liberties riddled with grotesquely disproportionate penalties. Even worse, it was drawn up in secret and held in reserve, ready for use by Marcos whenever he wished. It was Marcos's trump card, his personally crafted self-preservation firewall that outlawed virtually all methods and all avenues of dissent against him, and against his rule. The fact that it was a secret decree is telling. The day after he signed it in secret, he begrudgingly lifted martial law. Perhaps, at the back of his mind, he was reassured that Presidential Decree 1834 was his safety net, a fall-back position – legislation kept in reserve – that would allow him to wield even harsher control than he did during his martial law years. Afterall, presidential decrees were Marcos's legal weapon of choice.

Presidential Decree No. 1834 remained secret for more than two years, apparently never invoked, and when its existence was revealed, it was denounced by civil rights lawyers who demanded answers. The International Court of Justice said the secret decree, with its 'extremely drastic penalties' was specifically aimed to intimidate opponents of Marcos and suppress any opposition to his government. 'Obviously, there is hardly any democratic country in the world where demonstrations against the government would be considered to be sedition and (participants) threatened with a life sentence.'

The ICJ accused Marcos of using civil law as 'an instrument of terror' and hypothesised that under this law it would be a crime to 'reveal that the government is graft-ridden or that it is unable to cope with an economic crisis'.

Marcos admitted some of his decrees had not been published and blamed the government printing office. It was an acknowledgement that they existed. Not a pledge never to use them. He added, with menacing rhetoric, that the decrees could not and would not be enforced until they were published in the *Official Gazette*. He also denied the charge that he had signed more than a 1,000 secret decrees, general orders, and letters of instruction over the previous decade.

Marcos had lifted martial law, but a year later Amnesty International found little had changed. In fact, things had got worse. In jail were almost 900 political prisoners. 'Disappearances' and extra judicial killings were 'increasingly common while torture remained prevalent'. Marcos, in fact, had made it easier for soldiers to arbitrarily arrest and detain people. In a Letter of Instruction (14 months after lifting martial law), Marcos gave military officers even greater discretion to arrest suspects. They could bypass the courts and seek from Marcos a Presidential Commitment Order (PCO) that would allow them to seize (without warrant), detain (without charge), and hold (indefinitely) any person for 'national security' reasons.

Often, the PCOs were sought days, sometimes weeks, after detainees had been placed in detention. Amnesty International reported that many of those detained for 'subversive activities' were involved in non-violent activities such as 'trade union organisation, participation in church sponsored action groups, and opposition to particular government projects'. Marcos luxuriated in the power presidential decrees gave him. On several occasions, when faced with mounting opposition in the streets and from Church pulpits, Marcos issued thinly veiled intimidatory reminders to the Filipino people that the alternative to his decree-making powers would be the reimposition of martial law.

With his overworked, untouchable safety net of decree-making powers in place, Marcos felt emboldened to try to add another cloak of pseudo legitimacy to his rule – he announced presidential elections would be held in June 1981. His timing was significant. It was an opportunistic, shrewd political strategy: Marcos wanted to capitalize on a pending papal visit.

Papal Politics

Pope John Paul 11 had announced his intention to visit the Philippines in February 1981, one month after martial law's scheduled lifting, something the Roman Catholic church had long sought. Marcos undoubtedly reasoned that an election timed to occur four months after the pope's visit would win him papal praise. An election, he probably thought, would soften any criticism the pope would make of his authoritarian rule. Also, Marcos almost certainly believed the election would boost his democratic credentials in Washington with newly elected US president, Ronald Reagan.

Marcos no doubt believed that in the predominately Roman Catholic nation he would win popular kudos if the pro-government media reported that he and Imelda Marcos were the ones who invited the pope. But they were not, and the Church would have none of it. The Archbishop of Manila, Cardinal Jaime Sin, immediately issued a clarification. The invitation to the pope to visit was issued by the nation's bishops, he said, not the president and his wife. When this clarification went unreported in the pro-government media, bands of Catholic nuns flooded the nation's churches with copies of Cardinal Sin's letter. They won. In the eyes of millions of church-going Filipinos, it was clear who won the Church-State jostle for credit for the papal visit. And it wasn't the Marcoses. Shortly after, the cardinal quipped that the three fastest forms of communication in the Philippines were 'telephone, telegram, and tell-a-nun'.

Curiously, a 21-gun salute, a jetfighter fly-past, and a 5,000-strong security force was Marcos's tarmac welcome to the pope. On the one hand, Marcos no doubt hoped for some form of papal praise or endorsement of his rule now that he had lifted martial law and had scheduled elections. Imelda Marcos, on the other hand, was probably equally hopeful of the pontiff's blessing, preferably in public.

As governor of Metro Manila, Imelda Marcos ordered her 10,000-strong army of street-sweepers, called Metro Manila Aides, to cheer and wave flags as the pope drove past. They were rewarded with ready-made sandwiches and paid a few pesos. The Metro Manila Aides were used to being bused from one pro-government rally to another – mostly to cheer for their boss, Imelda – and so the street sweepers dutifully lined the boulevard into the city, waving flags, cheering, and holding banners.

Throughout the pope's six-day visit, Imelda Marcos – in a choreographed show of pomp and piety – shadowed the pontiff in his country-wide tour. She insisted the pope stay in a specially built multi-million-dollar Coconut Palace – 70 per cent built of coconut by-products and 100,000 coconuts – but he declined, calling it 'too opulent', and instead stayed at the papal nuncio residence.

Showing the sort of inappropriateness observers had come to expect of the Marcoses, gold and silver commemorative coins featuring the profiles of the pope and the president were issued. Earlier, Imelda Marcos had turned her attention to Manila's sprawling slum district, Tondo. She said it had to be 'beautified' to impress the pope who had scheduled a visit to what was regarded as possibly Asia's worst slum district.

Prior to the pope's arrival, Imelda Marcos oversaw months of construction work. First, she had hundreds of families relocated, taken to nearby provinces in dump trucks, and unloaded with the disassembled and broken remnants of their shanties. Then, she unveiled plans to convert a chosen slum district into a desirable housing community. It was another of her fabricated fantasies.

Shanties were flattened by bulldozers. High walls were built to block any roadside views of the sprawling, decrepit shanty village behind. Old walls were whitewashed. Fences were rebuilt and brightly painted, and unsightly views of illegal wire-tangled power poles were blocked by wooden facias with pretend walls and fake windows that were held upright by wooden support poles. Instant grass was laid, potted plants delivered, and fully-grown palm trees appeared overnight on land that was once a garbage dump.

The tone of the papal visit had been set within minutes of the pope's arrival. Sharing a stage, Marcos sat stony-faced as the pope declared that human rights violations could never be justified, even to meet exceptional security needs. It was a subtle rebuke, counterbalanced moments later, when the pope told militant priests and nuns not to take 'an exaggerated interest' in politics.

Before the pope's arrival, Cardinal Sin had insisted the pope's tour be regarded as a 'pastoral' visit and not a 'state' visit as Marcos had demanded. Also, Sin had wanted the pope to try to rein in the left-leaning clergy, while at the same time admonishing human rights abuses in the Philippines.

For more than a decade, there had been an uneasy relationship between the Roman Catholic church and the Marcos Government. It had grown wider, and the pope's visit had only drawn attention to the worsening economic inequality and the entrenched social injustice in the country. In the years ahead, dissident priests and nuns would be in the front ranks of the anti-government vanguard.

In June 1981, six months after the lifting of martial law, the first presidential election in 12 years was held. There was no credible opposition – only two relatively unknown figures stood – and Marcos made his re-election a virtual certainty. He ignored the opposition's boycott threat and rejected their demands for basic electoral rights and safeguards, including a purge of disputed voter lists, a minimum campaign period with equal time and access to mass media, and a reorganisation of the government appointed Commission on Elections.

The opposition's election boycott was inevitable, just as inevitable as the president's landslide 'victory'. Marcos proclaimed the birth of the Fourth Republic, but it was a pyrrhic victory that lasted less than five years and ended with him being hounded out of the country. Marcos's jubilance in his lopsided electoral win was short-lived, because in the years ahead he would face the challenges of ill-health; economic recession; a mounting communist rebellion; workers' protests; and massive popular protests over the assassination of his most prominent critic, Benigno Aquino, in August 1983.

In Death, Aquino Lives On

I was at Manila Airport when Aquino was shot. He was on his way home. He wanted to return to Philippine soil, to challenge an ailing Marcos after spending three years in self-exile in the United States where he had undergone medical treatment.

Aquino had been a political prisoner, snatched at the very beginning of martial law and detained in a military cell in Manila for eight years until he suffered a heart attack. Then, with the personal approval of Imelda Marcos, he was allowed to fly to the United States for heart surgery. Now he was heading home. Denied a passport, he had obtained a bogus one, and he had chosen to ignore friendly, and not so friendly advice, not to return. The government warned he faced impending danger if he did return.

The airport had been secured hours before Aquino's arrival with at least 1,000 troops. The moment Aquino's plane drew to a halt, soldiers came onboard and in front of startled passengers and disbelieving television crews and journalists, arrested Aquino. Grim-faced, Aquino was escorted out. Instead of the connected passenger air bridge, he was directed down a service staircase. Muffled shots were heard. Aquino's dream to return to Philippine soil ended with a bullet in the head as he descended the last few steps of a metal staircase with soldiers behind him, in front of him, others waiting on the tarmac. Aquino had wanted to touch Philippine soil, instead he lay dead on concrete, face down, sprawled, and bloodied. Nearby, was the body of his alleged assassin, Rolando Galman.

Several hundred metres away, confined with hundreds of Aquino supporters inside the airport's arrival area, and hemmed in by armed soldiers, I saw nothing. But word spread with lightning speed. 'They've killed him!' someone shouted. 'They've shot him!' The shout came from the back of the crowd of Aquino supporters who earlier had arrived at the airport, led by Aquino's brother, Butz. They had been chanting and waving banners of welcome. Combat ready armed soldiers had corralled them, and me, inside a stifling waiting room.

'They've shot him. He's dead!' The shout brought silence and gasps of disbelief. Everyone knew, instinctively, that 'they' meant the military. Everyone knew that 'he' was Aquino. The man whose shoulders bore the weight of so many people's hopes and expectations was no more. Dead. And he was just 50 years old. Most Filipinos dreaded, expected, half expected, or feared that Aquino would be killed if he returned to do battle with Marcos. And that's what happened. And when it did happen, a shocked sense of incredulity overwhelmed everyone in the cramped room where I was. The disbelief reverberated throughout the nation and around the world. The killing was so callous, audacious, brazen, and so utterly contemptuous of the nation's people, and a watching world. Among Filipinos, especially diehard Aquino supporters, their emotional reactions flittered from stunned disbelief to furious anger, to stifled vows of revenge.

On the day of Aquino's funeral, 10 days later, it seemed the public's affection for 'Ninoy' was the overwhelming emotion, although anger simmered close to the surface. For days, thousands of people had filed past Aquino's body which lay in an open casket in the lounge room of Aquino's suburban home. It had not been embalmed, no makeup had been applied, his face was bruised and blackened, and his safari-type shirt was deeply stained with blood which had dried a dark brown, almost black, and spread across his chest. That was the way Cory Aquino, his widow, wanted it. She wanted everyone to see what the military had done to her husband, she told me as we stood before the coffin. Hour after hour, thousands of Filipinos from all walks of life, filed past the open coffin in her lounge room to glimpse glassy-eyed; to stare disbelieving; to sniffle in prayer; to see for themselves what had become of their hero.

Soon after, Cory Aquino invited me into the kitchen for a drink and made me a cucumber sandwich. In three years, Cory Aquino would become the eleventh president of the Philippines, but on this day, she was concerned I might be hungry. 'Noynoy', her son, poured me a glass of water. Twenty-four years later he became the fifteenth president of the Philippines.

Ironically, it was four years earlier, in 1979, that I first met Benigno Aquino. We sat in his modest suburban home, in the same lounge room in which his body now lay. I was impressed. How could I not be? Charismatic and intelligent, he spoke with an immensely powerful, machine-gun-like delivery. Pro-government commentators often declared Marcos the nation's finest orator. Aquino was better, far better.

Aquino was showered in firsts – the country's youngest-ever mayor, the youngest-ever governor and, at 35, the youngest-ever senator. As an 18-year-old reporter, he covered the Korean War for the *Manila Times*. I met him by chance. And luck. He had been in a military stockade for seven years prior to our meeting and it was only due to the quirky nature of Philippine politics, and Imelda Marcos, that our meeting was possible. Imelda Marcos granted him a three-week furlough to celebrate his twenty-fifth wedding anniversary. He was home and I went to see him. I suppose there were plainclothes military guards, but I didn't see them. Why had Imelda Marcos shown some compassion to him, I asked. His answer took me by surprise. 'We dated when we were young,' he said with a smile, and changed the subject.

Even after spending eight years in jail, isolated from his supporters and unfamiliar to a younger generation, and then another three years abroad, reduced to long distance politicking, Aquino had remained the Philippines most popular opposition leader, and the strongest rival to Marcos. Now, he was dead, and so too were the hopes of many of his supporters. At the morning mass at the Aquino family's neighbouring church of Santo Domingo, Cardinal Sin, the nation's leading churchman, eulogised the slain father of five children as the 'personification of courage' in the face of oppression. It was a stronger than normal homily, in keeping with the national outpouring of grief.

What followed next was the biggest funeral in Philippine history. Millions of Filipinos lined the 30-kilometre route, at times 10 to 12 rows deep, to pay homage to a man many had once seen as the 'hope of the nation'. A flatbed truck, strewn with yellow flowers, carried Aquino's coffin. Slowly, at walking pace, the vehicle inched its way through the surging crowds at times held back by marshals, their arms linked to clear a path through the tearful, angry, sullen crowd. Amid chants of 'Ninoy', were occasional competing chants 'Marcos killer', and placards asking, 'Who killed Ninoy?'

Shortly after 9 p.m. – ten hours after it began – the funeral procession ended at a southern suburb cemetery where Aquino was interred. That night, on government television, the nation's biggest-ever funeral, in fact the biggest mass event in Philippine history, was hardly mentioned – a cursory 10 seconds, if I remember correctly. Instead, they led the bulletin with a story about bus fares.

With Aquino's death, the Philippines had got its martyr. The assassination was the impetus for a coalesced opposition movement with a single focus – the toppling of Marcos. The three years that followed, saw mounting public protests about political, civil, and human rights;

rising disaffection in the military; and an invigorated communist movement.

Troubles Here, There and Everywhere

Marcos's hold over public sentiment seemed to be slipping and the growing public alienation was obvious with an increased opposition vote at the May 1984 parliamentary polls, nine months after Aquino's killing. Of the 183 seats contested, the opposition won 60. The result was much better than they had hoped and far exceeded the 20 seats that Marcos had predicted. Imelda Marcos was shamefaced; she had overseen the government's election campaign in Manila where the opposition vote recorded a significant increase. Without doubt, public scrutiny contributed to the opposition's improved election results. The non-aligned electoral lobby, NAMFREL (National Citizen's Movement for Free Elections) fielded up to 200,000 poll watchers nationwide to check voter registration and voting procedures, and to investigate allegations of voting irregularities.

The death toll preceding the election and on polling day exceeded 200. And like all elections held during the Marcos years, there were complaints of widespread electoral fraud. Over-enthusiastic officials of the government-run Commission on Elections (COMELEC) reported a 100 per cent vote for Marcos-backed candidates in some regions. Filipino voters were expected to believe that in these provinces not even the opposition candidates voted for themselves. Neither did their spouses, their children, their relatives. Not a single friend. No one. In a country where dead people and infants vote, no one was surprised.

The aura of Aquino's assassination nine months earlier still pervaded the national conversation. There was common distrust of the government, and almost universal scepticism that Aquino's murder would ever be solved. This scepticism was understandable. Three days after the assassination, Marcos, reacting with knee-jerk speed, appointed a four-member commission of inquiry which met only twice before it was disbanded following a public outcry. Marcos tried again, and finally, two months after Aquino's assassination, he appointed a five-member Fact-Finding Board, but not before saying a few days earlier – even before it met for the first time – that he believed 'communists' were responsible for the killing. His prejudicial comments, apportioning blame to the communists, were repeated often during the inquiry and subsequent trial.

After a year-long inquiry, the Board surprisingly rejected the government's claim that a lone communist gunman, Rolando Galman, killed Aquino. Instead, a majority report blamed the assassination on a military conspiracy and named the Armed Forces chief of staff, General Fabian Ver, 24 other military men, and a civilian as responsible. All 26 men were formally charged three months later and tried by a Marcos-created anti-corruption court, the Sandiganbayan, whose three judges were all Marcos appointees. They did as the public expected, and what Marcos wanted: they reversed the previous findings of the Fact-Finding Board. The Sandiganbayan not only acquitted General Ver and all 25 other defendants but agreed with the military's version of the killing that Galman, acting alone, had managed to evade more than 1,000 soldiers, and had shot dead Aquino as soldiers escorted him down the airport service staircase. Moments later, according to the military, Galman himself was shot dead.

A Supreme Court appeal, lodged by Marcos opponents, which claimed the Sandiganbayan verdict should be overturned because of procedural 'irregularities' and 'bias' was rejected by the justices of the Supreme Court, every one of them a Marcos appointee. To most Filipinos, who long ago had lost any confidence in the judicial system, the Sandiganbayan verdict was rigged, just like Philippine elections of the past, the present, and undoubtedly the future.

Rumblings of Dissent

The people, as always, felt disempowered, disaffected, and disillusioned. This time, however, there was blowback from another direction – businesspeople. Most of them had been silent witnesses to Marcos's power grab over the years, but they now saw the Aquino killing as the 'last straw' moment of the Marcos Government. Enough. Enough of political intimidation and terror, the corruption, and the economic mismanagement. It had to end, they demanded.

The political upheaval caused by the Aquino assassination was matched by the deep economic hole into which the Philippines fell. By the end of the year – four months after Aquino's assassination – foreign investors pulled more than US$800 million out of the country. For the next two years, 1984 and 1985, the gross domestic product contracted by more than seven per cent each year as jittery international financial markets assessed the country's political stability and economic resilience.

For the first time, protests were staged in Makati, the business heart of Manila. Tens of thousands of well-dressed men and women marched, holding high protest banners, and chanting for Marcos's resignation. Office workers in high rise-buildings along the route peered down, cheered, and showered them with hastily shredded yellow confetti, the colour of protest in the Philippines. It was a protest that was to be repeated many times, for many months, and was enthusiastically dubbed the 'middle class revolt'. The attitude towards the Marcos regime within the upper middle class had shifted radically: from uncomfortable, but tolerable acquiescence in the very early days of martial law, to defiance and committed rejection, in the downward spiralling years following the Aquino assassination.

International pressures were closing in. The buoyant economy of the seventies – boosted by high commodity prices and underpinned by international financial market borrowings – was now drowning, due to free-falling commodity prices, skyrocketing oil prices, and a mounting foreign debt exceeding US$26 billion in 1985. Economic stagnation had set in. Politically, Marcos appeared beleaguered and vulnerable. Calls for him to stand down were growing louder and more frequent, emboldened by rumours of Marcos's declining health. Behind the scenes, there was jockeying for power, especially among the two most likely successors of Marcos – his wife, Imelda Marcos (supported by Gen. Ver), and the defence minister, Juan Ponce Enrile.

Mounting political pressure at home and abroad, particularly from an increasingly uneasy United States, compelled Marcos to call an early election, in February 1986, more than a year ahead of time. It was not a well-reasoned decision to call an early poll – the palace is believed to have been caught off guard – but it appeared to be an impulsive show of bravado by Marcos when he was asked on a US television program about his mandate to continue in power. His ego had been piqued, and his rash announcement of a 'snap election' would later be seen as a grave misperception of his popularity and a miscalculation of his power base. The opposition's confidence was growing stronger, while Marcos's health was growing weaker, and more apparent.

Ill-Health on Display for Everyone to See

Marcos had enjoyed a god-like omnipresence – seen everywhere, every day, with comments for every occasion. Now, he disappeared for days at a time, even longer on some occasions. 'His face grows fatter the sicker he gets,' I recall one opposition leader saying. His speech was mildly slurred and thick, his walk slow and careful, he wore what looked like thick pancake makeup to cover blotches or rashes. Opposition leaders, who claimed to have been briefed by 'insiders', said what was on public display were the side effects of the kidney disease commonly believed to afflict Marcos, Lupus Erythematosus. Sufferers can experience sensitivity to sunlight resulting in rashes, itching, and burning, as well as joint pain and fatigue.

In 1984, there were rumours that a kidney transplant operation had failed, and a second transplant was necessary. Marcos's non-appearances, sometimes for many days, fuelled speculation that he was seriously sick or dying. Palace claims that he was busy writing or resting after a hectic round of meetings, or suffering from a cold, were met with general disbelief. The image that Marcos so dearly wanted to project and had done so for years – the tough, superhuman, macho man of the Philippines – was now seen as a sham and, like Marcos himself, it was an image beyond recovery. Doubts about Marcos's health grew stronger the longer he remained out of sight, which was difficult with an election to contest.

Marcos probably thought his impulsive decision to call an early election was a shrewd political ploy, in fact considering his health, it was a liability, with his ill-health on display for all to see. He limited his public appearances and avoided being caught up in crowds. On one occasion, blood was seen to trickle down his hand from under his shirt. After that, he often wore a bandage on his hand. Sometimes he wore a floppy golf hat and was regularly shaded by an umbrella. At one rally, a frail looking Marcos was carried to an outdoor stage on the shoulders of impassive looking security men through a parting wave of supporters. Government television described it as a triumphal procession with Marcos borne aloft on the shoulders of enthusiastic supporters. It was not. To me, he looked like an ailing man, incapable of walking without assistance.

Marcos never acknowledged he was suffering from Lupus disease, but hours after he fled the country, reporters discovered in his ransacked bedroom in the presidential palace a hospital-like room containing a dialysis machine for purifying the blood of kidney patients. There was another dialysis machine in Marcos's 12-metre-long hospital bus – parked with 25 luxury vehicles in the palace garage – and it functioned as a mobile hospital. It contained an operating table with overhead lamps, an x-ray machine, oxygen tanks, and other medical supplies. A third dialysis machine – believed to be the only other one in a country of 55 million Filipinos – was reported to be in a high-class hospital in the financial district, Makati.

Marcos was a sick man desperately clinging to power. If he thought his sudden election announcement would catch the bickering opposition flat-footed, he was mistaken. The opposite happened. For once, the opposition agreed that the best possible opponent to do battle with Marcos was Aquino's widow, Cory. She was the 'people's choice', and she had a petition, signed by one million people, to prove it. The behind-the-scenes powerbroker who convinced Aquino to run was Cardinal Sin.

A Cardinal of Convictions and Clout

The Archbishop of Manila had met separately with Aquino and the other prominent opposition leader, former senator Salvador Laurel – both from different parties – and had brokered a deal that had Aquino the presidential candidate, and Laurel her vice-presidential running mate. Sin, wryly described as 'one of the country's most powerful politicians', had once again shown himself to be a formidable political manipulator, whose outspoken support for Aquino and the People Power revolution months later, helped drive Marcos from office.

Portly, round-faced, and bespectacled, Sin's appearance, coupled with a soft voice and a beguiling chuckle, belied a man of great intelligence and understated power. He was wily and he knew he wielded influence because, as the spiritual head of more than 40 million Filipinos, he presided over the most powerful institution in the Philippines, after the government.

A self-confessed moderate, Sin became archbishop of Manila two years after martial law was imposed. Initially, he talked of 'critical collaboration' with the Marcos Government, but it soon it became 'critical confrontation' as reports of corruption and human rights abuses flooded the nation's churches.

Frustratingly for a journalist, Sin often spoke euphemistically. It was criticism with a light touch, rather than biting, blunt rhetoric. Sin had an air of self-importance, even mild arrogance, which was assuaged by his well know joviality. 'Welcome to the House of Sin,' was his regular, though well-worn greeting when I first met him at his suburban archiepiscopal.

In an interview with me one day, he warned for the first time that civil war was possible if corruption and military abuses did not stop. It was a warning without nuance, without ambiguity: Marcos would be responsible for nationwide civil unrest unless he changed his ways. It was a significant hardening of Sin's earlier appeal for Marcos to end martial law. The exclusive BBC interview, in mid-1979, made international headlines, but Sin had no comment a few weeks later when I met him again. In fact, he seemed totally distracted as we sat on opposite sides of a small breakfast table in his study for a pre-arranged interview.

With a cup of coffee to one side, Sin had spread before him a broadsheet newspaper, munched on a piece of toast, and read, giving scant regard to my questions, and responding with unusually curt answers. He appeared to be half-listening and distracted. On at least three occasions, he turned the page, hitting the microphone with a thud, rendering the recording useless. Each time it happened, I had to repeat the question. 'Obviously, I'm wasting your time,' I said, standing. 'You don't want to do the interview. So, you're wasting my time too.' As I moved to leave, he expressed puzzlement but offered no apology for his supercilious behaviour. His press secretary called several hours later, and I accepted his offer to reschedule the interview.

A forerunner of this aborted interview had occurred more than a year earlier. It was the first time we met and I was there, tape recorder over my shoulder, prepared to conduct an interview for the BBC. In the study, near where we sat, was an air-conditioner that didn't hum but blasted a loud grinding noise. I explained it would make any recording impossible. This was a recording for the international service of the BBC, I said and suggested he turn off the air-conditioner, or we could move to another room. He raised his voice and sternly rejected both suggestions. It was a gruff uncharacteristic admonishment. Instead of him turning off the air-conditioner, I turned off my tape recorder and took notes. It was a bad start, but over the following years he and I met several more times and I watched as he became the opposition's behind-the-scenes 'power broker', a man who early on saw the 'neutral-ground, moral leadership' potential of Cory Aquino, and crucially convinced her to run against Marcos in 1986.

ELECTION SHENANIGANS

Even by Philippine standards, the fraud, intimidation, violence and cheating in the 1986 presidential election reached new lows. Reports of Marcos's ill-health had risen in tempo and volume. Now, they were given serious news coverage, even in pro-government newspapers, prompting strong denials from the presidential palace. Unfortunately, for his apologists, the silence, and the non-appearances of Marcos made matters worse. His campaigning was infrequent and short, and quickly a pattern emerged. Marcos avoided mingling with crowds, he stood only for short periods, but mostly he sat in a shaded chair. His speeches were short, and his voice lacked volume and depth. Most telling of all was his lack of resilience. He managed to visit only nine of the country's 73 provinces, whereas Aquino and Laurel visited 61.

The spontaneity, hoopla, and colour of the Aquino rallies were in marked contrast to the stage-managed, subdued uniformity of the Marcos rallies. Aquino, in her trademark yellow, was welcomed at every rally by chanting supporters swathed in yellow hats, caps, T-shirts and any other piece of yellow clothing they could find.

At the Marcos rallies, identical T-shirts with identical slogans were everywhere. So, too, were the banners – mostly the same size, and with two or three identically worded printed slogans. Few of the pro-Marcos banners had any of the originality, sometimes crudity, of the banners held aloft by the Aquino supporters. Like in previous elections, the government resorted to 'rent-a-crowds'. Buses were commandeered to drive to towns or cities where election rallies were to be held, and adults lured onboard by offers of free T-shirts, lunches, caps, and money.

Money – usually about 20 pesos – was offered as an inducement to someone to get on the bus and to be driven to the pro-government rally. More than once, Cardinal Sin advised the 'rent-a-crowds' to take the money but vote for Aquino. The 'rent-a-crowds' were offered free bottled water, and encouraged to choose a professionally printed banner, placard, flag, or poster, among a selection stashed on every bus.

Marcos volunteers, who acted like cheer squad leaders, operated in full view, disdainful of any criticism. Like tour guides, they ushered the needy and the hungry into orderly lines at the front door of the buses where large bamboo baskets stood ready. There was the T-shirt basket, the cap basket, and the sandwiches wrapped in plastic basket. Everyone got one of each. Then, the moment they stepped into the bus, the newly bribed Marcos supporters were handed 20 pesos.

The minders probably didn't think what they were

doing was wrong. In any case, they didn't care. Their only purpose was to have the nation's television viewers see hundreds of people at Marcos's rallies. For both sides, movie stars and singers were popular drawcards. The biggest movie stars and the most popular singers seemed to gravitate to the Marcos rallies, fully aware that it could be a career-breaking decision if they had the effrontery to ignore or decline an Imelda Marcos invitation to a rally.

Many people died long before the first vote was even cast. In the 57-day campaign, more than 500 people are believed to have been killed. On polling day, officials reported more than 20 deaths. A few days before the vote, Marcos reneged on his earlier commitment to keep troops in their barracks on election day. Now, soldiers would be stationed at polling booths, and at town and city collection centres where the votes would be tabulated and transmitted. It was an intimidatory move, repeated in many polling centres on election day.

'Vote early. Vote often' is a common tongue-in-cheek summation of Philippine elections. Exasperated Filipinos have a snappy list of terms to describe the various forms of election cheating so common in their country: flying voters; ghost voters; vote buying; ballot box stealing; ballot box stuffing; voter intimidation; voter list tampering; voter list purging; and illegal de-registrations. Most are self-evident, but two are wonderfully descriptive: 'Flying voters' are voters-for-hire who move from one polling booth to another and get paid each time they cast a vote, and 'Ghost voters' are resourceful money-makers who check cemetery headstones for names to sign on ballot papers.

As expected, voting in the 1986 presidential election proceeded along familiar lines. Once again, the government appointed Commission on Elections (COMELEC) was in charge, despite allegations of partiality. Marcos, in a move to placate his local and international critics, agreed that two other election monitoring groups be given observer status. They were the privately-run National Citizen's Movement for Free Elections (NAMFREL), and a 44-member international observer team from 19 countries. With COMELEC's endorsement, NAMFERL was allowed to conduct a 'parallel' vote count, and permitted to monitor the election campaign, and observe election day activities.

The scrutiny was unprecedented, and almost certainly a consequence of mounting international pressure on Marcos to allow free and fair elections. The non-partisan NAMFREL, supported by more than 250 private organisations, fielded a record 500,000 volunteers to most of the country's 86,000 voting precincts. After polling day, NAMFREL claimed about 20 per cent of the official vote was 'questionable' and said about two million opposition voters had been disenfranchised, including in Manila, where 10 per cent of names had disappeared from electoral rolls on polling day. Without comment or any explanation, COMELEC, tabulated the highly improbable: towns recording not a single vote for Aquino, but a 100 per cent vote for Marcos. And the certainly impossible: a 103 per cent vote for Marcos in one southern Philippines town.

There was indisputable evidence of cheating. In some towns, ballot boxes were found crammed with Marcos votes hours before voting even began. Some polling centres didn't open at all, and at others, armed men scared people away. Elsewhere, vigilant 'poll marshals' discovered widescale preparation for voter fraud when sheaves of Marcos ballots were discovered, pre-signed by COMELEC officials. All that was needed were the voter's names.

The election's most public and incriminating instance of election fraud occurred two days after the official vote count began. At least 30 computer operators suddenly and dramatically walked out of the government-controlled vote counting centre in Manila claiming that their computer tabulations were wildly different to what was appearing on the public tally board.

There was widespread evidence, from multiple sources, of a rigged and fraudulent election. Among its findings, the International Observer Delegation reported: 3.5 million voters were disenfranchised (their names were missing from electoral rolls); the marking of fingers with indelible ink was 'ignored or unenforced' in many areas; vote buying was widespread; there were numerous reports of 'fictional polling places'; in many areas, polling results were 'completely fabricated'; outlying provinces reported military intimidation of voters; and in many provinces, election officials were denied access to polling centres.

Despite the damning findings – from international election scrutineers; the government-accredited 'citizens' election body, NAMFREL; and the Catholic church – Marcos was proclaimed the winner by the government-controlled parliament.

Of the 26 million registered voters, only 20 million ballots were cast. The COMELEC count gave Marcos 54 per cent of the votes, Aquino 46 per cent. NAMFREL's count was almost the reverse, with Aquino credited with winning 52 per cent of the votes and Marcos 47 per cent. The late-night proclamation that Marcos had won the election prompted a parliamentary walkout by all 50 opposition members. At the same time, a defiant Aquino proclaimed herself the winner, denounced Marcos for having stolen the election, and vowed to hold a 'victory rally' the next day in Manila's largest park.

Rumblings of Revolution

Events were moving fast. The rally attracted hundreds of thousands of Aquino supporters, more people than at any other rally during Aquino's two-month election campaign. It was an impressive show of support for Aquino, and a stunning public rebuke of Marcos. To the chanting, boisterous crowd, Aquino was the obvious winner and Marcos was the conniving cheater, and they cheered their approval when Aquino announced a seven-point nationwide civil disobedience campaign.

Delay paying your utility bills, Aquino told the crowd. She called for a national boycott of the country's largest bank, Philippine National Bank, and six other banks, either owned by the government or by Marcos cronies. Close your accounts, withdraw your money, don't make any new deposits, she implored them. Aquino also urged a boycott of pro-government newspapers, the government-run Channel 4 television station, the nation's largest company, San Miguel Corporation, and its largest department store, both owned by Marcos associates.

The boycott strategy was immediately and enthusiastically embraced by Aquino supporters, disheartened by the 'stolen' election, but not discouraged. And now, on Aquino's urging, they were convinced, more than ever before, that sustained, popular pressure would force Marcos from office. In targeted pro-Marcos companies, sales dropped immediately and substantially. Heavy bank withdrawals were reported in pro-Marcos banks. The peso dropped 10 per cent in value. Advertising revenue for pro-government newspapers was down, and even sales of the Philippines most popular beer, San Miguel, declined.

In addition to the business boycott and the civil disobedience campaigns, the Aquino camp scheduled the nation's first-ever national strike on 25 February – Marcos's planned inauguration day – and called on factories, offices, and schools to organise protest rallies.

From pulpits around the country came invocations of support. Much of the credit for Aquino's success in taking up the political mantle of her slain husband, lay with Cardinal Sin. His unequivocal public endorsement of Aquino as the 'unifying moral symbol of opposition to Marcos' had been crucial. In addition, the priests and nuns who regularly stood in the front lines of her rallies were a constant and very visible affirmation that Aquino had the backing of the Catholic Church which, for the highly religious Filipinos, was extremely important. The priests and the nuns had taken the side of Aquino in the struggle against Marcos and for many Filipinos that rekindled their faith in the Church.

In a landmark statement – the most blistering, unequivocal 'political' statement ever released by the

Catholic Bishops Conference of the Philippines (CBCP) – the bishops denounced the election and condemned the fraud. 'A government that assumes or retains power through fraudulent means has no moral basis,' it said. 'Such an access to power is tantamount to a forcible seizure and cannot command the allegiance of the citizenry.'

Two unconnected events of immense importance occurred at this juncture which were a portent of things to come. There was a confluence of opinion from two sources ordinarily of divergent views – the Catholic Church and the Reform the Armed Forces Movement (RAM), a band of disaffected military officers.

The election was denounced as fraudulent by both sides – an unprecedented meeting of minds – and they even agreed on what needed to be done. The Church advocated 'active resistance of evil by peaceful means', and RAM supported a 'non-violent struggle' by the people. Aquino went one step further. In her victory rally speech she appealed for the first time for active non-compliance by the police and the military. 'Do not support a government that is not supported by the people,' she told them. 'It is not against the law of man or God to disobey unjust laws.'

Her speech was eerily prescient. A chain of confused but ultimately connected events followed. Nationwide, Aquino's call for a civil disobedience campaign was gaining adherents, and the business boycott call was gaining traction. The two instances were inexorably linked. Filipinos were itching for action. And when it came, the spark of ignition – a botched military coup – was unexpected and caught them off-guard.

At a huge protest rally, the day after the disputed poll,

Aquino had nominated 25 February – nine days away – as National Strike Day. But the strike never happened. Three days before it was due, Aquino's plans were gazumped by a military coup that took centre stage and ultimately precipitated the end of the Marcos regime. It was a military coup to dislodge a dictator that initially failed but ultimately succeeded. It won because vast numbers of people – far exceeding anything ever seen before – took to the streets in support of the anti-Marcos military rebels, and together they turned the failed coup into a successful revolution. The revolution's heartland – where the rebel soldiers held their ground, besieged in a military camp, and supported by more than a million people – was a stretch of highway, Epifanio de los Santos Avenue, commonly known by its acronym, EDSA.

In the end, Marcos was overthrown not by design, but by happenstance. The failed military coup only survived by the timely intervention of the Catholic church through Cardinal Sin's active encouragement. It mutated into a popular revolt. Sin's endorsement of the plotters brought more than a million people onto the streets, it provided a crucial injection of people power to aid and protect the besieged military renegades, and it gave them time to muster vital support among the armed forces.

The military defections that followed, exposed Marcos's weakness and vulnerability, and denied him options to counterattack; he risked bloodshed, mayhem, and condemnation if he tried, because the biggest civilian uprising in the nation's history was protecting the plotters, and the audacity of the People Power revolution had captured the world's attention and support.

The military insurrection and the People Power revolt were parallel events, involving different methods, with a single objective: the ousting of Marcos. Together, the military renegades and the people had the means and the tactics to make it happen. They needed each other to succeed. And they did. Over four days, a military uprising and an anti-government mass protest movement would merge in the most unlikely alliance, with each side's victory attributed, in some way, to the other.

The EDSA revolution was a win for People Power and People Power was a win for RAM. Marcos fled into exile and died three years later.

ADDENDUM.

Between November 1986 (nine months after the People Power revolution) and July 1987, there were six military coup attempts against Aquino. One of them (July 1986) involved the ill-conceived seizure of the Manila Hotel which ended, without bloodshed, after a day-and-a half. Another coup plot (November 1986) implicated the defence minister, Juan Ponce Enrile and RAM officers. Previously, they were pivotal to the success of the People Power revolution, but now they were accused of plotting the overthrow of Aquino as a counterblow to her efforts to reduce the role of the military in government. Enrile was sacked. These military rebels were also highly critical of the government's 'mishandling' of the communist insurgency. The coup attempt was thwarted.

The other three plots in January, April, and July 1987,

were low-level, poorly planned, and badly executed. Dismissed as military 'adventurism', they were quickly quashed with little or no violence. It was the sixth, and final coup attempt against Aquino (August 1987) that was the most worrying for the government. It lasted only one day and involved coordinated attacks on various targets. Fifty-three people died and more than 200, mostly civilians, were wounded.

Although Enrile and RAM had played a key role in the overthrow of Marcos and Aquino's assumption of power, disillusionment with the new government quickly emerged. The military renegades had triggered popular backing and had forced Marcos from power, but they had grown used to the military's encroachment into civil government under Marcos's rule – it was something they secretly countenanced and coveted – and now, having helped secure Aquino's ascendency, the 'RAM Boys' believed they deserved to be rewarded with an even greater share of decision-making powers. In particular, they wanted carriage of an intensified anti-communist crackdown. Aquino moved to do the opposite. Right-wing military elements despaired at their loss of power and opposed many of the new government's reform policies, particularly its handling of the communist insurgency. A rapacious series of conspiracies and power-grab attempts hobbled the Aquino Government from its earliest days.

POSTSCRIPT.

The Filipino people had lived for 21 years under a system

of government so cynically and repeatedly modified and manipulated to entrench one man in power, that they were left with nothing but a constitutional shambles, a mishmash of rules so befitting an autocracy that democracy was left gasping for life. Marcos robbed the people of their birthright so completely and for so long that Filipinos were oblivious of a non-Marcos world where the choice of government was theirs to make, and where freedoms were enjoyed not denied. It had become a dystopian world where Marcos and the presidency were inter-changeable; they had come to mean the same thing. Under Marcos, the Philippine constitution was unique in the world – it was custom tailored for just one man.

SIX

THE DEPOSING OF A DICTATOR.

To watch a revolution, I had the window of choice.

Not only could I see the presidential palace where Marcos, his family, friends, and trusted aides were hunkered down, protected by combat ready troops, but I could also hear the distant sound of small arms fire.

My window was on the eighth-floor office of the international newsagency, United Press International (UPI), and it opened wide enough for me to lean out with my long-cord telephone and capture the sounds of Manila's People Power revolution.

As a foreign correspondent for half a dozen national broadcasters and several newspapers, I found the window to be an invaluable observation post to an almost bloodless four-day coup. Hundreds of thousands of Filipinos, actively encouraged by the Catholic church, had poured into the streets to protect rebel soldiers in open revolt against the brutal, corrupt, and despotic 21-year rule of President Ferdinand Marcos.

From my vantage point, I could place the phone on the window ledge and lean out as far as the cord would allow me and report live to overseas radio stations with the sounds of battle in the background. It made for great radio. At key moments, over those four days, BBC listeners heard live gunfire between rebel and government troops; listeners to Canada's CBC heard me describe a helicopter rocket attack on the presidential palace; and when President Marcos fled Manila in a US military helicopter that flew directly over the building, listeners to Germany's Deutsche Welle heard the whoosh-whoosh-whoosh of the rotor blades.

What I could not see from the window were the hundreds of thousands of anguished and angry Filipinos who were protesting several kilometres away in the biggest mass protests the nation had ever seen. The people had blocked the entire eight lanes of Manila's main thoroughfare, Epifanio de los Santos Avenue (EDSA) where rebel troops had barricaded themselves in two adjacent camps: Camp Crame, the headquarters of the paramilitary Philippine Constabulary, and Camp Aguinaldo, the headquarters of the Armed Forces of the Philippines.

The rebel troops – who numbered in their hundreds on the first day – were members and followers of the Reform the Armed Forces Movement (RAM) whose plan for a pre-dawn attack on the presidential palace had been leaked, and at least 15 of their fellow plotters had been arrested. The quick, surgically precise military coup had been thwarted, and as more renegade officers and troops joined the besieged rebel officers and soldiers in their military camp boltholes, it was clear that the failed coup had become a mutiny. No longer was it a group of plotters whose goal was to remove the president; it was a group of military renegades intent on changing the government.

Their numbers had grown considerably, for this wasn't some amateurish quest for power, it was a rebellion led by the defence minister, Juan Ponce Enrile, and the Armed Forces vice chief of staff, Lt. Gen. Fidel Ramos. Enrile, who had long harboured leadership ambitions, and in recent years had fallen out of favour with the Armed Forces chief of staff, Gen. Fabian Ver, encouraged the early clandestine efforts of disillusioned RAM officers.

Enrile's aide-de-camp, Col. Gregorio Honasan was a leader of RAM, and many other RAM members were among Enrile's most loyal officers. Enrile's 20-year allegiance to Marcos had been under strain; now it had snapped. Less than three years earlier, in July 1983, in a very public display of his disenchantment, possibly distrust of his defence minister, Marcos revoked Enrile's power to give orders to the military, effectively removing him from Marcos's all-important chain of command. It was a demotion, and a humiliating public display that Marcos's previous rock-hard confidence in Enrile had waned.

Ver took Enrile's place in the chain of command and that made him the second most powerful person in the Philippines. Marcos also stripped Enrile of his responsibility for the Integrated National Police and gave it to himself. In the same year, 1983, Marcos withdrew some crucial police powers from Gen. Ramos and transferred them to Gen. Ver. In the historical, protracted power play between the nation's two most senior military chiefs, it was no surprise that Ver, best known for his unflinchingly loyalty to Marcos, won the president's imprimatur.

Ver was a zealot who had shown year after year through his fawning and deferential character, that he was singularly focused on winning and retaining the president's approval. Marcos, in turn, maintained his unflinching support for Ver who, in October 1984, took a leave of absence after being charged as a conspirator in the assassination of former senator, and fierce Marcos critic, Benigno Aquino. The vice chief of staff, Gen. Ramos took his place.

Fourteen months later, Ver was acquitted and within hours Marcos reinstated him to the nation's most powerful military post, despite allegations of unprofessionalism, incompetence, corruption, and rampant abuses in the Armed Forces. Marcos had chosen loyalty and unquestioning obedience, over competency. Patronage was preferred to performance and professionalism. Ver had created a powerful, elite military force within the Armed Forces, specifically to protect and serve Marcos, not the people. In the process, he had alienated a large body of professionally trained officers. To them, the Armed Forces of Ver's making did not represent the nation's soldiers, and they did not serve the people. They had signed up to be defenders of the people, not the protectors of Marcos.

Ramos, a US West Point graduate, respected and popular among his men, was resentful, but most of all he was worried about the military's reputation and the country's future with Ver back in control. In speeches, Ramos vowed to restore the military's tarnished image, eliminate human rights abuses, raise troop morale, and improve training standards. It was the same sentiment, the same set of goals, that had inspired the formation of RAM among dissatisfied and disaffected officers, many from the Philippine Military Academy. Internal dissention within the Armed Forces spread and grew louder following Aquino's assassination. The reform-minded officers were rankled that the assassination had tarnished the reputation of the Armed Forces because Aquino's killing was widely seen as a political vendetta, and the assassin was most likely a soldier. More particularly, RAM believed the killing had unfairly besmirched the characters of the reform minded officers. It was another issue the soldiers added to their growing list of grievances.

What they found most galling was the fact that so many professional officers had been overlooked, reassigned, denied promotion, or even dismissed in favour of Marcos's hand chosen, fiercely loyal senior commanders. Under Marcos, the Armed Forces had not only become politicised, but the military had effectively become another tier of government with senior officers occupying key public utility and public sector posts. Sometimes, the purpose of their promotion to top civilian posts was to entrench Marcos's domination of key government ministries, and sometimes it was an unmistakeable reward for loyalty: a prestigious, high-level, civilian posting which became, for so many generals, the source of readily tapped wealth and power.

This blatant 'corruption in the ranks' was one of many

deficiencies highlighted in a photocopied RAM pamphlet that had been furtively distributed months before the coup attempt. It listed RAM's objectives: 'Reform the service; foster nationalism and patriotism; fight against corruption and criminal activities; (and tackle) the problem of favouritism, incompetence, and corruption in senior leadership.'

They were noble goals, but RAM's stated objectives were hard to reconcile with troubling accounts I had heard about nefarious activities linked to RAM. Rumours and unverified accounts of human rights abuses, of night-time 'hit squads' eliminating suspected communists were too numerous to ignore, but almost impossible to verify. As commander in chief, Marcos could oversee the most senior military ranks – officers he could dismiss, anoint and appoint – but beneath the military hierarchy, RAM's self-assured officers operated in a barely hidden shadowy world of impertinent defiance, accountable only to themselves. RAM had propagated an image of respectability; democracy loving white knights committed to restoring order and decency. To me, their commitment was questionable; their motives were selfish. These were ambitious men with barely concealed self-serving agendas. It was self-promotion, status, and a lust for power that motivated them, especially the most senior RAM leaders who gravitated to Enrile, hoping to ride his coattails to power.

Clandestinely, the 'RAM boys', as they were called, organised, enlisted supporters, and planned a three-pronged military attack on the presidential palace in late December 1985, only to delay it when Marcos announced, in November, plans to hold presidential elections in February 1986. Soon afterwards, RAM and their fellow conspirators, settled on a new coup date – 23 February – after the election.

Marcos had hoped the election on 7 February would be a vindication of his past two decades in office, and a popular validation of his rule; an endorsement for him to continue in office for another term. The opposite happened. In the hearts of Filipinos, and in the eyes of world, Marcos cheated his way to a pyrrhic victory.

Roundly condemned for widespread fraud, intimidation, and voting irregularities, the election was universally dismissed as a sham, and Marcos's subsequent proclamation as the winner by the government dominated parliament, was disregarded, and disputed by the increasingly belligerent opposition. Huge protest demonstrations followed, bigger than any held in the pre-election campaign, and a nationwide boycott of pro-government companies had an immediate impact on the economy. Plans were announced for a nationwide strike. Filipinos were angry and increasingly distrustful of a regime that had denied them so much and given them so little. Defiance had replaced docility in the middle class, and large sections of the once politically neutral business community were eager for change.

In the background – unknown to most Filipinos – simmered an even greater, more immediate challenge to Marcos's survival: a military coup of daring audacity. The RAM officers could see for themselves the public's growing anti-government sentiment: the Aquino assassination had galvanized the nation, and the exoneration of the alleged killers only fired their anger.

In the three years since Aquino's murder, the number of demonstrations had increased. They got louder and they got bigger, and they drew to their ranks angry Filipinos from all sectors of society. The election was yet more proof that under Marcos, free and fair polls could never be held. For years, demonstrations for change had been the people's only recourse. And every time police and soldiers used brute force and intimidation to control the growing anger. But what was happening in the streets now was different; these were the biggest street protests to date. Surely Marcos could see what was happening.

The successful boycott of pro-Marcos businesses, and plans for a national strike, were further proof that the march for change had become unstoppable. The chant was for Marcos to go, but was he listening? Manila was a city alive with rumours, fuelled by the increasingly bold 'underground' media that in recent years had risen to the surface. People spoke of feeling apprehensive and anxious. If you were going to stage a coup, this was the time to do it. RAM could see and sense the nation's anger.

The planned December coup had been put on hold until late February, but behind the scenes rumours circulated of 'information sharing' and 'strategic planning' among RAM officers and sympathetic opposition leaders. Secrecy was tight and, at the time, little was learned. Later, it emerged that the coup plotters envisaged the overthrow of Marcos, a possible year-long transitional civilian-military administration, followed by presidential and local elections.

Then, it all fell apart. The conspiracy was discovered, 15 plotters were arrested, and the coup was aborted. Government intelligence agents, aware that the coup attempt had been sanctioned by Enrile, were quick to alert Ver of the defence minister's culpability. On hearing rumours of his imminent arrest, a frightened Enrile fled his home, but only after he phoned his co-conspirators. The renegade colonels and their men stopped long enough to retrieve a hidden cache of weapons and ammunition before they sought refuge at suburban Camp Aguinaldo, the general headquarters of the Armed Forces, and joined other disaffected soldiers and Enrile. Soon, Enrile was to convince the Armed Forces vice chief of staff, Ramos, to join him.

Not only had the rebels palace attack been thwarted, but tanks and soldiers had been assembled in the palace grounds to defend the president. There were reports that government troops were preparing to attack. They didn't. It was a stand-off. The coup had failed, but the rebellion had begun.

Many, if not most Filipinos, responded to news of the insurrection with puzzlement and incredulity. For years, they had believed Enrile and Ramos to be unswerving Marcos loyalists. It was an image promoted and perpetuated by the government press office and the pro-government media. Enrile was the chief civilian enforcer of a dictatorship pretending to be a democracy. For years, he was the ruthless, unquestioning implementor of strict presidential decrees restricting civilian liberties, with limitless powers to arrest and detain government critics.

Enrile's presidential ambitions were well known but

now appeared shaky, if not totally out of reach. In recent years he had lost the confidence of Marcos, and his loyalty was questionable due to his links to RAM. Now, any pretence was gone; his coup plot had been discovered and an arrest order had forced him and his co-conspirators to barricade themselves in a military camp.

Enrile was afraid. He feared for his life. It was then, after all those years of faithful, merciless service to Marcos, that Enrile claimed to have had an epiphany. 'I searched my conscience, and I found I could no longer serve the president,' he said, announcing his resignation from his military camp bolthole. Enrile turned to the people he had so long held under the yoke of authoritarianism and appealed for them to come to his aid. It is beyond dispute that on this day, Enrile's strongest motivation was self-preservation; the old days of self-centred grandstanding were over, at least for the moment.

The public opinion of Ramos, however, was divided. Some Filipinos regarded him highly. Others couldn't reconcile Ramos's calm, professional aura with the fact that he led the Philippine Constabulary, possibly the worst human rights offender in the Armed Forces. It was with the approval and direction of Ramos that the arbitrary arrest and wilful jailing of thousands of suspected communists, left-wing sympathisers, and often innocent civilians occurred. Nicknamed 'steady Eddie' due to his unflappable nature, Ramos was an urbane, unassuming man, who enjoyed tittering notoriety for chomping on an unlit cigar. He was efficient, non-controversial, and to all outward appearances, a loyal Marcos man. But Ramos was also West Point trained and believed in civilian pre-eminence over the military. His loyalty was to the commander in chief, the *position*, not the commander in chief, the *man*.

It puzzled me how Ramos managed to escape the opprobrium of being associated with misbehaving soldiers under his command. Perhaps it was his understated mannerisms, his well-groomed public image, and his open demeanour that shielded Ramos from the many well-documented human rights abuses carried out by elements of the Philippine Constabulary. At the eleventh hour of an intelligence-porous and shabbily executed coup plot, Ramos did the same as Enrile: he admitted his long-term culpability in empowering Marcos and declared his readiness to atone for his mistakes.

Now, it seemed, ordinary Filipinos were expected to embrace the defectors and forgive them for all those years of institutionalised oppression and militarisation. Wasn't it more likely that military renegades had staged an unsuccessful coup, and had turned to the people for support, desperate to survive?

After all these years, Filipinos instantly embraced any sign of dissention in the Armed Forces as a chink in the Marcos armour, and so the people turned to RAM as their unlikely saviours. Support was immediate. At that moment, when the end of Marcos seemed possible, maybe inevitable, Filipinos could sense victory; they had no time for any doubts about RAM's true intent, and little reason to question their motivation. Right now, what was most important was the ousting of Marcos, and RAM and the protestors wanted the same thing.

Sequestered in the three-storey defence ministry

building at Camp Aguinaldo, flanked by Uzi-carrying officers in battle fatigues, Enrile and Ramos held a press conference to announce the only coup d'état in modern Philippine history. Sitting side-by-side before a clutch of local and foreign reporters, Enrile spoke first. Dressed in jeans and sneakers, with a jacket pulled over a bullet-proof vest, he no longer dressed like a politician. Instead, he was a coup leader, and he looked the part.

Until a few hours earlier, he had been the country's longest serving defence minister. Now he called on fellow cabinet ministers to join the revolt. 'I cannot in my conscience recognise the president as the commander in chief of the Armed Forces and I am appealing to the other members of the cabinet to heed the will of the people expressed during the last elections,' he said, referring to the bitterly fought and contested presidential election 16 days earlier. Then, in a direct appeal for public support, he added: 'Our loyalty is to the constitution and the country…you are welcome to join us.'

Then, it was the turn of Ramos. Gone was the military uniform. In its place was a safari suit and running shoes. His defection had been essential. His credibility, authority, and respect gave legitimacy to the uprising; in the following days, his prominence and leadership convinced many wavering troops to join him.

'The president of 1986 is not the president to whom we dedicated our service,' he said, speaking into the bank of microphones. 'It is clear that (Marcos) no longer is the able and capable commander in chief that we count upon. He has put his personal family interest above the interest of the people. We do not consider President Marcos as now being a duly constituted authority.'

A news blackout quickly followed. With most television and radio stations either government controlled or owned by Marcos cronies, it was left to the Catholic church-run, Radio Veritas (Radio Truth) to broadcast rolling news coverage to a stunned and mesmerised nation. Live radio coverage of a military insurrection made for compelling listening. The radio station enjoyed strong popular support, and its repeated, increasingly strident public appeals, persuaded thousands of people to go to EDSA. By their sheer numbers, the protestors could show their support for the troops and, if necessary, protect them. They brought boxes of food and crates of soft drink. Nuns formed food brigades and handed out sandwiches. To them, the rebel soldiers' cause had become the people's cause, and that made it a national cause. But, in fact, this was mostly a Manila-centric revolt involving the traditional political parties and organisations, and the middle class. Left-wing organisations and the communists, who had boycotted the election, were effectively isolated and marginalised during the four-day revolt. EDSA was the epicentre of the people's revolt. Elsewhere in the city, life carried on with an air of tense normality. Several times, I jumped in a taxi and asked to be taken to EDSA. Only when we got near did I have to get out and walk because of the crowds.

The civilian-rebel alliance was an unlikely one. Over the past two decades, the military had come to be seen as the instrument of state abuse, oppression, and harassment under the Marcos Government. It was the armed forces that had kept Marcos in power all those years, and the idea that a breakaway band of rebel soldiers could possibly be their liberators, and not their oppressors, was difficult to comprehend. But now, animosities were put aside to fight a common foe.

It surprised many Filipinos to learn that an anti-Marcos sentiment in the upper ranks of the Armed Forces had been growing for several years. Among some in the officer corps, simmering frustration had boiled over into outright anger. The excesses of the martial law years, coupled with the recent and widely criticised presidential election, were evidence of Marcos's desperation to hang onto power, no matter the cost.

One week earlier, hundreds of thousands of supporters of Corazon 'Cory' Aquino had crowded into Manila's sprawling Luneta Park to 'crown' her the winner of the contentious 7 February presidential election, in angry defiance of the 'official' result which declared Marcos the winner. They cheered her call for a nationwide non-violent civil disobedience campaign and pledged to support her call to boycott 'crony' pro-Marcos banks, industries, and businesses. Within days, heavy and sustained withdrawals were recorded in seven 'crony' banks, business slumped in pro-Marcos stores and corporations, and advertising and consumer boycotts of pro-government media and retail companies triggered a sharp decline in sales and in share market stocks.

RAM saw the anti-Marcos protesters as their salvation, for they believed a mass show of popular support for the rebellious soldiers could be enough to convince Marcos to relinquish power, without triggering bloody civil unrest.

As for Aquino and her supporters, the undeniable consequence and benefit of an 'alliance of convenience' with RAM could be the toppling of the Marcos Government. But from the start, Aquino knew she had to keep her distance from the coup leaders. She couldn't jeopardise the long sought-after goal of her supporters – the ousting of the Marcos Government – by aligning herself too closely with the military rebels, and thus be seen as a military proxy, the acceptable civilian figurehead of a military junta.

Enrile and Ramos knew they needed the support of the powerful Catholic Church if their nascent coup was to survive, let alone succeed. Three hours before they publicly announced their resignations, both Enrile and Ramos made separate, private telephone calls to the influential archbishop of Manila, Cardinal Jaime Sin, seeking his backing, and hopefully, his public endorsement. Enrile pleaded for help. 'In one hour's time, we are going to die. The president's men are coming to arrest us,' he implored the church leader. Moments later, Ramos telephoned the cardinal. They were in imminent danger, he told Sin. If the cardinal could help them make a stand against Marcos, then he could guarantee key military support to oust Marcos.

Three hours after their desperate calls to the cardinal, Enrile and Ramos resigned. And two hours after that, Cardinal Sin broadcast over Radio Veritas his support for the coup and called on the people to mobilise, to go to the streets, and back the uprising. 'Leave your homes now…I ask you to support Mr Enrile and General Ramos. Give them food if you like, they are our friends…I am calling on all our people to support our two good friends…Show your solidarity, your support in this very crucial period.'

Cardinal Sin's endorsement and, if possible, his blessing is what Enrile and Ramos had hoped for and needed, and that's what they got. The cardinal supported the rebels and condemned the government. That was his message. It was final. Incontrovertible. Irreversible. It was a landmark address, a highpoint in the tense, fractious church-state relations that had worsened in recent years – particularly after the assassination three years earlier of Aquino's husband and leading Marcos critic, Benigno. The schism had become a rupture, and now it was a chasm. In an overwhelmingly Catholic country, cowed by years of brutal authoritarianism, Cardinal Sin's call for mass mobilisation was enthusiastically answered by hundreds of thousands of Filipinos who ultimately spilled into the streets of the capital.

Ninety minutes after Cardinal Sin's radio appeal, Marcos appeared on government television. 'Stop this stupidity and surrender so that we may negotiate,' he appealed to the plotters. In hindsight, Marcos's hesitancy, or reluctance to quickly quash the revolt on the first night of the ill-prepared revolt, was a miscalculation. By failing to act, Marcos had lost his military option. It was obvious, as more and more people joined the EDSA human barricades – with the encouragement and the blessing of the church – that Marcos could not risk any military action that could possibly see thousands of civilian casualties.

Overnight, as they monitored military radio transmissions, Ramos and his renegade troops scrambled to consolidate their numbers. Undermanned and ill-prepared, the rebels knew that an attack then by government forces would have crushed the revolt. It didn't come. Instead, what came next, turned out to be a game changer. Ramos knew that unless the rebels could persuade other soldiers to defect, the rebellion was doomed. So he devised a one-on-one psychological pitch – a hearts and minds appeal – to government soldiers to switch sides. It was a simple top-to-bottom cascading appeal down the ranks imploring soldiers to join the uprising. Ramos said he would call military commanders, and it was the job of young lieutenants and captains to call their military classmates and friends. Their wives, in turn, would call the wives of soldiers thought to be pro-government to convince their husbands to defect. Even parents of rebel soldiers were enlisted to call parents whose sons were pro-government or whose allegiance was under strain.

Support the people, not Marcos, was the plea. And the growing defections and vows of support showed the 'appeal to the heart' was working. Both Enrile and Ramos secured the backing of several provincial and regional commanders. But many of these battalions were stationed in regions well away from the capital and would have no immediate impact on the unfolding events in Manila.

At a midnight appearance before several thousand supporters, Ramos told them: 'This is not a coup d'état. It's a revolution of the people.' Marcos countered at 1 a.m. on government television and presented 'proof' of the plot: a captured senior rebel defector. Then, at 3 a.m. it was the turn of Cardinal Sin. He told Radio Veritas listeners that the revolt had his full support. In fact, he hardened his position. He did not plea, instead he warned Marcos not to use force against the demonstrators. Unbeknown to most, Marcos had on several occasions ordered that the demonstrators be dispersed, but repeatedly his demand was ignored or deliberately stalled by the metropolitan police commander. With each delay the crowd grew bigger.

Logistically and strategically, it made little sense for the undermanned rebel force to be occupying adjoining military camps and Enrile readily agreed to join Ramos in the more easily defendable Camp Crame, the headquarters of the Philippine Constabulary, on the afternoon of the second day. Hemmed in by thousands of unruly, shoving supporters, Enrile and his armed military escorts formed a single line and pushed their way along an open human channel, formed by the linked arms of their supporters, including habit-wearing nuns.

Hours later, and more than a kilometre away, thousands of other protestors blocked the advance of armoured units. An angry stand-off of several hours ensued before the soldiers withdrew. Before daybreak, the rebels reported the defection of one helicopter division, while government sources said tank and troop reinforcements had taken up positions in the grounds of the presidential palace.

The conflicting claims, counter claims, rumours, and speculation left the protestors confused and jittery. For the soldiers, their loyalty was sorely tested. With its continuous, minute-by-minute live broadcasts, Radio Veritas had successfully cajoled more and more people to come to EDSA to support, aid, and protect the rebels. Some marched from outer suburbs behind a sea of banners, shouting, chanting, imploring others to join them. EDSA was choked with anxious protestors and their ever-growing numbers stretched as far as I could see. The daytime people's 'rally' of solidarity with the rebels became a night-time mass 'vigil' to protect the rebel soldiers, still only numbering in their hundreds.

Determined to stay the night, protestors arrived with plastic sheets and tarpaulins, camping stools and pillows. Food and drinks were brought from home. Makeshift kitchens were set up wherever space could be found. The atmosphere was festive. There were entire families, poor and rich, together; children of all ages; college and university students; nuns, priests, and seminarians; professionals, office workers and labourers; and large numbers of middle-class Filipinos, who in recent years had become more and more strident in their criticism of Marcos.

History was being made in the streets of Manila and my wife, Bet, and three of her friends joined the protestors mingling outside Camp Crame. 'I have to go,' Bet was adamant when she rang. 'It's up to all of us. This is our chance to get rid of Marcos. If they bomb us. We could die, and I'm prepared to die,' she said, referring to persistent rumours that the Air Force had been ordered to disperse the protesters.

There was no way I could dissuade her from joining the EDSA rally. I imagined planes strafing the demonstrators. Stay on the outskirts of the crowd, I advised her. Get near a wall. Lie on the ground. Find whatever cover you can. If there's firing, cover your head. And if there's tear gas, wet your towel and cover your mouth. Then, as an afterthought, I added the rather pathetic advice: if there's panic or a stampede, get out of there.

Bet reported the gates of Camp Crame were festooned with banners, placards, and yellow ribbons. Protestors, who had climbed onto the imposing camp gates and clung to the steel bars of the surrounding fence, shouted slogans, and slowly waved fluttering banners and flags. Directly in front of them, on top of hastily erected metal scaffolding, a rebel lieutenant addressed the crowd. Armed soldiers peered through the camp gates, cradling machine guns and rocket propelled grenades. The atmosphere was outwardly relaxed, inwardly tense.

Strangers greeted each other as long-lost friends, and real friends found each other in the crush of people. It was a day of common cause, sometimes joyful when they chanted well-rehearsed slogans, and sometimes fearful when rumours swept the crowd that tanks were approaching. The much-feared air attack never eventuated, but Bet does recall the moment when the crowd fell silent. The ground began to tremble and there was the deep rumbling sound of approaching tanks. Instead of fleeing or seeking shelter behind the knee-high sandbag barricade, some protestors moved around and stood in front of the barrier, locked arms, and dared the tanks to move forward.

The tanks did move forward, but at walking pace, then they slowed and stopped. Moments later, the tanks turned right and barged through a wire fence and onto open ground on the side of the highway. The tank crews emerged, somewhat bewildered, and sat on the ground or stood near their silenced tanks, apparently awaiting orders, which came an hour or so later. Return to barracks.

And they did, to the cheers of the crowd. Not a shot had been fired.

As the voice of the Catholic Church, Radio Veritas engendered unwavering support among Filipinos. Its methods were novel and spontaneous. It repeatedly appealed to listeners to bring food, medicines, and supplies to the rebel troops. Radio Veritas opened its microphone to both the military rebel leaders, who appealed to wavering soldiers to join the revolt, and to senior anti-Marcos politicians, who rallied civilians to the barricades. It was a momentous occasion. Ramos proclaimed it was the first time anywhere in the world that a civilian-run radio station was being used to relay military orders and to convey instructions to military units in the field.

Listeners to Radio Veritas also rang in to advise the radio's audience about troop movements in the direction of EDSA. It was like a morning radio traffic report, but instead of car movements and traffic jams, listeners were told about approaching tanks and armoured personnel vehicles – how many there were, which street, how fast they were moving, and whether soldiers were following behind.

With this tank movement information, Radio Veritas called on listeners to rush to the scene and form 'human barricades' with their bodies and hastily assemble barricades with whatever they could find. 'Commandeer buses,' advised one caller. 'Line them up across the road and then throw away the ignition keys.' Elsewhere, protestors gathered behind established barricades of abandoned vehicles, mounds of tyres, rocks, bricks, discarded furniture, and placards. Chants of 'Co-ry, Co-ry' were followed by cries of 'Laban' (fight) and the protestors flashed the opposition's signature 'L' sign, by extending their thumbs horizontally and pointing upwards with their index finger.

Everywhere, were yellow ribbons, the colour of protest in the Philippines, and a sea of placards and banners demanding Marcos's ouster. The blow-by-blow broadcasts of Radio Veritas had become indispensable listening on the front lines. Portable loudspeakers blared the radio's non-stop reports, commentary, appeals, and advice. Among the crowd, transistor radios could be heard on the exact same frequency. Radio Veritas had become a symbol of defiance, but also a target to be silenced.

Before sunrise on the second day of the coup, government troops destroyed the Radio's main transmission tower in nearby Bulacan, knocking out its provincial broadcasts. A stand-by transmitter allowed Radio Veritas to continue its broadcasts to Luzon, including Manila, but it too failed later that day. On orders of Cardinal Sin, Radio Veritas quickly found a secret broadcasting location and soon after midnight resumed broadcasts under the moniker Radyo Bandido.

When not on the streets, I reported from the UPI office near Manila Bay, overlooking the presidential palace. Regularly, I ventured out to EDSA and other 'hot spots' to tape my reports and record interviews. With no mobile phones or laptop computers, live on-the-scene reports were impossible unless you could gain access to someone's land line in a nearby shop or home, and only if the owner allowed you to make an international call. In many cases, a cash offer didn't help, and even if the person did take the money, there was no certainty the phone call would get through.

From the outset, this coup had nothing to do with brute force. Instead of bloody battles with casualties on both sides, this coup was a test of wills, of stubborn defiance, bravado, and above all an assumption, shared by both sides, that they could count on the support of the armed forces.

Marcos, his family, his omnipresent 'yes' men, and his inner circle of political allies, were confined inside the presidential palace protected by a bevy of elite soldiers. Enrile had the loyalty of fellow defectors, but he was a civilian, and he didn't have the same inherent military support base enjoyed by his co-plotter, General Ramos. Ultimately, the success of the revolt would be determined by allegiances yet to be formed.

Over the course of the next 48 hours, the generals closest to Marcos found that their orders often were delayed, countermanded, ignored, or simply dismissed as impractical, dangerous, or criminal. At one point, without warning, two air force planes buzzed Camp Crame and roared low over the heads of the EDSA crowd. A wave of fear swept over the demonstrators. Were they going to be strafed?

Personal appeals went out over Radio Veritas from Air Force wives and their children that set hairs tingling on the back of my neck. I recall one wife, in a wavering voice, make an impassioned plea to her husband, an Air Force officer and pilot. She announced his name and gave his rank. 'I just want him to know that I'm here at EDSA with our children, and if the planes fire on us we could all be killed.' Then a little girl was heard to say: 'Daddy, don't do it. Come home.' It was heart-wrenching.

There were similar calls from spouses and family members. Young children of government soldiers pleaded on Radio Veritas for 'daddy' to join them at EDSA. Parents urged their soldier sons to defect and join the revolt. The most decisive turning point for the rebels came on the third day when the pilots of seven helicopter gunships of the 15th Air Wing defied orders to bomb Camp Crame. Instead, they flew in formation and landed inside the camp at dawn where they were met with cheers and hugs from the rebel troops and the coup leaders. Later that day, three of the helicopters strafed the nearby government controlled Villamor airbase and destroyed five helicopters on the ground.

The Air Force was in rebel hands. The Navy defected that same morning. The Army and the Police were on the verge of outright defection, according to Ramos. He told a press conference, military commanders in 40 provinces in all 12 regions, and in the four districts of Manila, were on the rebels' side.

Many of the most dramatic confrontations occurred on the streets approaching EDSA where tanks and armoured personnel carriers were stopped by thousands of protestors behind hurriedly assembled roadblocks of cars, trucks, and rubble. More than once, protesting nuns moved out from behind the barricades, lined up, linked arms, and knelt in prayer in front of the approaching tanks, forcing them to slow and then stop, just metres away. Prayers were said. Flowers were offered to the soldiers, many of whom wore no name badges and had removed their insignias.

On each occasion, protestors surged towards the tanks, surrounded them, and tried desperately and frantically to coax the soldiers to join them, or at least return to barracks. The protestors chanted, some wept. They demanded to know why the soldiers were trying to suppress a popular revolt. Some sang the protest song *Bayan Ko* (My Country) and everyone, it seemed, appealed to the soldiers to show loyalty to the people, not to a dictator. Every confrontation ended the same way – either the tanks and soldiers turned around, or they refused orders to break through the protestor's ranks. Some soldiers openly supported the demonstrators.

With ill-discipline, disobedience, or outright rebellion in many sections of the armed forces, Marcos's hold on power had dramatically loosened. From Washington, the White House questioned the 'credibility and legitimacy' of the Marcos Government in an obvious attempt to distance itself from a once favoured ally. In a desperate bid, Marcos offered the rebels amnesty. It was rejected immediately by the increasingly confident coup leaders who were buoyed by overnight rumours falsely claiming that Marcos and his family had fled the country. They celebrated prematurely. Some mistakenly proclaimed victory.

In the morning, however, Marcos put a decisive end to the speculation by appearing with his family on government television. He announced his intention to be inaugurated president the following day and then, in a forlorn, desperate assertion of power, he declared a 6 p.m. to 6 a.m. curfew. It was never obeyed because it was never enforced.

Marcos's 'proof of life' press conference to disprove

overnight rumours that he had fled the country, left his critics demoralised, but only for a short time. Flanked by his wife, Imelda, and his three children (his son, Bongbong in army fatigues), Marcos appeared to waver between agitation and anger and, for the first time I could recall, he appeared to lose control of his own press conference.

In an extraordinary live television exchange with Gen. Ver, who seemed to be itching for a fight, Marcos appeared flummoxed when the normally unflappable Ver angrily remonstrated. It was a heated exchange, an argument without the shouting. Ver approached the seated Marcos and assertively recommended that Marcos order an attack on Camp Crame. Ver did what no one had ever seen before – he badgered the president. Two F5 planes were at that moment circling above the besieged camp, Ver said. All that they were waiting for was the president's order to strike. It was a surprising show of assertiveness and frustration from the Philippines most senior military official, and the president's most loyal defender and supporter. It was perceived by many as a reflection of the agitation and the confusion welling up in the ranks.

Marcos's response was stern. 'My order is not to attack. No, no, no.' Heavy weapons may be necessary at some time, Marcos said, but for the moment only small weapons should be used. Then, in mid-sentence, as he ordered that the demonstrators be dispersed, the unthinkable happened – the television went blank. The signal had been cut by anti-Marcos troops.

It was a profound moment. Here was the first-ever glaringly obvious sign in more than 20 years that Marcos and his henchmen no longer could control the dissemination of news in the Philippines. His message had been scuttled, sabotaged in a rebel attack on the government's own television station. The blank television screen was the harbinger of worse to come – his forced exile, less than 36 hours later.

The channel resumed broadcasts soon afterwards, only this time it was not Marcos on screen, but opposition leaders who appealed to all military officers and soldiers not to support Marcos 'because he is no longer president of the Philippines'. As a journalist, I remember thinking this was a milestone moment. Television, one of the most essential instruments of power, had suddenly been ripped from the man who needed it most, and whose survival depended on it. And the entire nation had seen it happen. It was a pivotal moment. The 'message' was no longer Marcos's to monopolise, massage, and manipulate. The man who had led the news bulletins every day, night after night, was gone from their television screens, or so they thought.

Marcos's power was ebbing away, and so was his health. At the height of the insurrection, Marcos – who suffered from a kidney disease – unexpectedly and regularly disappeared for hours at a time. His years of ill-health, once hidden and denied, were increasingly obvious and confirmed by long, inexplicable absences from public life. He was resting or sleeping, we were told. Not only was Marcos's physical stamina waning, but his increasing powerlessness to assert control over large sections of the military, and the police, made him especially vulnerable. In his final 24 hours in the Philippines, Marcos suffered two glaring indignities that were a portent to his ignominious demise: a rocket attack, and a shambolic 'inauguration'.

With his political power and prestige diminishing, and unable to rely on his once bloated military machine, Marcos found himself besieged in the presidential palace with at least 50 heavily armed soldiers protecting him. Hundreds of marines were on full alert in the palace grounds. But even in his palace, Marcos wasn't safe. In an ominous display of power, the rebels ordered a helicopter gunship fire on the palace.

From my UPI window observation ledge, I watched the helicopter slowly rise above a swirling downdraught, it hovered for a few seconds, and then it fired a single rocket into one wing of the presidential palace. It then banked and flew off. Dust and smoke billowed from the building, but I was too far away to hear any sounds of gunfire. The damage was superficial. But the symbolism was undeniable. Behind the bravado and bluster, Marcos's hold on power was crumbling by the hour.

24 February was the last night Marcos would spend in the presidential palace. Wearing a denim jacket, and his son, 'Bongbong', in army fatigues, Marcos was joined by his wife and their two daughters for a televised address, shortly after 8 p.m. Twice in 24 hours, 'Bongbong' Marcos had appeared in army fatigues. Obviously, Marcos's son wanted to be noticed, and being by his father's side in army fatigues was the battle-ready image he wanted the public to see. Up to now, he had eschewed public scrutiny. The young Marcos had dressed for the occasion; he had dressed to impress. He wore military fatigues and a grim expression, and the image he conveyed – of a loyal son's devotion and defiance – was exactly what he wanted.

Condemning the two coup leaders, a furious Marcos

claimed they intended to assassinate him and his wife, even though Enrile had told the media the previous day: 'There is no intention on the part of anybody here to harm him or his family.' Then Marcos warned that Enrile and Ramos were planning to set up a 'third force' to take control of the country. Once more, he appealed to the people to support 'the legally elected' government. Marcos had the dubious foresight to bring with him a copy of the day's newspaper. He held it up, pointed to it, and pathetically declared: 'At 8.20 in the evening of the 24th of February, I am here.'

Even Marcos realised that his credibility, his believability, had sunk so low that unless he brought the day's newspaper, and indicated the date, vast numbers of Filipinos would never believe him. Afterall, he had shown himself in the past to be a master media manipulator.

'We have no intention of going abroad,' Macros then assured the nation. 'We will defend the republic until the last breath of life and until the last drop of blood in our bodies.' He lied. Even as he spoke, behind-the-scenes preparations and negotiations for his, and his family's departure were well underway. His 'inauguration' the next day was an elaborate, cynical ruse.

Right up to the very last moment, Marcos deceived the nation in a calculated, manipulative way. In secret, he planned to flee the Philippines in less than 24 hours, and in preparation he ordered crates of belongings be removed from the presidential palace overnight. But in public, Marcos did everything to project authority. He continued the defiant pretence that he was in power, besieged but determined to stay put. In fact, Marcos had been advised by Washington to leave the Philippines, and he, in turn, advised his family to pack. But there was no announcement, no national broadcast of his plans; only his closest aides knew.

Marcos had promised he would be inaugurated and there was no going back, despite the obvious collapse of his extraordinary empire of greed, so methodically planned and ruthlessly implemented over so many years. Was it denial of reality? Deception? Hope? Nevertheless, Marcos went ahead and prepared for his midday inauguration, even though Aquino's rival 'inauguration' at suburban Club Filipino, had been broadcast nationwide one hour earlier.

To quash any suggestion or criticism that she was beholden to Enrile or Ramos, Aquino had insisted that her inauguration be on neutral ground – the prestigious Club Filipino, and not a military camp – and she rejected the offer (for appearances sake) to be brought there in a military helicopter.

Aquino's was a televised ceremony of controlled exhilaration. Boisterous applause and chants of 'Co-ry! Co-ry! Co-ry!' greeted her on arrival. On the periphery, armed renegade soldiers maintained a tight cordon sanitaire around invitees, dignitaries, and diplomats who shuffled for the best view of Aquino. Leading opposition figures stood at her side. Enrile and Ramos were there with several bodyguards. Senior Supreme Court Justice, Claudio Teehankee solemnly recited the presidential oath of office and, with her right hand raised, Aquino repeated the words. It ended with thunderous applause which drowned out the distant buzz of a military helicopter. Enrile and Ramos joined the mass singing of the protest song 'Bayan Ko' ('My country') and then, along with everyone else, raised their arms, extended their thumbs and forefingers to form the letter 'L' for Laban ('fight'), the opposition's sign of defiance. The symbolism could not have been greater; the finality of the Marcos government incontrovertible.

Undeterred, Marcos went ahead with his own inauguration, and the contrast could not have been greater. With the city in turmoil, and ensconced in his palace, Marcos had no choice of venue and he proceeded with his inauguration without the pomp and ceremony he so loved. All three of his previous inaugurations – 1965, 1969 and 1981 – were held in the city's biggest park. They were grandiose affairs in front of massive crowds, diplomats, church leaders, and politicians. There was a ceremonial grandstand covered in bunting; a troop review; the singing of the national anthem; an ecumenical invocation; a musical interlude; and a 21-gun salute.

This time, there was none of that. There were no foreign dignitaries, and only seven members of his 23-member cabinet in attendance, along with half a dozen generals. Outside, assembled on the palace grounds, were about 1,000 members of the most loyal pro-Marcos groups. Marcos's military minders had anticipated trouble. After rebel troops attacked and seized control of the government's television station the previous day – cutting transmission of Marcos's press conference – the government had established an emergency microwave connection to three remaining pro-government television stations.

It was a precautionary measure, but it failed

spectacularly at the inauguration ceremony's most poignant moment. Just as Marcos raised his right hand for the oath taking, television screens went blank. Once again, rebel soldiers had cut the transmission lines. Once again, Marcos's vulnerability, his inability to control events, was starkly evident for all to see. Here was proof that something, finally, was beyond his control.

It was a fiasco; the second time in two days Marcos suffered the ignominy of a sabotaged broadcast. But this time it was different. This was the last time Marcos would ever be seen on television. In fact, for most Filipinos, this was the last image they would ever have of Marcos. Embarrassed, Marcos angrily halted proceedings, took a break, and then demanded that the ceremony be re-enacted for the film crews and the video recordists present, even if the nation would never see it. On a palace balcony, Marcos and his family looked out over a small gathering of loyalists who had passed through barbed wire barricades, heavily armed palace gates, and pushed through a swelling crowd of Aquino supporters, to get to the inauguration ceremony.

Inside the palace grounds, the Marcos loyalists were protected by soldiers. Marcos addressed them. He was angry and defiant, arm waving and bellicose, adamant he was president. Imelda Marcos serenaded the crowd with her husband's favourite love song; there were shouts of support and encouragement, and then the pretend inauguration was over; the Marcoses retreated inside the palace.

Of all the Marcos family members who were dressed in white, only 'Bongbong' Marcos stood out in his green army fatigues. He stood on the balcony, going through this pretence, knowing that in just a few hours he would join his father on a helicopter flight into exile. He was a 28-year-old man. He knew what was happening. He knew what was at stake. More importantly, he knew what had happened in all those preceding years – aged eight to 28 – when he grew up inside the palace, so sheltered and so impervious to the reality of everyday life for everyday Filipinos.

For 21 years, Marcos had cultivated an image of invincibility. On this day, Filipinos witnessed his fallibility. The man who once controlled so much, now controlled so little. The military was split and in open revolt; the people were baying for his removal; and the church was praying for his ouster.

Besieged, barricaded, and beaten, Marcos was now the diminished and demoralised victim of circumstances well beyond his control. Marcos had become what he hated most – a beaten man. It was a profound moment. It's poignancy not lost on anyone. This blank television moment was Marcos's final indignity, for everyone to see.

Marcos desperately clung to power, and for a short time the Philippines had two people who claimed to be president. For Marcos, the pretence lasted nine hours. He spent those hours liaising with Enrile and Ramos about the terms of his departure. He wanted safety guarantees. From the Reagan administration, the US ambassador, the CIA, and the US Airforce he won assurances his 'evacuation' – others called it his 'expulsion' – would be in the form of a smooth military airlift out of the country and into exile in the United States.

At 9 p.m. on 25 February, nine hours after his 'inauguration' charade, an ailing Marcos and his family boarded a US helicopter that lifted off from the palace grounds. It passed directly over my UPI window lookout. I craned my neck as the helicopter's looming black underbelly, with flashing undercarriage lights, rose steeply from the confined space of the palace grounds. It loomed large as it grew closer, and noisier, and passed directly above. It was a deafening, giant shadow, and I swivelled my head to watch it go. I was on a 'live cross' to the German radio station, Deutsche Welle, and the shuddering helicopter roar almost drowned out my words as I leaned out the window to describe the moment: historic, momentous, extraordinary.

Radio and television news reports of his ignominious departure came soon afterwards. Joyous, cheering crowds surged into the streets to celebrate, their whoops and shouts drowned out by honking car horns and firecrackers. Crowds, that earlier had converged near the presidential palace sensing victory, immediately scrambled and jostled through the gates and up the stairs into the ornate building. It was now the people's palace, at least for an hour or two.

Marcos issued no statement and made no announcement. Never again did he set foot on Philippine soil. He fled, leaving behind his mother, who for eight years had been confined at the Philippine Heart Center in Manila. (She died there, aged 95, in May 1988. The Aquino government paid her US$57,250 hospital bill.)

Marcos and his family flew to the US Clark Airforce base, 80 kms across Manila Bay, from where they transferred to a US Airforce military plane with Red Cross markings. Marcos was carried by stretcher aboard the plane, but when it arrived at the US territory of Guam, he alighted unaided, but very unsteady. Marcos remained in exile in Hawaii until his death three years later.

The Marcoses' fled into exile with a staggering number of items. The US Customs declaration form lists 23 crates, 12 suitcases, and numerous bags and boxes whose contents were enough to fill 67 clothes racks. There were 413 pieces of jewellery (tiaras, earrings, broaches, rings, cufflinks, and chokers made of gold, silver, diamonds, emeralds, rubies, sapphires, and pearls); 24 gold bars (each one inscribed 'To my husband on our 24th anniversary'); 27 million newly printed Philippine pesos (US$1.3 million); hundreds of dresses; 500 black brassieres; 880 handbags; 71 pairs of sunglasses; 65 parasols; and 3,000 pairs of shoes. It is estimated that Marcos stole as much as US$10 billion.

Marcos stole a great many things. Material things. He, his family, and friends grew rich while the poor grew even poorer. He reigned like a despot, stole like a kleptocrat, ruled like an autocrat, and robbed the nation of its dignity, its pride, and its potential.

Shortly after the helicopter carrying Marcos disappeared into the night sky, my body told me to go home. I had watched four sunrises and four sunsets without a single hour's sleep, working for 10 radio stations and three newspapers on four continents. I had filed – I don't know how many – radio reports and newspaper stories. Occasionally, in a rush, I reported simultaneously to two radio stations by holding a telephone to each ear and delivering the same report, but with separate signoffs.

Every hour was a deadline somewhere. I never got to

sleep. Not once. I did grow a beard though. And there was a toilet in the UPI building, and a handbasin. Food was snatched wherever and whenever I could find it. Once, Bet (my wife), tore herself away from her EDSA vigil and brought me some food, a shirt, soap, a toothbrush, and toothpaste. She forgot to bring a razor, so my beard remained.

Finally, with Marcos gone, I could leave. *That's it!* I remember thinking. *That's enough! No more! Now I can sleep.* Adrenalin had kept me awake and functioning; now that my adrenalin maker had fled the country, it was time to sleep. Home was 15 minutes away. 'Don't wake me,' I told the maid on arrival and collapsed exhausted on my bed. 'I must sleep,' I sighed. Maybe she didn't hear me. Maybe it was 15 minutes later. I don't know. Whatever it was, the phone rang, and of course the maid woke me. It was Radio New Zealand. That much I remember. And I do recall they wanted an update on Marcos. I didn't say, 'Who?' But that's what I thought. I had no idea what they were talking about. Who was Marcos? My mind was blank. Totally blank. There was a rush of confusion, uncertainty, mixed with a tinge of embarrassment because I knew, deep down, I was a journalist, and I probably should know who Marcos is.

'I'll call you back,' I stammered and hung up. It's all I could say. I went and searched my office desk, shuffled through transcripts and newspapers. Nothing made sense. My mind was blank. What's going on? Why can't I remember? I was befuddled, bewildered. Surely, I must know who Marcos is. I just needed time – sleep time – to figure out what was going on.

Then, for some reason, I don't know why, instinctively I pulled the telephone from its wall socket. I returned to bed. 'I'm going crazy. I'm going crazy,' I repeated to myself. In fact, I may have said it out loud. This is what sleep deprivation is all about! It's a form of torture!

Get some sleep and it will all come back, I remember thinking, before falling into a deep sleep. I was right. An hour or two later I awoke, clearheaded. I remembered everything. Best of all, I knew who Marcos was. He was my daylight nightmare.

POSTSCRIPT.

Instead of being held in the Philippines, charged, and punished, and left to see his legacy deservedly wither, Marcos was allowed to flee the Philippines, avoid retribution and punishment, and spend the remaining three years of his life justifying the unjustifiable.

I will never forget the buzzing exhilaration of the first 'post-Marcos' day. How different it felt! It wasn't my imagination. On the streets, in huddled conversations, the people were animated and talkative. Gone was the man who had dominated all facets of life for more than two decades. The Marcos propagandists, the acolytes, and sycophants, had imbued all manner of greatness on Marcos. He was infallible with sage-like wisdom. Every utterance was important, and his opinion mattered more than anyone else's. For many – the children especially – he was a hovering omnipresent demagogue, a godlike character who appeared ad nauseam on TV, on radio, on wall posters, books, and magazines. He was the overbearing, overseeing, omniscient, 'father of the nation'. They had grown up with him. Now he was gone. What now? What next? They were impatient to find out.

There was excitement about the future, even among political 'fence-sitters' or 'Cory doubters'. For some Marcos diehards there was trepidation and regret. But in public, their opinions were rarely sought or given. Instead, people I spoke to were eager, anxious, and optimistic. On this first post-Marcos morning, they were experiencing something most Filipinos hardly knew – freedom.

PART THREE

REPRESSION AND RESISTANCE.

PART THREE

PROGRESSION AND EVOLUTION

SEVEN

MEMORIES NO EIGHT-YEAR-OLD GIRL
SHOULD HAVE.

The village of Sag-od in Northern Samar, in the central Philippines, unfortunately shared a border with the massive San Jose Timber Corporation.

Illegal activities were rife – unsurveyed logging, unmapped roads, disappearances, killings – but more ominously, the huge concession was owned by Juan Ponce Enrile, the longest-serving defence minister in the country, and one of its 'strongmen'.

A Marcos henchman, Enrile enforced martial law with a savage efficiency that saw thousands of people arrested, jailed, tortured, and often killed. Military 'hit squads' were tolerated, if not sanctioned, by the Armed Forces. And, through its silence, the government was complicit in the clandestine operations of these 'hit squads'. In fact, the Armed Forces contemptuously coined the euphemism 'disappeared' in an apparent effort to diminish the seriousness and the extent of these incidents.

Security at Enrile's logging concession was overseen by a renegade colonel, Carlos Lademora, who in turn gathered a group of armed misfits called the 'Lost Command'. This ragbag paramilitary group belonged to the Civilian Home Defence Force (CHDF).

Established by Marcos in 1977, the CHDF was nominally under the control of the Philippine Constabulary (PC), which itself was one of the four branches of the Armed Forces of the Philippines. Its reputation was abysmal. Poor military screening overlooked men with criminal backgrounds, and low pay attracted the desperately poor, or the long-term unemployed.

Regarded as a second-rank, second-class militia, the CHDF was starved of funds for weapons, military training, and even uniforms. Their salaries were often paid – fully or partially – by wealthy landowners, and powerful politicians. In many provinces, this unclear line of command meant that CHDF units served in two capacities: paramilitary soldiers, accountable to the Armed Forces; and members of private armies, in the employ of powerful landowners and politicians. Either way, the CHDF had a reputation for human rights abuses, brutality, and vigilantism.

Terror came to Sag-od on 15 September 1981. It was an unremarkable morning. A day that began like any other and quickly became a day like no other. It was a massacre of such savagery that Sag-od instantly won grim recognition as the site of the biggest civilian massacre in the Philippines since the Second World War. In a tiny village, whose population numbered just over 100, a staggering 45 people died – 18 men, 15 women and 12 children – killed by at least 18 members of the CHDF. Worse still, according to an Amnesty report, soldiers from an infantry battalion arrived a few hours later and set fire to some houses in which an unknown number of bodies had been placed. (Enrile said in a newspaper report, 18 days after the massacre, that 16 people had survived).

Instead of instant condemnation, public outrage, or saturation media coverage, the massacre of 45 innocent civilians went unreported for nine days. Finally, the *Bulletin Today* newspaper broke the story, but the details were vague and contradictory. Military sources told the Manila newspaper 'unidentified armed men' were responsible. Survivors said they were 'army troops'. From the outset, the story was cloaked by a curtain of secrecy drawn across the scene almost as soon as it happened. There was unimaginable grief – almost half the population of Sagod had been slaughtered – and there was unbearable fear of reprisals among survivors and witnesses if they dared identify the killers. After all, the CHDF were government paramilitary soldiers meant to protect the people from communist rebels of the New People's Army (NPA) who sporadically attacked military patrols and outposts.

But the Philippines was a militarised, lawless country where government troops, paramilitary units, private armies, and communist and Islamic rebels operated. Where villagers, caught in the middle, were often forced to take sides, thereby risking their lives and livelihoods. It was a choice no one should be forced to make –

collaborate with one side or the other – because no matter which side you chose, most likely you would be a victim.

Despite military checkpoints leading into and out of Sag-od, rumours swirled of a bloodbath, far worse than anyone had ever known. Curious farmers and townsfolk reported being turned away by soldiers at roadblocks on the barangay's outskirts. The physical barriers, however, could not stop the questions, nor halt the growing calls for answers. As usual, the most dogmatic and the most persistent enquiries came from 'social justice' nuns. In almost every town and province in the Philippines they were at the front line of the anti-government movement, demanding human rights, and seeking justice. For many, especially the more radical nuns, the sobriquet 'leftist nuns' was a badge of honour.

Throughout many regions, nuns and human rights advocates operated clandestine shelters for persecuted people or left-wing 'sympathisers', produced and distributed protest pamphlets, joined rallies, and occasionally used church halls and seminaries for protest meetings. For years, this fearless alliance of nuns and courageous civilians, doggedly investigated, logged, and publicised what the mainstream media routinely ignored or downplayed. So, it was not surprising that almost a week after the massacre, I received a telephone call from a nun, not from Sag-od, but from Manila.

Sister Mary said she had just come from the provinces. There had been a massacre. Forty-five people – men, women, and children – had been lined up and shot by the CHDF. We have a witness, a survivor, an eight-year-old girl. 'You're with the foreign media,' Sister Mary said. 'We want the world to know what happened.'

I met the survivor, Marela Yanay, when Sister Mary and three other nuns, brought her to my home the next day. She was small, underweight, timid, and appeared even younger than her eight years. The four nuns in workday jeans and blouses formed a protective half-circle around Marela, who sat between them, studied the floor, and said nothing. When I asked her to tell her story, she fidgeted, remained silent, and snuggled a little closer to the nun who spoke her dialect, and who held her in a light embrace.

It was cruel to ask her to re-live that moment. I hesitated. But the nuns urged me on. They had heard Marela's story – more than once – and as heart wrenching as it was, the nuns knew that by re-telling it, just one more time to this foreigner, Marela was doing honour to her mother's memory. Eventually, when Marela did speak, with the encouragement of one Visayan-speaking nun, it was a hesitant, innocent recitation of a mass murder I have never forgotten.

What happened to her mother, to her baby brother, to her friends, to the other women and children, happened just days ago. How could an eight-year-old be expected to describe a massacre? But she did. She wriggled a little, released herself from the nun's protective arms, and sat upright, stock-still in the chair, her feet unable to touch the floor. Not once did she look at me, or anyone. She spoke to the wall in front of her. For the next five minutes or so, Marela told her story in a flat, soft voice.

She recalled being roused early in the morning

by a commotion. Armed men in uniform, with rifles, had entered the southern end of the village and were noisily and roughly herding at gunpoint all the women – mothers, some with babies, and grandmothers – and young children along the track leading out of the village. At the same time, Marela said, other soldiers roughly shoved the men, boys, and the older children in the opposite direction, to the northern outskirts of the village. Marela said the women around her were sobbing, pleading for answers. At gunpoint, everyone was prodded into a tight group. Suddenly, off in the distance, a fusillade of gunfire was heard. It was like a signal for the interrogation to begin. The commander accused the women of being sympathisers of the New People's Army and demanded to know their whereabouts. Marela said everyone was terrified, crying, pleading their innocence. She explained how she had been pushed to the front of the group, where she sought out her mother's legs and hung on tight, if only for a few seconds. Marela said she looked up at her mother, who was cradling her infant son. Then everything happened. All at once. All in a blur. In a whirl of motion.

Pushed from behind, probably by her mother, Marela stumbled and fell to the ground. She said she twisted her body and looked behind. Bullets ripped into her mother's chest and cut in half the body of her baby brother, Jumar. Instantly, Marela was buried under her mother's body and the mangled bodies of others. Marela wiped something wet and gooey from her hair and forehead – her mother's brains. In a post-traumatic release of memories, she had told her story in an eerily calm monotone, expressionless, motionless, and without tears.

Without prompting, the nuns filled in some of the gaps in Marela's story. They believed Marela's mother shoved her to the ground instinctively, the moment she saw the troops raise their guns to shoot. According to the nuns, the long burst of gunfire the women and children heard when they were being led away, was the mass murder of Sag-od's men and older children, both boys and girls.

For several days, the nuns had conducted their own enquiries and, most importantly, had spoken to an eyewitness, a Sag-od resident who, on the day of the massacre, had risen before dawn to check his fields. He heard sporadic gunfire then momentary silence, followed by another burst of gunfire. Later, he told the investigating nuns, he crept towards the direction of the sound with the foreboding realisation that the gunfire came from his village.

Even in the early morning light, he could see the ragdoll-like contorted bodies of women and children; sprawled limbs and bullet-riddled bodies. The silence was eerie. No shouts, no wailing. It was then, he told the nuns, that he had a sickening recollection of a second burst of gunfire. Within minutes, he found another mound of bodies – this time mostly men and boys – at the other end of town. It was pointless to look for life, but he did anyway. Within moments, he saw an arm move beneath a pile of bodies. It was Marela.

Marela had survived one of the worst civilian massacres in modern Philippine history. Even in a country bathed in the blood of countless battles, this was a massacre of such callous barbarity that military and government attempts to cover it up, and to suppress media coverage, were utterly contemptible. A few days after meeting Marela, I sought an interview with Defence Minister Enrile, the owner of the San Jose Timber Corporation, and for whom the CHDF troops allegedly worked.

He agreed to meet me. He recalled my name because we had met before, including once at the Foreign Correspondents' Association of the Philippines where he had worked the room, shaking hands, engaging in chit chat. Now, I was meeting him again, face-to-face. His oversize office was dominated by a huge desk, flanked by two Philippine flags that almost touched the ceiling. Like many men his age, Enrile had bottle-black hair, and a welcoming smile that was so slight and fleeting that it was gone before I realised it was even there. He didn't shake my hand. Instead, he dismissively waved his arm towards one of two strategically placed seats at either end of his desk and beckoned me to sit. They were big, soft, low-slung leather seats built not for comfort, but for intimidation. Eye level was below desk height. Sunk into the seat, I could only see Enrile's upper chest and head, not even the top of his desk. That's what he wanted: people to look up to him, to feel uneasy. Immediately, to gain height, I perched myself on the edge of the seat and stayed there.

Over the years, Enrile's mannerisms hadn't changed. He was the master of martial law. The enforcer. He oozed power. He looked steadfastly into the distance, unflinching and rigid, with quiet arrogance, and steely aloofness. Without any pre-interview niceties, I began. 'I want to ask you about Sag-od,' I said. 'Is it true you own a timber concession in Samar and is it true that you employ a certain Colonel Lademora?' After each question, I paused for an answer. None came. Instead, there was silence, and he continued to look straight ahead, not at me.

Then the clincher. 'What do you know about the murder of 45 men, women, and children in Samar? Was this the work of the Lost Command?' Finally, he turned towards me, and for the first time, he answered my question with one of his own. It was chilling. 'What's your name again?' he asked. I was angry. Without hesitation and without thinking I rose, leaned across his desk until I was a metre from him and stared into his eyes. 'D-A-L-T-O-N.' I spelled my surname – one letter per second. I didn't blink. For six seconds I stared into his eyes, and he returned the stare. It was six seconds of insolence. I knew it was. I had overstepped the mark. Instantly, I regretted my indiscretion, my act of indignant bravado. Here I was, an upstart, in front of one of the Philippines most powerful and feared men, and I had shown impertinence and undisguised contempt of him. I had let my feelings get the better of me and immediately realised my foolhardiness. I regretted it, but equally there was a tinge of nervous pride.

I was annoyed that he pretended not to know me and refused to answer my questions. But most of all I was quietly seething. Such an imperious attitude! Such arrogance! Apparently, he didn't have to explain himself to anyone, especially to someone like me. Enrile was Marcos's chief henchman, the stern-faced, ruthless implementor of all those oppressive presidential decrees. He was possibly the most feared man in the Marcos government. He was beyond reproach. He was untouchable. In his eyes, I was an inconsequential, brash journalist who by my impudence had shown him deep disrespect.

Enrile had had enough. Not another word was said. Not by him. Not by me. Not by two men in civilian clothes with holstered revolvers who sternly entered the room and ushered me out without a word. It was the last time I met Enrile.

The drive from Enrile's office, in the back of an unmarked military jeep took about 40 minutes and ended in an abandoned construction site with scattered mini mounds of road fill. Little had been said. Up front, my two abductors shared glances and exchanged a few words. I was convinced I was on the road to oblivion.

When the jeep screeched to a stop in a cloud of dust, the military goon in the front passenger seat jumped out and joined me in the back seat. Without a word and with the bombastic flair of a *Dirty Harry* fan, he withdrew his revolver stuck in his jeans in the small of his back.

True to script, he withdrew each cartridge from the cylinder one at a time. It was all for show. I was their plaything, the human prop in their pantomime of intimidation. But then he went off script. Instead of putting one cartridge back and spinning the cylinder, he left the chamber empty – at least that's what I think I saw, hoped I saw – and held the barrel to my temple. 'Don't report anything,' he sneered. He didn't pull the trigger. He didn't need to. The pressure on my temple was enough. I felt the spreading warmth of pee in my pants. Seconds later, I was ordered out of the jeep and left to find my way home.

Postscript.

For several weeks after this incident my phone was bugged, a military vehicle was stationed outside my home, and I was followed on several occasions. Enrile ordered the commander of the Army's Eastern Command, Brig. Gen. Salvador Mison, to enquire into the massacre. Closed to the public, the military inquiry found the massacre was the work of the communist New People's Army and the case was closed. Never again did I see Marela. I don't need to close my eyes to picture her. And four decades later, I remember her name.

EIGHT

SPARROWS AND NICE PEOPLE AROUND.

I saw my first 'sparrow' propped up against a power pole, pants pulled to his knees, bare feet, his T-shirt drenched in blood, his limp head flopped on his right shoulder, his face coursed with rivulets of blood from a bullet that had shattered his skull and splattered his hair with brain matter. Behind his back, his hands were tied with thick rope. There was one unlit cigarette dangling from swollen lips, and two other cigarettes, one in each ear.

Maybe the cigarettes were meant to be a joke, but no one was laughing, or giggling, just staring, and murmuring among themselves. It was a spectacle with ghoulish spectators. There were men and women, and teenagers, passive, and staring. Incomprehensively, two women stood side-by-side, one with a child held to her chest, the other balancing a three- or four-year-old child on her hip. Both children had swivelled in their mothers' arms to get a better view. Other children stood nearby.

They seemed intrigued, not shocked, by the sight of the mangled corpse.

It was a deplorable, macabre sight I have never forgotten. This was a main Manila thoroughfare in the mid-1980s, and yet this horrific scene attracted little more than squeamish curiosity from passers-by who crowded around to see the city's latest street killing. Even the traffic, which had slowed to look, now whirled past, moved on by a soldier playing traffic cop.

An empty military jeep, metres from the pole, had obviously screeched to a halt. It was on an angle, one wheel on the footpath, the other three wheels on the road. The man giving orders to the soldiers wore jeans, a T-shirt, and had a gun on his hip, stuck inside his jeans. I recognised him as the officer I meet several weeks earlier; charming, quick to please, anxious to make an impression. Now, on seeing him, I knew he was the one who called me less than an hour earlier to say he had something to show me. He even gave me directions to this trophy street killing.

He was obviously pleased with himself. He had the cocksure swagger and the excited speech of a hunter showing off his kill, acting up to his civilian audience to impress them with his prowess.

A 'sparrow' – an urban assassin – had been killed in one of Manila's busiest streets, in one of the military's first recorded encounters with an urban guerrilla member of the communist New People's Army. More guerrilla street attacks would follow. Urban guerrilla warfare was a new tactic. Mostly using three- to four-man units, the lightly armed assassination squad would emerge from a crowd, shoot the victim in the head, and quickly disappear among the startled pedestrians and street sellers. Mostly, the 'target' was a policeman, a soldier, a businessman, or a store owner, and sometimes an informer.

The moniker was obvious. Sparrows hop and dart, here, there, and everywhere. They're never still. Try to catch them, and they fly off in the nick of time. Today's 'sparrow' killing was more luck than planning. On this occasion, I was told, three 'sparrows' had been tailing their prey – a uniformed and armed policeman – when they struck near an open street market filled with street vendors with barrows of food and assorted goods.

No one heard anything, or saw any signal, at least none that they could recall. But they did remember sudden movement from three directions. Only one 'sparrow' appeared to be armed. The other two acted as lookouts, possibly decoys. A single shot, fired with precision into the back of the policeman's head brought instant death and immediate panic as people fled for cover in all directions. The two backup 'sparrows' scrambled to safety in the confusion.

My military contact gleefully told me that the person who panicked most and momentarily froze, was the 'hit man' himself. It was long enough for another policeman, patrolling nearby, to give chase. The 'sparrow' stumbled along the footpath for a short distance, weaving between the abandoned produce carts, before he darted across the road, dodging all but one car that clipped him and threw him to the ground. Unconscious, his gun nowhere to be seen, the 'sparrow' was dragged by the policeman to the side of the road and dumped face down near a power pole. Without handcuffs, the policeman instead used rope to tie the man's hands behind his back. Only then did he roll him over and prop him against the poll, just as a military jeep screeched to a halt metres away.

Up to now, the story recounted by my military contact seemed reasonable enough, even though he had not actually seen it. He had arrived on the scene a minute or two after the soldiers. It was what he said next – or didn't say – that worried me. He ignored my 'what happened?' and 'why was the man killed?' questions. Instead, he proceeded to describe the scene, telling me how jittery the soldiers were about the 'sparrows', the merciless killers who stalked the streets, struck without warning, and killed without reason. He looked at me earnestly, lowered his voice, and spoke in a confidential 'man-to-man' tone, explaining how the soldiers arrived on the scene fearful, angry, revengeful. Then he stopped talking. That was it? No justification? Apparently, he believed his defence of the soldiers mental state – that they had a latent fear of the 'sparrows' and harboured adrenaline-fuelled aggression towards them – was enough to explain why they had executed the man moments after they arrived at the scene. Obviously, he believed his 'just-between-you-and-me' conversation moments earlier gave 'context' as to why the body had been so brutalised. By taking me into his confidence, he probably thought I would understand the soldiers' actions.

Understand? Understand what? Understand their reasoning to kill a defenceless man, possibly an unconscious man, with his hands tied behind his back? Understand the need to shoot him in the back of his head? The exploded forehead and brain splatter was evidence of that. And was I meant to understand the need to defile his body, to wrench his pants down to his knees, and to stick cigarettes in his dead lips and in his ears? Like a cat with a dead mouse, they publicly desecrated a corpse, contemptuously toyed with it, and in the process diminished themselves beyond measure.

Only a psychopath would be so proud of an execution that he would ring me, tell me of the killing, give directions, and request that I hurry. Only a psychopath would be so delusional to believe that I, a person he hardly knew, and a foreign correspondent, would somehow share his enthusiasm to crow over a mangled corpse with such smug satisfaction. Over the years, I met many soldiers like him: heartless, 'obey-all-orders' automatons who explained, almost with pleasure, certainly with pride, the number of people they had killed.

I remember surveying the brutal scene before me: a bloodied, twisted corpse; three soldiers in fatigues, ill at ease, smoking, waiting for orders; another soldier on the road directing nosy drivers away from the scene; my military contact; and gawking, silent onlookers. Someone must have seen what had happened. But no one would talk, especially with soldiers around. I recognised the similarity in this crowd's behaviour to reports I had read weeks earlier of crowd responses to similar 'sparrow' assassinations in the southern city of Davao, 1,500 kms south of Manila. It was the nation's third largest city, where dozens of street assassinations had occurred, most of them in the slums where more than 300,000 people – one third of the city – lived in poverty.

Davao was the NPA's testing ground of its 'sparrow' urban guerrilla strategy of targeted street assassinations. Manila would be next, we were told. Was the prediction correct? Was this body proof that the 'sparrows' Manila killing campaign had begun? Probably.

It was the NPA's strategy to embed their cadres into local communities, immerse themselves in the activities and the conversations of the people, and discover the common issues that united and angered them the most. It came as no surprise that the same issues were cited time after time: grinding poverty; poor health services; underfunded schools; neglected infrastructure; and greedy landlords. But their biggest grievance was 'bad cops'. They hated the way the cops intimidated and harassed them for no reason; how they took freely and regularly from struggling shop owners; the bribes they demanded to overlook minor offences; the bribes they demanded to make 'imaginary' crimes go away; or the bribes they demanded before they would investigate a 'real' crime. Next on the people's hate list were the corrupt businessmen whose deep pockets ensured 'sweetheart' deals with councillors, police protection, and immunity from prosecution by court officials who looked the other way.

'Soldiers' were ranked high on the people's hate list because of the abuse, the torture, and sometimes the deaths of innocent civilians who were caught up in military dragnets, set up to capture communist rebels or left-wing sympathisers. Often underpaid, soldiers hired themselves out as personal bodyguards to influential or corrupt politicians or businessmen, or they changed into 'civies' at night and were paid to be 'bully boy' street enforcers or bouncers.

These were not overnight grievances, but long-standing injustices. They were not trivial, but deeply felt and personal. In the squalid areas, the squatter communities had come to believe that the law was for others and it always had been until the 'sparrows' arrived and began to dispense their form of revolutionary justice. Those policemen, soldiers, and businessmen identified for their roguish, corrupt, brutal, and exploitative behaviour had become 'sparrow' targets. Every death came unexpectedly, in public, often in crowded streets or markets, and every time there was pandemonium. But the curious onlookers who quickly gathered around to see each new victim of 'street justice' did so out of curiosity, not fear. To them, it was deserved retribution. It was justice done.

Every death emboldened the NPA; every policeman and every soldier feared becoming the next victim. The NPA had grown bolder, more assertive. Davao, where 'sparrows' shot dead 70 policemen in 1984, was the big city testing ground and success there had encouraged the 'sparrows' to enter Manila. Defence Ministry figures revealed the truth of the communist insurgency: the communists had the upper hand. Nationwide, a total of 2,650 people, including 800 soldiers and 895 NPA rebels were killed in communist ambushes, raids, assassinations, and other incidents in the first 10 months of 1984, a 20 per cent increase over the same period in 1983.

The rise of communism in the Philippines stretches back decades, originating in the 1930s among unionists and rural workers; transforming into an anti-Japanese guerrilla army in the Second World War; and falling into 20 years of post-war ideological infighting between Chinese and Soviet factions until, virtually moribund, a reconstituted Maoist-aligned Communist Party of the Philippines was formed in 1968.

Its military wing, the New People's Army, was formed a year later, and its political wing, the National Democratic Front – an estimated 100,000-strong alliance of left-wing social activist, labour, rural, and human rights groups – was formed in 1973. NPA cadres proudly recall the guerrilla army's origins in Capas, a town 100 kms north of Manila, and they repeat the legendry claim that it began with 60 rebel fighters and 35 rifles, some left over from the Second World War. At its height, in the late 1980s, the NPA commanded up to 25,000 fighters in 62 of the nation's 73 provinces. Rebel numbers had grown 23 per cent a year since 1981, Defence Minister Enrile told a party caucus in January 1985. Unless checked, he said, the NPA would match the government's firepower in three to five years. At least 20 per cent of all villages in the country were communist influenced and the rebels claimed an arsenal of at least 20,000 firearms. A consequence of the rebels' hit-and-run strategies and the military's regular troop reassignments to these 'hot zones' was the disruption of civilian lives. Forced internal population movements to avoid being caught up in the insurgency war were commonplace but mostly went underreported. Red Cross figures show that from 1972, when Marcos imposed martial law, until the first quarter of 1984, a total of 5.7 million people in the Philippines had been displaced by the communist uprising.

The NPA's influence reached deep into the very heart of the nation's fabric: the barangay (barrio). These council-like bodies existed in every town and small city. Over the years, NPA cadres systematically infiltrated and indoctrinated hundreds of thousands of people who were active in the nation's barangays. The NPA formed so-called clandestine militias. They were a form of 'sleeper cells', a dormant but formidable army of sympathisers, supporters, and possible future recruits.

Armaments were always a problem for the NPA, whose members often claimed that a shortage of weapons, more than anything else, restricted the number of combat-ready fighters and curtailed their battlefield operations. Limited arms shipments from China in the 1970s ceased after the Philippines and China established diplomatic relations in 1975, and the Communist Party's modest money-raising efforts were mostly restricted to Europe, Japan, and the United States.

In the NPA's formative years, small-scale hit-and-run attacks on military patrols or poorly secured armouries netted some weapons. But a better, more reliable source was the government funded, trained, and armed civilian militia, the Civilian Home Defence Force (CHDF). These underpaid and poorly trained CHDF units mostly comprised a motely group of men, many unemployed and some with criminal records, who would frequently sell their weapons to the rebels, or drop their guns and run at the first exchange of gunfire.

The NPA's political dogma and battlefield tactics changed over time. Unlike other Maoist-styled 'liberation movements' elsewhere in Asia, the Philippines guerrilla movement was led mostly by university graduates, students, intellectuals, and disaffected urban workers who had fled the cities to the hills. To them, the armed struggle was very much a continuation of the decades' old agrarian revolution. They needed to build a bigger country-wide militia, with a better-informed rural mass-support base before they could even consider a nationwide revolt.

Over the years, the NPA's battlefield tactics evolved from guerrilla-style hit-and-run attacks by small, highly mobile 10-15-man squads; to larger platoon-sized conventional battles against military outposts, patrols, and isolated barracks involving 20-50 rebel fighters. The NPA could never maintain established bases, which were obvious targets for the armed forces, and so they decentralised their operations beyond rural towns. Each fighting unit became autonomous, self-sustained, and able to operate (preferable in the mountains) using the most suitable tactics, depending on local conditions.

Flat country, head-on confrontations were rare and almost always accidental. The rebels hard-earned lessons of guerrilla warfare had convinced them to bide their time in remote regions, gather intelligence, plan assiduously, restock, reconnoitre, and only then strike hard and fast before making a hurried withdrawal.

Martial law was the impetus for change – on both sides. Marcos had an uncontested, absolute monopoly of political power, complete freedom to make his own rules, and an unlimited military budget to impose the strongest-possible iron grip on the Philippines. Marcos worked hard to keep the allegiance of the Armed Forces by pampering to their wishes and bestowing patronage to secure loyalty. He boosted military spending and top-level pay. He created a military elite whose generals were chosen for their loyalty rather than their competency. And he rewarded some of his most loyal officers by extending their mandated retirement date, often indefinitely, or by appointing them to much sought-after corporate or political posts, many of which became notorious for corruption and incompetence.

Reinforced, revamped, and reinvigorated, the Armed Forces struck deep into the heart of the opposition movement with mass arrests, indefinite detention, and harassment. On the battlefront, the Armed Forces expanded the scope and the intensity of its military operations.

In the early 1980s, Mindanao, in the southern Philippines had become the communist rebels' heartland. Increasingly, the NPA chose the time and the location to do battle. For them, it was a tactical win over the military's superior firepower. Eventually, up to 60 per cent of government troops were stationed in Mindanao, the nation's second largest island. Not only had Mindanao become the military's 'hot zone', but it also was the testing ground for a new and ruthless tactic – 'hamletting' or 'zoning'. In rural areas infiltrated by the NPA, villages were ordered by soldiers to vacate their houses and to relocate to nearby 'hamlets' where, the soldiers told them, they could be better protected from the rebels. A social activist group, the Mindanao Documentation Committee for Refugees, estimated at least half a million farmers had been moved off their land in the early 1980s.

The villagers resentment at having to leave was

immediate and deep-set. In most cases, they believed it was unnecessary, with too few rebels in the area to justify such a radical upheaval. But what irked them most was the order to dismantle their homes which they were told would deprive the NPA of shelter. And once their homes had been demolished, the farmers had to destroy or remove equipment, anything that could aid the rebels.

In most cases, the nearby hamlets were not prepared, and the new arrivals suffered from lack of food, unsafe drinking water, and poor sanitation. Only during daylight hours could they leave the hamlets to work their fields. At night, they were confined to the hamlets by soldiers. The farmers believed they were being duped. Instead of protecting them, they believed the hamlets had been established to vacate the land, so that rich landowners could extend their holdings. In a rare legal challenge to the Marcos regime, the Integrated Bar of the Philippines (IBP) said hamletting's intent was obvious, the ramifications inevitable, and the impact far reaching and illegal.

The hamlets violated the villagers' freedom of movement and their freedom of liberty to live where they wished, the IBP said. To force farmers to demolish their own homes was a criminal and an unconstitutional deprivation of property. Despite an order from Defence Minister Enrile that hamletting stop, it continued. In fact it expanded in some areas for several more years. Enrile's inability to enforce his orders was a significant early indication of his declining influence over the Armed Forces.

Hamletting was hated. It was a policy of forced coercion, accompanied by military harassment and abuse.

The IBP called it 'involuntary servitude'. No single issue did more to alienate and antagonise the people, while simultaneously raising the profile and boosting the people's sympathy for the New People's Army. Under their breath, many people called the NPA, Nice People Around.

Inevitably, in the following months and years, the military's unbridled powers led to more frequent arbitrary raids and indiscriminate arrests. The killings, torture, arrests, and indefinite detention of anti-government critics, leftist sympathisers, and an increasing number of innocent civilians, triggered the opposite reaction to what the military expected. Instead of timidity and fear, there was a spurt in membership of the underground Communist Party, and a flood of recruits to the New People's Army.

Without doubt, military misconduct was the biggest recruitment tool for the NPA. In the conflict's early years, the NPA was outnumbered and outgunned and often avoided conflicts. On every occasion, it assessed its strengths and chose its battles. But, in the latter years of the Marcos regime, tactical offenses involving up to 200 to 300 NPA rebels were reported.

Diplomats viewed NPA activity as impressive. Candidly, local government officials were alarmed. Military analysts and academics looked to the 'foreseeable' future and opined that the rebel army could not overthrow the Marcos government, but neither could the government control the spreading influence of the NPA.

For Marcos, time was running out. He was a sick man. Problems were mounting, loomed large, and had the government teetering on the verge of collapse. The economy was worryingly fragile; international and domestic pressure was mounting on Marcos to reform the economy and sever links with his crony friends; poverty and unemployment were worsening; the once divided opposition parties were united, louder, and bolder; Marcos bore the brunt of public admonition, if not culpability for the Aquino assassination and the people blamed Marcos for the inevitable political backlash, the economic shambles, and the country's rapid reputational decline; divisions had splintered the once inviolate armed forces; in the southern Philippines, a fractious prolonged war by independence-seeking Islamic fighters was mired in a military quagmire with government troops; and nationwide, communist rebel attacks on government troops had become more frequent and more deadly.

Marcos's fundamental blind spot was that he saw the NPA as a military problem to be solved by force, rather than a political problem requiring economic solutions. These involved a people-focused economic realignment and new policies to tackle poverty and eliminate the gnawing inequities and injustices that buttressed his regime.

Marcos relied on military commanders (many of questionable loyalty) and troops (mostly alienated, badly paid and poorly educated) to fight the fiercely determined, ideologically driven, politically devout, rebel soldiers of the NPA. As Marcos's powers and influence weakened, the reach and the authority of the NPA strengthened.

When I put out 'feelers' that I wanted to visit an NPA camp, I was not surprised that Sister Mary, the leftist nun

I had known for several years, and a young man, earnest and shabbily dressed, volunteered to be my emissaries. We planned my trip in a nearby sari-sari (grocery) stall where we sat on old upturned wooden fruit crates on the footpath, drinking tea.

They believed Samar, a middle-sized island in the central Philippines, would be the best place for my NPA 'education'. It would be a field trip, secret and possibly dangerous. Samar was a notorious 'hot spot'. I knew it was. And so did Sister Mary. She was the Manila-based nun who several years earlier had alerted me of a mass murder in Northern Samar, in the village of Sag-od. Forty-five people had been executed by paramilitary troops in what was, at the time, the biggest civilian massacre in the Philippines since the Second World War.

A few days later, on Samar Island, an overloaded 10-seat commuter bus took me from the airport and let me off at a pre-arranged location. Then, within minutes, my special transfer bus pulled up. It was another 10-seater bus, but this time the only passenger was Sister Mary, in civvies. Soon, we turned off the highway and for the next 20 minutes headed towards distant hills, down a dirt track more suited to a buffalo-drawn cart. For the last five minutes, I was ordered to wear an eye mask. Sister Mary insisted. She didn't believe it was necessary, but she explained that the people I would meet that night were 'super cautious' and this was the first time they had spoken to the media, foreign or local.

Finally, we stopped outside an ordinary rural house in the middle of nowhere. I was ushered off the bus which quickly drove off, seconds after Sister Mary left instructions with the homeowner in a dialogue I didn't understand. Through broken English, I got the message: Settle down. Wait. Have a sleep. You leave tonight.

It was after midnight when the bus returned. Once again, seated alone in the back, Sister Mary looked seriously concerned. She cautioned me to obey all instructions and be 'extra quiet' especially when I was being escorted to the rebels' jungle camp. She handed me the same eye mask and once again insisted I wear it, immediately.

We were off. Down the dirt track. The bus headlights turned off. Leaning closer, Sister Mary explained in a low voice the need for caution. Government troops were in the area. They had been seen the day before, on patrol, on a path skirting the jungle. About 20 of them; fully armed, and being led by a local villager, whether willingly or not, they didn't know.

The night was even darker with my mask on. The normal creaks and squeaks from a rocking bus on a potholed track seemed louder than ever. Then, the bus stopped. The door opened. The low scraping sound of the sliding door echoed off into the jungle. Muffled voices, little more than whispers, grew louder and closer until I was told I could remove my mask. In front of me were three young civilian-dressed, gun-carrying, communist cadres who would lead me into the jungle, to their rebel encampment.

Then began one of the most frightening short walks of my life. As if on cue, the leader raised a single finger to his lips. Silence. Nothing, absolutely nothing was said for the next 10 to 15 minutes. Only hand gestures. There was no track. At least I couldn't see one. It was too dark to see anything other than the two rebel fighters in front who slowly, almost rhythmically, swung their rifles from side to side at waist level, aiming into the eerily dark jungle on either side of the path, ever alert for trouble. Look only at the back of the rebel in front of you, I had been told. Concentrate on his back. There will be someone behind you. Don't worry. You'll be fine.

The jungle closed in on us. The sounds I didn't hear before became a discordant cacophony, a night-time chorus of unfamiliar buzzing sounds, squawks, and eerie noises. The sounds enveloped me, unnerved me, and seemed incredibly close, made worse by the total darkness that scrambled my sense of safety and direction. At times, for short bursts, we were enveloped in silence. Only the slight crunch of leaves and twigs on the forest floor could be heard as we proceeded, ever wary of being ambushed by government troops who were somewhere out there. Occasionally, low-hanging vines and protruding branches sprang out at me or dangled down and brushed my face and body as I sidled past. I guessed it was about 1 a.m. The moon cast a feeble light.

Suddenly, the track that wasn't really a track ended and without hesitation we stepped unsteadily and ankle-deep into the darkest of streams. The water was not fast, but the boulders were slippery. I almost stumbled. Flailing, I grabbed the closest thing I could, the bandolier of my rebel guide (the cartridge-filled ammunition belt worn over one shoulder and across his chest) and I jerked it so hard he almost fell backwards into the stream. He steadied, righted himself, and looked back over his shoulder. He was furious, but silent. It could have been disastrous; a tumbled splash would have given away our position. Maybe it had. Maybe the backward stumble had been heard because, at that very moment, the lead soldier ahead suddenly stopped and instantaneously punched the air with a hand signal. Stop! All of us froze in mid-stream. Silent. Straining to hear. Peering into the night. Then, the NPA rebel beside me pointed, and through the darkness I could see the weak light of kerosene lamps and the moving shadows of two or three indiscernible figures.

'Soldiers,' the rebel fighter whispered without turning, his eyes fixed on what looked to be an improvised encampment just 50 metres away. Instinctively, I held my breath, as if breathing would give our position away. The shadowy figures were in the open and muffled voices could be heard. I could make out what seemed to be a makeshift shelter, probably a tarpaulin stretched across branches, and other black shapes of irregular size. It looked to be a makeshift military camp on the riverbank. So close. The soldiers were so close. I expected at any moment the thud of bullets smashing into tree trunks and branches, the explosion of foliage and bark, and then a panicked dive for safety. Instead, a sort of frozen silence overwhelmed us. Ten seconds went by. Ten heart-beating, eye-darting seconds. Ten seconds of acute sensory awareness that the tiniest sound, the slightest movement could reveal our position. Not a word was said. Just hand signals. Surely, we would have to abandon our journey, make a detour, and turn back. But no. Only the sound of the river could be heard as we slunk away upstream without looking back. We pressed ahead in utter silence for another 15 minutes over easier, undulating terrain until we again stopped on hearing distant voices. We had arrived.

In the faintest early morning light, I saw that the rebel encampment was much as I had expected. I would investigate in the morning, but for now I was directed to a hut and told to sleep until dawn. There were two huts for sleeping, relaxing, strategizing, and possibly preparing the weapons of war. Finely woven bamboo sleeping mats covered parts of the bare earth. I couldn't sleep. I didn't even try. I just lay on my back, eyes wide open, my ears, like mini radars, searching out the slightest sounds. Morning came slowly. And when it came, I could see around me the shabbiest, primitive encampment.

These were crude huts built for a purpose – shelter, sleep, rest, and recuperate. These were quick 'get-up-and-go-and-leave-everything-behind' huts, filled with basic, bare necessities: mats, blankets, and grubby flat pillows; hygiene objects; several cardboard boxes of personal possessions; a rope clothesline; books; plastic bottles of water; and in one hut, a battered guitar. There was an unroofed latrine at one end of the small jungle clearing and an unattended cooking area at the other end. It was a temporary waystation, a battle-ready camp for battle-tested fighters.

This was a military camp for NPA guerrillas, not government soldiers. Arms were nearby, always at the ready, not locked in an armoury. Rank was battlefield earned, not college bestowed. There was no saluting, no discernible sign of rank. Instead, everyone seemed to know what job they had to do, and they moved with purpose around the camp.

Weaponry was a problem. The NPA relied on guns

confiscated in raids on military armouries; weapons stripped from troops killed in battle; weapons bought or confiscated from civilian militiamen; guns bought on the black market; and even vintage guns from the Second World War and the Korean war. It was a weapons hodgepodge that I saw that day. Dirty, well-worn, much-prized M-16 rifles – the same used by the Philippine military – were the most valued. Almost as popular were the AK-47s with their distinctive curved cartridge magazine, the weapon of choice of guerrilla movements the world over.

Many rifles looked so battered, almost makeshift, they could have been homemade. Some were. I could see no weapons display arsenal, no weapons stored in a crate. Instead, the rebel fighters seemed to be in a permanent state of readiness, able to erupt with practiced speed, with each rebel fighter knowing which carefully positioned rifle to grab in order to be ready for battle at a moment's notice. Inside one of the huts, I saw what looked like several boxes of ammunition, one or two handguns, a large machete, but nothing more. Only two or three rebels had rifles slung over their shoulders. I assumed they were 'on watch' while their compadres were resting, reading, conversing, sleeping. The camp was surprisingly, unusually calm.

The three rebel soldiers who had shepherded me here had gone after briefly introducing me to the two NPA leaders I had come to see. Both men, once prominent leaders of anti-Marcos Manila protest rallies, looked to be in their mid-twenties. One was an engineering student, forced out of university after organising one too many demonstrations, and the other was a factory union organiser, a left-wing agitator who management was keen to get rid of. Both had similar stories of harassment, police surveillance, and military brutality going back several years. The union organiser recounted being frogmarched out of his workplace by guards, handed over to the police, and interrogated and bashed because of his views.

The former radical university student told me of a military raid on a student café in the very early days of martial law when soldiers prowled the streets, emboldened by limitless powers of arrest and detention. On this never to be forgotten night, soldiers shoved his head on the table and used scissors to roughly hack off chunks of his long hair. As other soldiers blocked the café exit, the soldiers did the same to two other long-haired young men. Years later, it was snidely referred to as Marcos's 'attack on the long hairs', a throwback reference to the Nazi's 'night of the long knives'. In the first blush of martial law zealotry, anyone with long hair was a dangerous leftist; an enemy of Marcos's New Society. That personal attack had an irrevocable impact on the NPA leader seated before me. It was his 'radicalisation baptism', he told me.

Nationwide, rallies followed – increasingly angry demonstrations against martial law powers and abuses – and they were brutally suppressed by soldiers and police. Thousands of people were arbitrarily arrested and indefinitely detained. Increasingly, the choice for dissidents was to stay and suffer, or to flee and fight. Both men had fled to 'the hills' and, with their organisational skills and political nous they had risen quickly in the NPA's ranks to become commanders.

Looking around, I could see possibly 15 NPA fighters,

including three young women, who enjoyed equal status. The rebels wore no uniforms, just casual clothes – jeans, cheap shirts, T-shirts, and sneakers. Some declared they were Maoists, but there were no red star badges pinned to their clothes, no revolutionary flags fluttering in the breeze, no assemblies for rote sloganeering, and no saluting because this army of idealists was a people's army with no formalised system of rank. Instead, this isolated jungle clearing to which I had been brought resembled a rough encampment for civilians, anxious to be trained and re-birthed as rebel soldiers. The guns, and the basic paraphernalia of war were there, but little else. The camp obviously had been created out of necessity – a way station with spartan surroundings – hidden in the jungle.

The rebels' wellspring of revolutionary fervour came from the poverty, the abuses, and the injustices they saw and experienced under Marcos. And they believed that it was in the country's rural heartland that the war to restore basic rights and freedoms would be fought. From there, it would spread nationwide. It was an austere, demanding life of sacrifice they chose. They were committed to a cause with far-off rewards, and to achieve them, deprivation was the price. Past lives were abandoned for the harshness of jungle living – poor food, unattended sickness, primitive sanitation, loneliness and, most of all, danger. Fear prevailed: fear of discovery, of battles, of injury, of death.

On meeting the two NPA commanders, I left unsaid one of my first impressions. Why was this camp on hilly terrain where it was relatively exposed, rather than in some mountain hideout? I had been brought to a tongue of forested land surrounded by open dry rice fields.

Even I could see the risk! Instead, over what passed for breakfast – warm rice, fried eggs, and instant coffee – we talked NPA tactics. The cornerstone of the NPA's strategy begins with the slow and deliberate infiltration into rural communities of intelligence scouts whose job it is to assess the villages' amenability to strangers with new ideas. 'Win the trust, win the hearts, win the minds,' was the rebels' mantra – in that order.

No village or barrio in the Philippines lived in such isolation as to be oblivious of the NPA; their battlefield skirmishes with soldiers and para-military troops were common scuttlebutt. Less well known were their ideological hearts-and-minds propaganda lectures in carefully chosen isolated barrio halls and remote open-air meeting places, well away from preying eyes and twitchy ears.

Possibly inspired by the 'barefoot doctors' of Mao Zedong's China, NPA cadres fanned out, like left-wing Peace Corps workers, to the most remote villages in the Philippines on targeted missions to provide help, advice, and protection to what they saw as underserved, often neglected rural communities. They helped with farming, provided basic health care, and offered advice. Once accepted for who they were and what they did, the NPA cadres gradually took on the work of proselytizing advocates of a communist revolution.

Rudimentary seminars were held, mostly about corrupt local and government officials, exploitative landlords, unfair taxes, poor services, and often harsh policing. The rural folk were attentive, mostly primary school graduates, a minority were young women. Invariably, there were lashings of politics, condemnation of capitalism and imperialism, and praise for Marxism and communism. I was told it was routine for each lesson to end with a free-for-all airing of complaints. By drawing out the villagers' grievances, by understanding their complaints, the NPA cadres were better able to empathise and to offer help.

In most cases, the catalogue of complaints was the same, province after province: the bullying landlord; the stealing of stock and grains; the unreasonable rents; the military harassment; the bribe-taking policemen; and the nagging, unmet demand for reliable water and electricity. On behalf of the villagers, the NPA took retaliatory action in various ways. Sometimes, it was a rebuke and a stern warning to the abusive policeman, the corrupt official, the greedy landlord, or the violent thug. For serial offenders, more serious reprisals could be a petrol bomb attack or destroyed equipment. Other times, repeat offenders were given 'three times and your dead' warnings, which usually worked.

The NPA rebels were tough, but they were tough on themselves too. Good behaviour was expected, misbehaviour was not tolerated, and discipline was strict. For NPA offenders, punishment was public and, in many cases, harsh – a reprimand, sometimes an expulsion, and in exceptional circumstances, execution. Examples had to be set for their sincerity to be believed.

Overall, revolutionary justice was popular with the people but hated by the military. To revenge a NPA killing, for example, the military frequently overreacted with a night-time or early morning raid, roughhousing of families, abuse, and sometimes the killing of innocent civilians. It was collective punishment for the actions of others. The military reprisals were often so savage and ill-targeted that the NPA was proven right, time after time: soldiers were the enemy and could never be trusted. Rural communities became mistrustful and radicalised.

Often, a covert network of peasant supporters shared sparce food supplies with the rebels and took the risk of housing them overnight. Civilians were lookouts too, constant observers of troop movements. Isolated in their camps, the NPA fighters were reliant on the support of sympathetic villagers and townsfolk to deliver limited food supplies, often at great risk to themselves. Government troop patrols were commonplace, and suspected food couriers risked harsh punishment.

The rebels' geographic isolation left them anguished and on edge. Worse, they existed in a communication void. Their only knowledge of what was happening in the outside world was via their battery-operated radios. Mobile phones and laptop computers were still to be invented, so the rebels relied on civilian supporters to personally bring them news, or instructions, or vital information about troop movements, or even evacuation orders.

These 'news' couriers – most of them young boys – would become essential go-betweens, often risking their lives to convey messages to the rebels in their jungle hideouts and then relaying the rebels' response to NPA agents or commanders in nearby towns. It was a fragile two-way communications chain, easily broken by roving military patrols or jeopardised by informers. Many civilians, from all walks of life, provided invaluable intelligence about troop deployments or roaming patrols, or relayed believable rumours. It was not until the late 1980s that a few hard-to-get Walkie Talkie radios reached rebel hands. Most were scavenged from slain soldiers.

With its nationwide penetration, the Catholic Church had immense influence over the people, and the left-leaning clergy was a formidable force. The church hierarchy estimated that possibly half the country's 4,000 priests and 15,000 nuns were sympathetic to the anti-Marcos cause, and the most radical of those were active members of the underground alliance, the National Democratic Front, a communist linked umbrella group of social activists, students, unionists, and workers.

From the pulpit, many priests denounced government policies and growing militarisation in the countryside. Often, activist nuns provided safe houses and shelter to innocent victims of military raids and attacks, sometimes for merely attending anti-government rallies. Together and individually, priests, nuns, and laypeople routinely went to the slums, the workplaces, the rural, and fishing communities, to offer support and to help organise protest movements for workers' rights and conditions, and to denounce human rights abuses.

Over the years, at least 15 priests were so radicalised that they put down the bible, picked up a gun, and became rebel priests. The most prominent was Father Conrado Balweg. In the early '80s he joined rebels fighting for tribal rights in the Cordillera region in the northern Philippines. He was a charismatic teacher of Marxist philosophy, and when I first met him in a tiny mountain village, he was delivering an outdoor classroom lesson to an enraptured group of about 20 people, some no doubt attracted by his notoriety. Later in the day, he changed from his civilian garb into what looked to be scrounged combat fatigues. Most memorable was the rifle he cradled in his lap and the cartridge filled bandolier across his chest. He was a fighter and a priest. Fighting for the people was the 'highest form of mass' he told the BBC Television crew I was with.

At the grassroots level, the church played a pivotal role in galvanising the people's spirits and directing them, often leading them, in rallies, big and small, that culminated in 1986 in the church-endorsed People Power revolution that swept Marcos from office.

My questioning of the two commanders suddenly stopped, interrupted by a teenage boy I assumed to be a courier. He was running towards us, frantic, breathless, and even before he reached us, he blurted out what could only have been a warning. Panic. Everyone scattered. There was no time for shouted commands. I was told the soldiers were coming. Run. Where? On the shouted order of one of the commanders, a cadre grabbed my arm and pulled me aside. He had been ordered to look after me. 'Come,' was all he said, and we rushed, pell-mell in a mad sprint for cover, just as the first gunshots peppered the corrugated tin roofs and splintered the wood frames of the rebel huts. Dust and grit flew everywhere from bullets that burrowed ferociously into the ground. Never had I experienced the chaotic, frenzied, raucous ferocity of battle and for the first time in my life I was terrified. Befuddled. Helpless. What *should* I do? What *could* I do? Run. That's what I *must* do. Run. Run like hell.

The log, behind which we sheltered, was useless. There were four of us. Me and three rebels who were armed but in obvious panic, not knowing where to shoot. The jungle was our best chance. The latrine was close, about 20 metres away. In a flash of saneness, I visualised my escape, but before I could get to my feet, a fearsome roar and an ear-shattering explosive thud shuddered the ground and sent a huge cloud of dirt and rubble rocketing into the air. A grenade? A mortar? It must have been a mortar. What else shakes you like a ragdoll and leaves your ears ringing?

Instantly, I thought of last night – the soldier's camp near the river. We must have been seen! This attack was no coincidence. I couldn't think. I couldn't see. All I could hear was the zinging, whizzing, ricocheting, supersonic shockwaves of gunfire, so loud that even shouting was useless. Soldiers were attacking us, shooting into the camp. Just a minute ago, I was talking to the two commandos. Were they alive? What about the others? That one mortar shell had changed everything. What chance did we have against mortar fire. Surely a barrage of mortar fire would follow. When? In seconds? How long does it take to reload a mortar? I scampered, bent down, towards the latrine. There were shots, but they were on the other side of the camp. Without hesitating, I threw myself to the ground and did a belly crawl to the safety of the forest. My NPA bodyguard joined me. For a moment, it was strangely quiet. The firefight had stopped, replaced by indistinct shouting, but no second mortar blast, just the one. Why just one?

Stunned, frightened, the two of us said nothing. Hand gestures were enough. We were off, crashing our way through the jungle. What was happening? We heard occasional small arms fire behind us as we ran headlong through the bush. Then, a dull, muffled explosion. Another mortar round.

We continued running. It must have been five minutes before we stopped, gasping for air. Only when we regained our breath, did we pause to listen. Nothing. How could the battle be over? Had the others escaped like us? Had they run helter-skelter, the moment they could, into the jungle? We blundered noisily through the bushes, trees, and undergrowth, along the same track we had so carefully and quietly trodden hours earlier in fear of being discovered. Now, we didn't care. We just wanted to get away, safely. Eventually, it felt safe enough to walk. Only when I saw Sister Mary in the distance, waiting, did I feel a sense of calm return. She gave a single wave. In her other hand was a plastic bottle of water, for us. Somehow, she knew. She had returned in the same van, to the same drop-off point. She had questions to ask. But the answers would come later.

POSTSCRIPT.

The firefight left three NPA guerillas dead. A fourth was wounded and captured. Over the years, Sister Mary and I became friends. I thought it was by chance. She told me it was planned. She said the news tip-offs about human rights violations, and arrests, and anti-government rallies were part of a strategy by a small cloister of left-wing nuns who chose to become informants to the foreign press. Sister Mary chose the BBC. I'm very glad she did.

NINE

Mendiola mayhem.

In a massacre, there are bodies. I could see five. Two young men close together, sprawled, dishevelled, contorted, face-up, in the middle of Mendiola square in a dark, almost black pool of blood that had crept out from beneath their bodies; a teenager in a bloody T-shirt on the footpath, slumped in a frozen squat against a shopfront pillar that supported his body and stopped it from toppling over; a man spreadeagled, a weeping dark bullet hole in the back of his head; and, off in the distance, at least 50 metres away, was a human mound of clothing beneath a shattered banner. A leg poked out.

I didn't see the other seven or eight people who died that day, although I did see several of the 100 or more protestors who had been injured, some shot in the leg or arm, stumbling, hobbling, aided by friends, desperate to flee the massacre site. And others, some of them women, who had been pummelled by batons, writhing in pain, or standing dazed, transfixed, petrified.

Footwear! Never in my life had I seen anything like it. Dozens of flip-flops, rubber sandals, and plastic slippers of all shapes, sizes and colours littered the massacre site as if they had fallen from the sky in a catastrophic downpour. It was the most disturbing evidence of mass panic imaginable. A volley of gunfire had ignited such terror that these panicked people had literally jumped out of their rubber flip-flops and plastic sandals in a frantic stampede to safety. What I saw, when I stood up, was the pitiful evidence of terrified flight. Tellingly, I didn't see leather shoes or sneakers, or any form of footwear with laces, the footwear of the well-to-do. Before me, was the footwear of the poor, the farmers, and the self-described peasants.

Mendiola, the scene of the massacre, has a violent legacy in Philippine history. It is the urban heart of Manila, the site of four universities and colleges, and the battleground of many student demonstrations and mass protests since the 1960s. This bloody clash, on 22 January 1987, became known as the Mendiola Massacre. To this day, the number who died in this slaughter and running street battle is disputed. Some say 12 or 13 on the day, rising to possibly 19 the following day when injured protestors died of their wounds.

Ordinarily, Mendiola is a deceptively quiet street. It is the nearest pedestrians can approach the presidential palace, which fronts the nearby Pasig River. A permanent military roadblock diverts traffic from getting too close; it can be closed fortress-like in moments, and it regularly is. That's what happened on this day when 10- to 15,000 farmers, their families, and supporters, radiated into Manila's heart from carefully chosen rallying points on the city's outskirts.

Chanting, shouting, and brandishing crudely made banners and placards, they implored the Aquino Government to implement the long demanded but never delivered agrarian reforms promised by the Marcos Government.

For years, it was widely acknowledged that anti-government demonstrations were often infiltrated by agent provocateurs from either ends of the political spectrum. Dressed in battle-appropriate garb, wearing balaclavas, shouldering suspicious looking rucksacks, and often armed with crude wooden batons, these crowd provokers left little doubt about their true intentions. Despite ominous government warnings, I saw few of these agitators in the crowd that approached Mendiola that day. Likewise, I saw little evidence of the less obvious civilian-dressed police infiltrators, or the short-haired easily detectable military intelligence agents within the crowd.

The protestors advancing on the presidential palace that day were mostly farmers dressed in their rural work-clothes, side-by-side with mothers and other women, some holding umbrellas high above their heads to shade themselves and the many children marching with them. They demanded justice for millions of landless peasants denied comprehensive land reform in a country where the vast bulk of the land was owned by oligarchs and corporations, and where worker exploitation dates back to the Spanish colonial period.

A sprinkling of students, labourers, urban workers, catholic priests, and nuns had joined the protestors, but they were far outnumbered. All day, there were reports on government aligned radio and television stations that this was the protest vanguard heading towards the presidential palace; there were repeated unverified and unsubstantiated 'sightings' of thousands more sympathisers lurking in nearby suburbs, ready to join the march at short notice.

Consequently, military preparedness for a major confrontation began early that morning. No one was to get past Mendiola Bridge and it was closed off by an impenetrable phalanx of police, soldiers, marines, trucks, water cannons, and fire engines. The first line was khaki dressed police carrying aluminium shields and armed with truncheons and gas masks. More than a metre behind them were the paramilitary Integrated National Police in riot gear and armed with truncheons, shields, and gas masks. Another metre back were the marines. They, too, had shields and truncheons. They also had M16 rifles. Behind the security lines were six army trucks, parked head-to-tail to block off Mendiola Street. Two water cannons were positioned on either side of the street, and eight fire trucks were on standby if they needed to be resupplied. The military came to the demonstration prepared for war.

Intimidated by the formidable police and military barricade, the demonstrators stopped and hesitated long enough to shout abuse and hurl rocks and pieces of timber before summoning the courage to surge forward. They pushed against the security forces. Punches and scuffles followed, until several tear gas explosions forced the demonstrators to retreat 20 metres or more. A stand-off followed. For several minutes, the protestors chanted, pumped their fists in anger, and screamed abuse before the hubbub subsided; on one side, a seething mass of anger, and on the other side, three silent lines of stoic, almost transfixed soldiers, and police.

Suddenly, an unheard command sent the first line of

police to one knee, allowing the marines behind to aim their M16s and fire into the crowd. There was no warning. I heard no appeal for the demonstrators to disperse, either shouted or through a megaphone. The sudden volley of fire was aimed at the demonstrators, not above their heads. They fell to the ground screaming, terrified, scurrying for cover in a square that offered none.

The utter confusion didn't deter some fearless demonstrators to ignore the volley of gunfire, get to their knees, and defiantly hurl stones, pieces of timber, and whatever they could find at the ranks of soldiers and policemen. Everyone else dropped to the ground, pressed their bodies hard against the road, cowered in fear, screamed, covered their heads, lay on top of their children as human shields, or tried desperately to scamper away on all fours. Absolute panic robbed everyone, including me, of thinking beyond personal survival. I confess, it was a moment I thought of no one but me. I saw shelter behind a planter box and in my blind rush to safety, I pushed my way through everyone blocking my path, including mothers and children, I'm ashamed to say.

The ten-seconds fusillade was followed by sporadic gunfire. Once the firing stopped, there was momentary silence, then the wailing and the moaning could be heard. I counted at least five twisted, lifeless bodies lying in pools of blood. Most shot in the upper body. One in the head. One in the back. Many others, wounded in the arms and legs tried to drag themselves to safety, aided by friends who ignored the gunfire, the swirling tear gas, the panic, and the confusion.

The ground was littered with scores of rubber sandals and plastic shoes as well as discarded umbrellas which only moments earlier had been protecting mothers and children from the sun. Pamphlets lay scattered like confetti; discarded banners, clothing, and hats littered the ground. Clouds of choking tear gas slowly dissipated and drifted skywards.

As the shooting tapered off, tear gas cannisters were thrown or fired at the fleeing demonstrators who had scattered in various directions, disorganised, and panicked. Wounded demonstrators, men, and women, young and old, who had huddled in barricaded shop fronts, behind pillars, wherever they could hide, slowly emerged dazed from their hiding spots. I saw the limp body of one bloodied protestor hastily dumped on the hood of a jeep and driven away.

In seconds, the disciplined police and military lines had given way to a confused melee. In tear gas filled Mendiola, automatic weapons fire and single gunshots rang out as the marines with M16s and mask-wearing, truncheon-wielding police, pursued the fleeing demonstrators down adjoining streets, well away from the presidential palace. Even though they no longer threatened to breach military and police lines (and never did), the demonstrators had become prey, to be hunted down and caught.

Intermittent, indiscriminate gunfire forced me to shelter in a side street. I pressed hard against a shop's concrete pillar – the width of my body – for safety. I was a foreigner, obviously a journalist, with a tape recorder hanging from my shoulder and a microphone in one hand. I stood out, not so much as a bystander, but as a witness. For two young men, fleeing the ruckus, I would be their salvation.

Both were men in their late teens. There was nowhere for them to shelter in safety. The abandoned streets near

Mendiola were deserted, litter strewn with discarded banners and pamphlets, and blanketed with rocks perfect for throwing. All the shops and buildings appeared to be shuttered. From the safety of first floor windows, scared residents and shopkeepers peered out. The scene was reminiscent of urban warfare, with armed military and police in street-by-street engagement.

The two young men saw me, ran to my hiding spot behind the pillar, and hung on. Each grabbed an arm. They held tight and I could feel them trembling uncontrollably as they pressed hard against my body. From our vantage point we watched, unobserved, as two other protesters ran past into a shop opposite and once inside, pulled the concertina steel door shut behind them. But they had been seen. Two khaki-wearing policemen, with handguns drawn, savagely wrenched open the door, momentarily disappeared inside, and then reappeared seconds later dragging the two demonstrators by their shirt collars into the street. Frantically struggling, the protestors wriggled violently, kicked the air, whimpered, and yelled.

In desperation, one of the policemen who was struggling to pin his captive to the ground, raised his handgun, pressed the muzzle hard into the protestor's upper body and fired. Was it aimed at the shoulder, or lower, near the heart? Was he dead? This was no accident. The muzzle had been pressed hard against his body. Was he alive? Dead? From this distance I couldn't tell. But he didn't move. He looked to be dead. Startled, the other policeman reeled back in apparent horror, the fight had gone out of him long enough for the other protester to get up and scramble to safety.

The three of us, from our hiding place, had witnessed what looked to be an execution, and now, as witnesses, we feared for our lives. Up until that moment, the two policemen had been so focused on their human prey, they appeared to be oblivious of everything else – particularly their surroundings, and especially whether they had been seen.

For the first time, they looked up, looked around, and immediately saw us. Up until then, the lawlessness of the streets was their cover to do as they pleased. Not now. Three people had seen what they had done; three witnesses, and what made it worse, one of them was a foreign reporter.

Without a word – as if they read each other's thoughts – the policemen turned and walked away. They didn't hurry. They walked slowly away, leaving the body in the middle of the street. As they did, my two companions, who had not said a word, loosened their grip on my arms. Still fearful, we watched in silence, but with growing relief, as the policeman reached the end of the street, turned the corner, and didn't look back.

'Thank you, thank you,' the young men stammered, almost breathlessly. Shocked and exhausted, they gave me a quick hug. Then they ran down the street in the opposite direction to where the policemen were last seen.

POSTSCRIPT.

I don't know if the protestor died. I do know that no one was ever punished for the deaths of the farmers. Survivors and relatives of the victims did not receive any compensation.

TEN

EVEN A SMALL CHICK CAN GROW INTO A FIGHTING COCK.

DRAWN FROM INTERVIEWS WITH ELEVEN-YEAR-OLD JOSE.

'Quick. Up the tree. Now.'

The farmer hollered to his son, Jose, the moment he saw three soldiers, guns drawn, advancing towards him through the field. Confused. Fearful. Instinctively, he knew he had to save his son.

The coconut tree was Jose's only escape. It was 20 metres away, but he was able to scurry through low undergrowth and shimmy up the tree without being seen. Only when Jose was halfway up did the farmer return his gaze to the soldiers who were now upon him, shouting and pointing their weapons directly at him.

Jose clambered through the confusion of fronds as far as he could and clung to the largest swaying frond, heaving, and gasping for breath. He hugged the frond so tight his chest hurt. He heaved for breath. Scratches left trickles of blood tracking down his bare legs; his feet were cut from his frantic ascent.

The fronds below obscured his view, but Jose feared to look anywhere but straight ahead in the disoriented belief that to look down would give away his hiding spot. But he needn't have worried. Jose's scramble to his tree-top lair had gone unnoticed, no commotion could be heard, and he was hidden by a lush canopy of fronds.

For now, he was safe but scared, terror was giving way to confusion. Why had a normal day in the fields with his father become a day of terror? He summoned the courage to peer below. Still, the soldiers were there. Jose's white-knuckle grip on the frond was loosening, he feared he could lose his hold and topple onto the soldiers below. He was too shocked to sob. All he could do was wait until the soldiers moved off. Only then, he believed, could he gingerly make his way down.

Suddenly, the sound of yelling. Then screaming. It was his father's cry. Jose stared open-mouthed. He could see what they were doing to his father: a rifle barrel pushed into his chest, a rifle butt smashed across his jaw, then a knife held to his neck. Jose could look no more, but the piercing cries continued. Then, agonising whimpering. Then, silence.

Instinctively, Jose looked, unable to bear the silence, and immediately his stomach convulsed. He vomited, then dry-retched with a noisy guttural spasm, luckily not loud enough to be heard. The crumpled and bloodied body of his father lay directly below, limbs contorted in death. A sort of paralysis had captured Jose's body. He wanted to move, he wanted to cry out, but he couldn't.

His immediate instinct, to scramble down the tree to his father was almost overwhelming, but even for an 11-year-old he knew that to reveal his tree-top lair would be more than stupid, it could mean death. So, he stayed, silently swaying with the branch, as his befuddled brain thought of the bloodiest, most gruesome revenge he could enact against his father's killers.

Minutes went by until he became aware of the silence below. He couldn't see anyone, but still he took his time, fearful that the soldiers had known all along he was up there and were waiting in ambush. But they weren't. They had gone. Jose descended the tree at a speed he never thought possible. He was running the moment he touched ground. And he ran the familiar route home, the same route he had taken that morning with his father.

Once in his mother's arms, Jose spluttered out what he had seen from his tree-top lookout. The bloody, swirling images buzzed through his mind. Without warning, his mother's tight grip suddenly loosened, her arms fell away, and she collapsed wailing inconsolably. This morning had changed everything, Jose realised. It was just him and his mother now. Usually, the three of them worked the fields. What were they to do?

Only rarely had Jose seen soldiers near the village. Usually, they stayed away. When soldiers did pass through the village, people hid from sight, for fear of interrogation, or being forced to provide food. Sometimes, the soldiers stole chickens, or bags of rice.

From an early age, Jose had been warned to keep clear of soldiers. They were bad people, he was told. Now, Jose had seen just how bad they were. They were killers, and Jose wanted revenge; to kill them. It was Jose's uncle who intervened. He had come running on hearing of the murder, and only after Jose finished telling what happened, did his uncle offer a suggestion. Jose's uncle was the village intellectual and what he said made sense. Jose was only 11, his uncle reminded him. He had never held a gun. He wasn't big enough. His uncle suggested the best thing he could do, if he wanted revenge, was to tell people what happened.

How? Jose wanted to know. He rarely ventured into the neighbouring town. There was an army camp on the town's outskirts and Jose had been told to keep clear of the soldiers who always seemed to be roaming nearby. Jose didn't know how he could tell people what happened to his father when the place he could tell the most people was off limits to him.

Jose's uncle had the answer. He knew people who knew people who could help organise a press conference, and then everyone would hear how Jose's father died. Once again, activist nuns got involved. Word spread. And once again, I got a telephone call from the same nun, Sister Mary, who years earlier had inviting me to interview an eight-year-old girl, who had survived a massacre of 45 people on the nearby central island of Samar.

This time, the press conference was to be a small outside gathering of vetted 'sympathetic' journalists who could be relied upon to report the story fairly. Up until now, only snippets of information had been reported in the overly timid local media.

By the time I arrived and crossed the rice field to the designated spot – the base of the coconut tree that had been Jose's lifesaver – I found three other reporters waiting, talking among themselves. The unusual clandestine news conference began with the introduction of Jose, who had gained more confidence each time he told his story. This time, he filled in some gaps.

The local district was coloured red on military maps because it was infiltrated by rebel fighters of the New People's Army (NPA). Only once had Jose and his father seen rebels – five of them – as they cautiously walked through the village early one morning months ago. They didn't stop, but the villagers gathered to watch them pass.

At this point, the conference organiser interrupted. He wanted us to understand what happened the day before Jose's father was killed. Apparently, the NPA had raided a paramilitary arms cache at a military camp several kilometres from the farm, and fled with guns and ammunition, after killing one CHDF soldier.

Furious and vowing revenge, the paramilitary command ordered the rebels be tracked down and killed. Among the soldiers who fanned out into the nearby farmlands were three paramilitary soldiers who headed in the direction of the farm owned by Jose's father.

There was a lot at stake for the paramilitary troops. Even among regular soldiers, they were looked down upon, ridiculed for their poor training and abusive behaviour. Worse still, the paramilitary troopers faced possible military discipline for losing weapons to the communists. They were hellbent on face-saving retribution. Instead, they ended up extracting revenge on an innocent man.

Jose then took up the story. He defiantly recalled the last minutes of his father's life. The words spilled out. What he said was gut-wrenchingly horrible. He recalled the soldiers yelling, accusing his father of being a communist, of killing the soldiers' comrade, and then stealing weapons from the army cache. Although browbeaten and submissive, Jose's father at first argued his innocence, but his loud denials soon petered out and he fell to whimpering, repeatedly pleading for his life. Jose told how the soldiers yelled, shoved, and savagely hit his father with rifle butts.

The angriest soldier among them drew closer, a large knife in his hand. He caught the farmer off guard, tripped him up, and once on the ground managed to pin his arms to his side. Seconds later, he twisted the farmer's head to one side, grabbed his hair, yanked his head back, and with a several frenzied saw-like motions severed his head, which fell to the ground.

Terror-struck, Jose said he was petrified. He couldn't move. Vomit burst into his mouth. He wanted to wail but couldn't, for fear of revealing his hiding spot. He wanted to shimmy down the tree but couldn't, to do so would risk death. So he stayed, clinging to a coconut branch far above the spot where his father's body lay. There was nothing he could do. He was a witness to his father's animal-like slaughter which, until then, Joe never even thought was possible. He seethed with rage; he wanted to kill the killers.

Jose recalled he couldn't hear what the soldiers said after his father's beheading. They were jabbering, arguing. One soldier angrily finger-butted the killer who still held the bloodied knife. Slowly, with trepidation, one soldier moved forward and tentatively poked the head with a big stick. Again, he did it. Then cautiously he kicked the head.

But it was heavy, too heavy to roll, except for half a metre or so. Once again, he kicked it, harder this time, as if he was a soccer ball. But the head barely rolled. Dispirited, the soldier and his comrades covered the head with leaves and left in a hurry.

There was a moment of silence. It appeared the press conference was over. But Jose had a few words to add. Once he descended from the coconut tree, he said, he couldn't bear to look at his father's remains. He had to run. Get away. Tell his mother what had happened. He returned hours later, once he had summoned up the courage to show villagers where the soldiers had hidden his father's head. Did he want revenge? Jose nodded. 'I want to avenge my father's death. Even a small chick can grow into a fighting cock.'

ELEVEN

SUGAR'S BITTER AFTERTASTE.

So far, the count was two skulls and three skeletons. Everyone agreed that the third skull would probably never be found.

It was a small mass grave on the grounds of a sugar plantation on Negros Occidental in the central Philippines, and if the skull couldn't be found after an extra 15-minute search in the muddy hole, then it probably wasn't there.

The volunteer diggers had wiped excessive mud from the two skulls and had casually placed them, side by side, on the edge of the hole where they worked. Nearby, were assorted bones of various sizes, dumped unceremoniously in a small pile, separated from barely recognisable pieces of clothing and the remnants of a belt. Inquisitive bystanders, about 10 adults and several children, looked on in curious, respectful silence.

Except for the familiar smell of damp turned earth, there was no stench of death, not even a whiff. The grave diggers, mud smeared, shirtless, and barefooted, wore no masks. Only a few women held scarves or small cloths over their noses and mouths; a medical officer, not a doctor, was in charge, but stood to the side.

Beyond the civilians, away from the mud, and seated on two small wooden crates that barely held their weight, were two soldiers who, nonchalantly, surveyed the scene. The job of supervising the exhumation was obviously not to their liking, but they instantly rose from their seats the moment I arrived at the scene on the back of a motorcycle.

My driver and guide was a Catholic church layperson, well-known for campaigning against human rights abuses by soldiers and paramilitary troops. That explained the soldiers' unease. My being in his company, added to their suspicions. A foreigner was always a curiosity among civilians, and a person of suspicion among the military. My presence was not welcome, and the soldiers glared but stayed their distance, and asked no questions.

I had been told before I arrived, that several people gathered at the graveside had an extra interest in the exhumation because they believed the remains might be relatives who had disappeared several years ago. Apparently, they had been highly vocal campaigners for workers' rights, and that made them targets to be silenced.

Disappearances were common on Negros. So, too, were killings. And most of them could be traced back to the island's feudal-like structure, born in the Spanish colonial years, that had condemned Negros to be the economic and social basket case of the Philippines, where wages were the lowest in the country; poverty levels among the highest;

malnutrition so bad that it caused the deaths of more than 100 children each month; and a communist insurgency that was growing faster on Negros than anywhere else in the country.

I had been to Negros the year before, in 1984, to visit a jailed Australian Columban missionary, Father Brian Gore who, along with an Irish and a Filipino priest and six church lay workers, had been arrested on trumped up charges of killing a local mayor and four of his companions. The case drew extensive international and domestic publicity and criticism, and they were eventually released 14 months later when a court found insufficient evidence against them. But the trial turned a spotlight on the province's chronic poverty, its indentured workforce, and a virulent communist insurgency.

Negros was an island of crippling inequality, where several hundred of the richest families held at least half the island's wealth, and where four out of five households had incomes below the poverty level, according to a 1983 government survey. Among the people, there was festering discontent and anger with a system so unfairly weighted against them.

They were poor, landless, and impoverished. The sugar plantation owners – the island's dominant landowners – were rich and in powerful alliance with the island's business elite. Their chosen candidates filled council chambers, they got to choose the local police chief, and together with the Armed Forces they helped arm the estimated 5,000-strong paramilitary Civilian Home Defence Force (CHDF), which often acted as the landowner's private armies.

Long before Marcos, sugar growers wielded considerable clout in national politics. They could be relied upon to deliver the 'Negros vote' to whatever administration, or candidate, they chose. That power of influence became a tool of extortion, to win favourable outcomes, or to derail any legislation – local or national – intended to curtail their stranglehold on the island, the Philippine's fourth largest.

In contrast, the people's hope for justice and representation lay with the Catholic church, and with missionaries like Father Gore whose Basic Christian Communities (BCC) could muster thousands of loyal supporters. The BCC were self-motivated, self-sufficient community groups that demanded fair pay and better working conditions for the people, campaigned against illegal logging, and unfair trade practices, and established communal food farms.

The missionaries were the peoples' voice for justice. It was the missionaries the people went to with their grievances, which aroused the ire and rancour of the plantation owners, who previously had enjoyed the status and the privilege of all-powerful hacienda overlords. Now, they believed, their influence was being undercut by left-leaning clerics. These hacienda owners were angered by the changing power equation; they blamed activist missionaries and church members, and denounced them as leftist sympathisers, if not outright communists.

Sometimes, disempowered by uncaring landlords or brutalised by their armed 'goons', the people did align themselves with the communist New People's Army

(NPA), who meted out quick justice. The communists viewed Negros's smouldering volcano of discontent as rich recruitment grounds for their war against feudalism and exploitation.

From an advance guard of 30 to 50 guerrillas in 1982, the NPA had an estimated 1,000 fighters on Negros in 1985. Defence Minister Enrile said insurgent numbers had grown by nearly 40 per cent over the year before, and he admitted that Negros was the country's second most active communist war zone after Mindanao, the nation's second largest island to the south.

Over several years, combat-hardened rebel fighters from Mindanao were sent to reinforce NPA units on Negros. With bolstered firepower, the NPA attacks became more frequent and bolder. In March 1985, a 20-man NPA raid on the Visayan Maritime Academy in Bacolod, the capital city of Negros, netted 400 rifles, nine submachine guns, and large quantities of ammunition. It was, up to then, the largest single haul of weapons by the insurgents nationwide, and it exposed the vulnerability of Negros itself.

Public sympathy and allegiance to the NPA was growing. In some areas, the NPA was confident enough to form parallel or 'shadow' governments. The hacienda bosses were worried that their innate authority and control over the population was being challenged and undermined. When they could, and where it was possible, the plantation owners tried heavy-handed measures to reassert control over an increasingly disgruntled population fed up with entrenched generational poverty. The sugar workers were becoming a receptive audience to union activists and communist agitators, and that made them targets of intimidatory attacks and reprisals by the landlords' armed 'goons'.

The mass grave I had come to see that day was almost certainly gruesome evidence of how bloody and ruthless the fight for control of Negros had become. The victims and their killers were unknown, although given Negros's history – its legacy of near-serfdom and social and political injustice – the deaths of the three farm workers seemed dreadfully predictable, perhaps cruelly inevitable; to demand change you risked death.

No region in the Philippines was like Negros, the heartland of the sugar industry. From the mid-nineteenth century to the mid-1970s, sugar was the nation's most important agricultural export. In 1980, Negros accounted for half the area planted to sugar in all the Philippines and it produced two-thirds of the country's sugar. Of its 2.2 million people, about 600,000 were directly employed in the sugar industry, and 90 per cent of its economy was directly or indirectly dependent on sugar. It was a monocrop dependency so overwhelming, that eventually it would prove catastrophic.

Sugar production flourished under the feudal land ownership system of the Spanish colonial era. Over time, sugar plantations became a generational inheritance of rich Filipino sugar planters. They were the richest, most elite members of Filipino society. In sprawling haciendas (attended to by maids, handymen, gardeners, drivers and child-minding nanays), the plantation-owning families enjoyed unrivalled power, status, wealth, and privilege. Negros was one of the most conservative regions in the country, dominated for centuries by local oligarchs.

Nowhere else in the Philippines was the discrepancy between the rich and the poor so obvious, so pronounced, and so entrenched. Academics described the island as semi-feudal, with workers existing on near-slave wages and labouring under inhumane working conditions.

Generation after generation, the poor uneducated sugarcane workers toiled under a system of owner-labourer dependency. In recognition of the seasonal nature of their work, many sugarcane workers lived on haciendas rent-free and received free medical care, electricity, water, and off-season pay advances and loans. When these loans were 'called in', or when harvests failed, this life of subservience and dependency became even more tenuous and oppressive.

A government survey in the mid-1980s found two-thirds of sugarcane workers were not receiving even the paltry minimum wage; for many it was 50 per cent of the mandated amount. Oxfam, the international famine relief organisation, reported that most sugar workers received less than half the minimum 'farm wage' of US$1.60 a day.

Negros's priests and nuns who sided with the poor were ostracized by the rich. Often chided by government officials and the military for their increasingly outspoken support of the poor, the church leaders routinely were the vanguard of social action groups and protest movements seeking a 'living wage' and civil rights for workers. 'The workers have a right to organise unions,' the outspoken Archbishop of Bacolod, Antonio Fortich, told me earlier that morning before I visited the mass grave. 'Violence can be unseen. You can be violent by not giving people what is due them.'

Lauded as the 'defender of the people' by some, and as a 'communist' by others, the cardinal was a friend to most, especially the poor, and the enemy of some, mostly the land-owning clique. How polarising the archbishop had become was obvious in the span of three years. In 1987, a right-wing group exploded a grenade outside the bishop's home, beneath his bedroom window. It was a warning, not an assassination attempt, the police claimed. Then, in 1989, Bishop Fortich was nominated for the Nobel Peace Prize for his advocacy of the rights of the poor and his peace keeping efforts in Negros.

It was Bishop Fortich who lobbied Pope John Paul 11 to visit Bacolod in 1981 to see the plight of sugarcane workers for himself. Not only did the pope see conditions in Negros, so too did an international television audience. To the chagrin of the Marcos government, the pope affirmed the workers right to organise. He told the Bacolod faithful that 'the church should not hesitate to be the voice of those who have no voice.' He continued: 'For to be so poorly paid that you can hardly support yourselves and your families, that you become slaves rather than free and responsible workers - this too is not just.'

In the 1980s, about 350,000 hectares of land was devoted to sugarcane production by 11,000 planters. But the numbers hid a shocking inequality. According to the National Federation of Sugarcane Workers, almost half of this land was owned by just nine per cent of the planters. For years, under a Preferential Trade Agreement with the USA, the Philippines had enjoyed a predictable and profitable return on its sugar exports, usually above the world price. Sugar was the Philippines biggest source of foreign exchange.

In 1974, things changed. The trade agreement expired, and the Philippines was forced to compete on the volatile world market where sugar prices plunged from US65 cents per pound in 1975 to US4 cents in 1984. In just five years, from 1975 to 1980, sugar's percentage of the nation's total exports dropped from 25 to 11 per cent. The country's foreign exchange earnings from sugar plummeted, from 27 per cent in 1974 to eight per cent in 1983. From the mid-1970s to the late 1980s, world sugar prices yo-yoed, reaching their lowest point in 1985. Philippine sugar production costs were US 13 cents per pound, but the sale price was just US 4 cents per pound.

Years earlier, when prices were at record highs, over-eager landowners converted rice and corn fields, and other basic food producing lands, to sugar. In many cases, workers were prevented from growing food crops in fallow lands. To boost productivity, mechanisation was introduced. Yields increased, but it caused a dramatic slump in workforce numbers. On some haciendas, half the workers lost their jobs. Immediately, a quarter of a million workers found themselves without work, without money, and without the means to provide for themselves and their families.

Marcos had long held plans for the sugar industry. First, he moved to take control of its power base. An American CIA analysis at the time described how 'many of these (sugar) families watched their fortunes decline as Marcos set out to destroy the power of the sugar bloc and largely replace its influence with personal and politically loyal associates whom he allowed to acquire large tracts of land on Negros'.

Next, Marcos moved to control the industry itself. In 1974, two years after imposing martial law, Marcos used his decree-making powers to nationalise sugar trading in the domestic and international markets. He created a monopoly, and through presidential fiat, Marcos made his long-time friend, fraternity brother, and political ally, Roberto Benedicto, the sugar czar of the Philippines. This fraternal closeness was starkly apparent years earlier when Benedicto was chosen to be the godfather of Marcos's son, Ferdinand 'Bongbong' Marcos.

Benedicto dominated every facet of the sugar industry and he moved quickly to take full advantage of his exceptional powers. No longer the 'sugar baron', to many Filipinos, he became the 'robber baron'. Through specially written presidential decrees, Benedicto was given control of the nation's policymaking regulatory body, the Philippine Sugar Commission (PHILSUCOM) which decided sugar production levels. He also controlled the international and national marketing body, the National Sugar Trading Corporation (NASUTRA), which had exclusive rights to buy sugar from Philippine planters, and exclusive rights to sell it abroad.

Benedicto also owned the Republic Planters Bank, from which Marcos ordered all sugar producers to obtain their loans, and Benedicto owned the Philippine Sugar Corporation, which owned most cane crushing mills. The Benedicto-owned Traders Royal Bank was reported to have siphoned sugar profits and transferred them abroad into a 'special' presidential fund.

But Marcos wasn't done helping his friend. He directed that NASUTRA be exempt from government audit. It was a blatant and deliberate money-making devise for a Marcos friend, and Benedicto made the most of it. With total control over sugar growing, marketing, and pricing, and shielded from any government audit, Benedicto and his associates reaped enormous profits. According to a US Embassy report, Benedicto made more than US$ 1 billion 'through trading with overseas sugar brokerage houses that he owns'.

A 1984 study by the University of the Philippines School of Economics calculated the Marcos devised sugar monopoly had resulted in losses to producers of between US$1.2 billion to US$1.5 billion from 1974 to 1983. 'Benedicto's financial fiefdom is a substantial, and growing, drain on the country's economy,' the US embassy reported.

Benedicto did well during the Marcos years. Among his assets – just in the Philippines – were: 85 corporations, 106 sugar farms, 14 haciendas, 17 radio stations, 16 television stations, two telecommunications networks, seven buildings, and 14 hectares of land in Bacolod City. Also, he held shares in an oil company and several golf and country clubs. He owned 10 ships and five aircraft. There were more assets overseas. The director of the Records Management and Archives Office of the Philippines found Benedicto owned a sugar mill in Venezuela, a trading company in Spain, and several mansions, limousines, and bank accounts in California.

With Marcos's imprimatur, Benedicto had special powers to buy and sell sugar; to set prices paid to growers and millers; to purchase companies connected to the sugar industry; and to market sugar domestically and internationally. Nevertheless, Benedicto oversaw, probably precipitated, the collapse of the Philippines sugar industry. He did it through mismanagement, price manipulation, fraudulent dealings, political kickbacks, inventory manipulation, and exchange rate speculation.

Underpaid and disempowered, many of the nation's sugar planters went bankrupt or sank into debt. Many haciendas were abandoned, their owners choosing to live in Negros's cities and towns whose populations were swollen by thousands of jobless sugar cane workers. Some of the richest landowners relocated to Manila.

For sugar workers, it was a brutal choice. Hacienda born and bred, they knew no other life. They lacked the knowledge and skills to seek other employment, and they had grown up in a cradle-to-the-grave social and economic system of landowner dependency. At the age of 10, many children were employed as casual workers and stayed on haciendas for their entire working lives. Even in good times, food was a day-by-day lottery, depending on income. Every year, the workers struggled through the no-work 'dead season' (between sugar planting and harvesting) by taking loans from the landlords. It was a cyclical, institutionalized arrangement that was at best satisfactory. Not anymore.

The workers scraped by. But not this year (1985). Only half the area planted to sugar was harvested. Work hours contracted – often the only jobs were weeding and clearing. Hunger took hold. Malnutrition followed. Then, children, especially infants, began to die.

The more resourceful workers tried to grow rice and other food crops in tiny over-used plots around their huts, even on narrow stretches of land along the side of roads. But it wasn't enough, and it was too late. Even as the industry floundered, some diehard plantation owners refused to allow workers to grow food crops on idle sugar lands, perhaps expecting better times, when in fact worse was to come.

The 1984-85 harvest was predicted to be 1.6 million tons, but the sugar quota was only 312,000 tons. And even though the following year's harvest was predicted to be lower, at 1.3 million tons, the sugar quota also was further reduced to 215,000 tons. The mountain of unsold sugar was growing, and it seemed the sugar industry was imploding.

I had come to Negros to witness a crisis caused by man, not nature. Hundreds of thousands of people had lost their livelihood. Each month, about 100 children were dying, if not for lack of food, then from tropical diseases worsened by severe malnutrition. Shortly before I arrived, a UNICEF survey of Negros children under the age of 14 found that 40 per cent of them – 350,000 – were 'severely malnourished' (their body weight 65 per cent of normal). A year later, it was worse. In the first half of 1985, infant deaths at Bacolod City Hospital jumped 67 per cent over the same period the year before. Three-quarters of all children in some parts of the island were 'malnourished'. Stark evidence of the island's famine – distended stomachs of children and the gaunt, emaciated figures of adults – affected more than one million people, according to international relief agencies.

Jobs were hard to find. Beggars appeared routinely on the streets of Bacolod and other towns. They lived where they could, on the urban fringe, in lean-to hovels. In the countryside, it was commonplace for displaced, penniless workers and their families to live in crude hessian and bamboo huts, or abandoned buildings, and eat field rats, wild root crops like camote, and freely grown edible plants such as bananas.

Oxfam feeding centres provided one meal per day for an estimated 85,000 children under six, with moderate to severe malnutrition. Another 20,000 people – adults and children – received daily meals from Catholic Relief Services.

The independent Union of Catholic Asia News (UCA News) said Philippine wages had declined in real value over the past 50 years. For many, rice was unaffordable. Before the Second World War, the daily wage (60 centavos) bought 10 kilos of rice. In the late 1960s, the daily wage (four pesos) bought seven kilos of rice. The year I visited (1985), the daily wage (28 pesos) bought four kilos.

But a sugar worker's legislated daily wage was fallacious. Even the Department of Labour admitted the minimum wage law had never been enforced. The National Federation of Sugar Workers said 90 per cent of sugar workers received a daily rate of just 12-15 pesos, about half the amount mandated by the government.

The situation was bad, and predicted to get worse, because the industry was locked into a never-ending cycle of bewildering confusion and deliberate manipulation. Landowners did not know to whom their sugar had been sold, and at what price. And most grating were glaring discrepancies between the sale price and landowner's reimbursement.

Through NASUTRA's mismanagement, planters were owed money or were underpaid. And that meant they had little or no money to finance their planting and refining operations. Banks wouldn't lend them money for the next crop, and so crops were left unharvested or fields unseeded, mills were shut down, and several hundred thousand labourers were thrown out of work.

The sugar families of Negros were starving because of the government's incompetent handling – some say criminal mishandling – of the sugar industry. This was exacerbated by the landowners' intransigence to change (clinging instead to discredited and inefficient work practices), and their refusal to discard colonial estate holdings through sweeping land reforms.

Convinced of the need for change, a few enlightened landowners converted sections of fallow land to alternative crops, and some allowed workers to grow self-supporting patches of rice and other food crops, but most landowners spurned change. Even though this piecemeal food crop conversion provided sustenance, supplemental income, and employed many displaced workers, it was resisted by most of the monocrop traditionalists.

The sugar industry was under scrutiny. Nationally, the famine exposed questionable practices and bad management. Internationally, the world focused on landlords who acted as warlords, and an industry in crisis bogged down by its anachronistic feudalistic powerbase. The clamour for change had radicalised the plantation workers and had won them the support of the New

People's Army. In addition, hovering in the background, was the island's radicalised, leftist-leaning Roman Catholic Church whose advocacy role as the 'people's voice' had been denounced by the Marcos government. 'Crop substitution and market diversification' was the mantra of an unlikely alliance of progressive sugar planters and unionised sugar cane workers, who believed that only fundamental structural change would save the industry.

At the height of the sugar crisis, instead of clarity, the presidential palace added to the confusion. Records of the Sugar Regulatory Administration show that in a single year – 1984 – Marcos issued one presidential decree (PD1905) that ended the government's monopolistic marketing agency, NASUTRA, and restored free trading. Then, a few months later, he issued another presidential (PD1918) that postponed implementation of the earlier decree. Finally, another sugar decree (PD1939) restored NASUTRA to its previous position. Marcos had done a confusing 360-degree political manoeuvre. The status quo was back, despite industry criticism and allegations of criminality. And Marcos's friend, Roberto Benedicto remained chairman of NASUTRA, despite being investigated by the nation's National Assembly for fraud, cheating and smuggling.

The International Monetary Fund had recommended the sugar monopoly be eliminated as a condition for restructuring the Philippines US$25.6 billion foreign debt, but little had been done, and the same people remained in control. All this toing and froing came to an end in February 1985 with another presidential decree (PD1971) which countermanded all the others. It 'revitalized' the sugar industry by converting NASUTRA into a private corporation called the Philippine Sugar Marketing Corporation (PHILSUMA), to be fully owned by sugar producers. It was too little, too late. The People Power revolution was one year away, and it was left to the incoming government of President Corazon Aquino to try to rationalise the industry.

The last years of the Marcos regime saw Negros descend into a tinderbox of discontent with frustrated and angry sugar workers clamouring for agrarian reform, land distribution, fair wages, and proper working conditions. They were spurred on by communist cadres and NPA rebels who had expanded their infiltration of haciendas, villages, towns, and cities. Sometimes they organised clandestine meetings, other times they openly rallied the people. The mass base of the communists was expanding faster on Negros than anywhere else in the Philippines. Many anxious landowners, in the vulnerable outlying regions where the rebels roamed more freely, abandoned their already distressed farmlands and moved to urban centres for safety, and to escape NPA taxes.

Other, older and wealthier haciendas sought protection by hiring civilian militias, mostly members of the government armed and trained Civilian Home Defence Force (CHDF) whose reputation was little better than ruffians in uniform. On occasions, the landowners helped pay for some of their weapons.

On Negros, it was the CHDF and undisciplined soldiers who were guilty of most human rights abuses, ranging from intimidation, stealing, arson, rape, assault, and indiscriminate killings. Negros was militarized, and in many areas its people were terrorized. Often, people told me they were more frightened of the military than the NPA, to whom they sometimes gave shelter and food. It was a volatile tussle for allegiances and in many areas the government and local authorities were losing.

The CIA reported in 1985 that 'in many areas of the island, the local civilian authorities have been supplanted by military commanders or the insurgents.' The report carried an ominous prediction: 'Negros later this year, in our judgment, has at least an even chance to join Mindanao and become the second politically strategic island in the archipelago where communist influence rivals that of the central government.'

A few months after my return to Manila, Negros was back in the news. In the town of Escalante, 95 kms north of Bacolod, the thirteenth anniversary of martial law's imposition was marked by a protest rally. An estimated 2,000 people – workers, farmers, fishermen, urban poor – gathered in the town's central plaza with protest banners and placards. Encircled by soldiers, CHDF troops, and police, the protesters weren't deterred. Tear gas and water hoses didn't stop the anti-government chanting. But bullets did. Without warning, a volley of gunfire killed more than 20 protesters and wounded at least 30 others. It was one of the Philippines biggest-ever civilian massacres.

Of all the places I've visited in the Philippines, nowhere is the chasm between rich and poor so wide and so deep as it is on Negros.

TWELVE

Workers' rights. What rights?

To Marcos, low wages were intrinsically good. Marcos saw low wages as something to boast about in speeches and in government brochures. He saw it as an advantage the Philippines had over other Asian countries, and with his anti-strike labour laws, he aimed to ensure that the Philippines had a docile labour force as well.

He didn't see his country's chronic low wages as a negative reflection of the state of the economy, but as a positive advantage – an attractive lure to international investors. Martial law gave him the chance to act. Within two months of its imposition, Marcos signed presidential decree No. 66 creating the Bataan Export Processing Zone (BEPZ), 170 kms by road from the capital. It was specifically established to attract foreign industries and businesses. Among various inducements – 100% foreign ownership, an initial six-year tax holiday, and other tax concessions – companies were permitted to pay workers below the minimum wage, and the government promised that any labour disputes would be settled by compulsory arbitration, effectively outlawing strikes.

In the early 1980s, about 80 per cent of the BEPZ's 20,000-strong workforce was female, mostly poorly educated rural workers, and half of them were below 25 years-of-age. Surprisingly, the vast majority were union members. It was a mass sympathy strike involving 14,000 workers that brought me to the BEPZ in 1982.

The mass walkout had been sparked by a strike in one company where some workers complained that they had been sacked for their union membership and for complaining about poor working conditions. The Ministry of Labour and Employment declared it a 'vital' company in an 'essential industry' and said the strike was against the 'national interest'. And what did this company produce that was so vital to the national economy? Plastic bags.

The strike and picketing continued. Fifty-four protesters were arrested and detained. Picketers were attacked by police. That was the breaking point. That's when the majority of workers at the BEPZ went on a 'sympathy strike'.

Young workers, whom I met off site, told me of living in cramped, non-air-conditioned dormitories, of being refused sick or bereavement leave, working 12-hour shifts almost without a break, and of rationed toilet breaks which left some girls with no alternative but to stuff toilet paper or pieces of torn cloth in their panties so they could urinate standing up.

The lowest paid worker I met was a 16-year-old girl. She knew she had been exploited. She told me she had been a trainee for 18 months – three, six-month periods. Just before her first six-month traineeship ended, she was moved to another part of the factory and had to begin an entirely new six-month traineeship. Then, it happened a third time. She was paid the equivalent of US$1 an hour.

Strikes were counteracted with 'union busting' activities such as worker 'lockouts' and mass dismissal of unionists. On one occasion, a company sacked several hundred unionists two weeks after an industrial court awarded the workers their right to join a union. The conditions were so onerous and abhorrent that even the Ministry of Labour and Employment admitted that the cause of most of the strikes were violations of labour standards, underpayment of wages, illegal dismissals, and unfair labour practices.

The International Labour Organisation (ILO) reported the results of a mid-1980s survey that found that seven per cent of workers were paid below the minimum wage, and that across the workforce, cost of living allowances and overtime pay were lower than officially mandated. Another survey of 230 workers quoted by the ILO, found 50 per cent of the workforce worked more than the standard 48-hour week. (The average was 54 hours). Forty-six per cent said they worked two successive shifts. Eleven per cent said they were given no rest period. A 1984 survey by the Ministry of Labour and Employment found seven companies at the BEPZ provided no rest day at all.

Throughout the eighties, the BEPZ was battered by industrial relations problems, cost increases, unfulfilled business returns, market shortfalls, and most significantly bad publicity – domestically and internationally.

The BEPZ never lived up to the ambitious economic projections, and the over-egged spruiking of the Marcos government. In fact, things went backwards. The BEPZ's 1980 target – to convince 113 firms to relocate to the 345-hectare site – was only half met. Just 56 companies set up business at the BEPZ, and five years later the number of companies had dwindled to 50. Thirty per cent of the BEPZ companies were South Korean- and Taiwanese-owned textile and garment factories, known locally as 'sweat factories'.

But most surprising of all was the failure of Marcos's grand strategy: the export-oriented industrialisation of the Philippines through foreign direct investment. It was the raison d'etre for the establishment of the BEPZ. But 10 years after its establishment, the BEPZ had not attracted the hoped-for surge of interest from foreign companies. Just 32.7 per cent of companies were foreign owned, and 26.9 per cent were Filipino owned, according to a 1982 survey by the Ministry of Labour and Employment. The principal motivation of these Philippine-owned companies to re-locate to the BEPZ was legalised wage exploitation, devised and enforced by the Marcos government: the mandated daily wage for Filipino workers *inside* the zone was considerably less than *outside* the BEPZ.

To potential foreign investors, the BEPZ's initial underlying attraction was its cowed workforce and government assurances of controlled wages, significantly below prevailing mandated rates. But, as investors found out, brochure promises often differed from on-the-ground reality.

Outside the confines of the BEPZ, the government tried

to muzzle the growth of trade unions and demands for better pay and conditions, by a diversionary tactic: divide and rule. Working surreptitiously, it tacitly supported the formation of a pro-government union federation, the Trade Union Congress of the Philippines (TUCP), which ostensibly campaigned for workers' rights, but whose conservative leadership actively worked to isolate militant unionists and fragment the nation's trade union movement.

Whenever it could, the Marcos government acted with leniency towards the TUCP – seen by many rival trade unionists as a government aligned 'front' organisation – and saved its strongest anti-labour rhetoric for the more militant left-leaning Kilusang Mayo Uno (May First Movement) that actively competed against the TUCP for membership. It was a shrewd government strategy: give qualified support to 'legitimate' government-approved trade unions, but crackdown on militant labour leaders whose growing popularity threatened to mobilize the workforce and generate wage demands.

From the moment of its birth, in 1980, the KMU was denounced as a communist front; its offices regularly raided, and its leaders harassed and often jailed. KMU leader and founder, Felix Olalia was the doyen of Philippine trade unionism. Beginning as a 13-year-old apprentice in a shoe factory in suburban Manila in the 1930s, Olalia quickly became an assertive and influential union official.

A life-long communist, Olalia won a landmark case that reduced the mandated daily work roster from 12 hours to eight hours, making him a national hero among working people. He was an outspoken critic of Marcos

– a 'firebrand' the government called him – and it was no surprise that he was arrested, without charge, and detained for five months in a military stockade when Marcos imposed martial law in 1972.

What is surprising is that his son, Rolando, a 38-year-old trade union official, was also arrested with his father. He was detained in the same military stockade as his father, only he was released after three months. Both father and son were never charged. It was an act of intimidation by a president with unconstrained powers. But instead of a deterrent it was a spur to action. Upon his release, Olalia Sr. set about organising the KMU which eventually attracted 300,000 members, mostly agricultural and industrial workers. It was the nation's most successful 'grass roots' union, with a national profile, and Olalia became the worker's symbol of anti-government defiance. It also made him a government target, and Marcos set out to make him an example of what happens to trade union leaders who garner a national profile.

In August 1982 – almost exactly 10 years after Felix Olalia was first arrested at the onset of martial law – he was again arrested. And just like the first time, he was seized by soldiers. There was no warrant. He was not charged. He was hauled off the streets and confined to a military cell. So, too, was his son. Their incarceration was an exact repeat of what happened to them 10 years earlier. The military also seized 40 other KMU officials in simultaneous raids.

Days later, Felix Olalia was charged with economic sabotage for threatening to call a general strike. Threating! Not instigating. Not organising. He had called for a nationwide strike for higher wages and better conditions.

For that, he was accused of inciting sedition and rebellion. Olalia was taken to Camp Crame, the headquarters of the Philippine Constabulary in the heart of Manila and forced to lie on a bare concrete floor during hours of interrogation. Olalia was 79.

Frail and suffering heart and blood pressure problems, he was held in a military stockade for nine months, some of that time in solitary confinement. Responding to a report from human rights lawyers that said Olalia's health was deteriorating rapidly and he risked dying in custody, Marcos agreed to release him. Olalia could go home, but he would be kept under house arrest.

Seven months later, in December 1983, Olalia died of heart failure and pneumonia. He was 80 years old. Eulogised as one of the founders of Philippine trade unionism, Olalia had enough strength to write a letter to his supporters the day before he died. In it, he condemned Marcos and described the Philippines as 'one big stinking prison cell'.

On the death of his father and imbued with the same unionist zeal, Rolando Olalia replaced him as chairman of the KMU. It was a seamless transfer. Not only was Rolando steeped in trade union ideology, but his movement up the union ranks was a testament to his father's tutelage. Under Rolando's chairmanship, KMU membership increased by 200,000 to half a million. For once, the son had outdone his father.

Rolando was possibly the most prominent and most popular trade unionist in the country. And, just like his father, that made him a target. In November 1986, two years and 11 months after his father died, Rolando along with his driver was abducted. It happened less than 48 hours after Rolando, responding to rumours, vowed to call a national strike if dissident soldiers loyal to Defence Minister Enrile attempted a coup against the Aquino government.

Olalia Jr. and his driver were found dead the following day, shot, and stabbed multiple times. Rolando was shot four times in the head, twice in the chest, stabbed four times, his eyes gouged out, and newspaper shoved into his mouth. Both bodies were mutilated beyond recognition. Rolando was only identified by a scar on his leg.

They were a team, the Olalias! An incomparable 'father and son' team. They lived for their beliefs and died for their beliefs. The killers of Rolando Olalia and his driver were rumoured to be members of the Reform the Armed Forces Movement (RAM) which had helped usher Cory Aquino to power eight months earlier.

In the Philippines in the 1980s, trade union and student activism were perilous pursuits.

'You have to be prepared to die,' Lean Alejandro, one of the country's most prominent student leaders told me the first time we met. And he was right. Less than two years later, his prophetic acceptance of the inevitable came true. He was murdered. He died for his beliefs – a bullet in the head – at the age of 27.

Alejandro was a natural born leader. Like the Olalias' revered status as the nation's leading crusaders for workers' rights, Alejandro enjoyed notoriety as the Philippines most prominent advocate for students' rights. He was a self-assured, charismatic student protest leader who had outgrown campus politics to become a persuasive advocate of a national campaign to topple the Marcos regime and to restore the people's human, social, and economic rights.

He could harangue and he could cajole. To his supporters, he was a rabblerouser who they would gladly follow to the barricades. But the police and the military regarded him as a dangerous troublemaker. When I last saw Alejandro, I was on the edge of a crowd of placard carrying protesters who had thronged the imposing Post Office steps for an anti-government rally.

Lean Alejandro was the Prince of Protest. No one could work the crowd like he could. Positioned half-way up the steps, bullhorn to his lips, he spoke, sometimes shouted, in Tagalog and in English, and the crowd with their bobbing sea of placards and unfurled banners, listened quietly, sometimes rowdily, always intently. At various times during Alejandro's haranguing address, they cheered, booed, and chanted. They were frustrated, angry, and bitter, and it showed.

A lot of faith had been placed in Alejandro. Too much, perhaps. He was a young firebrand in the protest movement, which was dominated by old-style pre-martial law unionists, who yearned for the old days, and probably the old ways. Jailed for two months in 1985 for student activism, Alejandro had always lived under the Marcos dictatorship. For him, he could only imagine what a functioning democracy was like. Like all Filipinos his age and younger, Alejandro's quest for a better, freer life had nothing to do with restoring past freedoms, because he had never known the sort of freedom many older people spoke of with such nostalgia. For almost his entire life, Alejandro, and millions of others, had grown up in a Marcos dominated world. Marcos is all he had ever known.

He was five years old when Marcos was elected president. And he was 12 when Marcos declared martial law. And then, for the next 14 years, right through Alejandro's teenage years and into his early adulthood, Marcos was always there. If you set aside Alejandro's first five years as an infant, he enjoyed only 19 months of a Marcos-free life (after Marcos fled into exile) before he was assassinated in a roadside ambush blamed, at the time, on a soldier.

Before his death, Alejandro was known as a notoriously active critic and protestor. He was one of the key leaders who marched in the front ranks of the so-called 'parliament of the streets.' Alejandro was a child of the protest movement. It was happening before his birth, and it continued after his death.

From its beginnings in the 1960s, the nascent student movement exploded in the early 1970s with an outpouring of rallies that yearly grew bigger, more boisterous, more demanding, and frequently violent. Others joined – disgruntled urban and rural workers and office workers – and clamoured for change. Rallies shook the nation. Marcos responded with severe crackdowns on freedom of speech and assembly. Eventually, he clamped the nation under martial law in 1972.

Once confined to campus politics, student activists became more nationalistic, more left-wing. Their narrow focus on student issues, widened and they launched nationwide campaigns against unemployment, rising poverty, and they demanded a restoration of civil and human rights.

In cautious defiance of martial law, like-minded alliances were formed with landless and exploited farmers, underpaid and unemployed urban workers, and slum communities. Sympathetic priests, nuns, and laypeople followed suit. There was a common cause and a compelling reason for these protest movements to unite: the economy was in the doldrums. In the mid-1980s, inflation, unemployment, and underemployment skyrocketed, and the economy either stagnated or underperformed. One in four residents in Manila was officially classified a squatter. It was worse in the countryside, with health, welfare, and public housing either underfinanced, or virtually non-existent.

Military raids and roundups at worksites, campuses, union premises, and offices netted thousands of suspected 'communists', or 'left-wing sympathisers'. Many were jailed, without charge, and indefinitely detained. With such extraordinary carte blanche authoritarian powers, the police and the military were roundly condemned as human right abusers. Basic liberties were swept aside, and protests suppressed. And as the protests became commonplace, the general public grew increasingly troubled by what they saw: the law enforcers were more often than not the law breakers whose immunity from prosecution was virtually assured by a pro-government, Marcos-appointed judiciary.

Many students and academics were swept up in the government ordered clampdown on dissidents. The more disillusioned headed to 'the hills' where they joined the communist New People's Army, took up guns, and fervently plotted the overthrow of the Marcos regime.

It was to such a turbulent world that Alejandro committed himself. He fought his way up through the student ranks and emerged a persuasive master campaigner and a charismatic leader who could galvanise a crowd to action. After that Post Office rally, I didn't see Alejandro again. Several weeks later, in September 1987, he called a press conference to announce plans for a nationwide workers strike against wage stagnation, trade union intimidation, and creeping militarisation sweeping the land. Marcos had gone. Corazon Aquino was in power. But the injustices remained. The press conference, held on a Saturday, declared a national strike for the following Monday, which coincided with the 15th anniversary of the imposition of martial law.

Alejandro lived for about one hour after his press conference. He had become a leader and as such, like so many others before him, that made him a target to be silenced. To be killed. Driven to his office on the other side of the city, Alejandro's car (with him in the front seat) was blocked by a white van as it was about to enter the compound. Alejandro was shot several times 'in the face and the neck and died instantly', the military said. Speculation was that his assassin was a 'right-wing soldier'.

The deaths of the two highly prominent and popular leaders – Alejandro, the activist, and Olalia, the unionist – which occurred within a year of each other, are compellingly similar. Both were believed to have been killed by renegade soldiers linked to the Reform the Armed Forces Movement (RAM) which was involved in the ousting of Marcos and the installation of the Aquino government. However, within months of Aquino taking office, dissatisfied RAM officers, who felt ostracised and unrewarded by the Aquino government, began plotting against her and were involved in several coup attempts. Alejandro was killed three weeks *after* an attempted military coup against the Aquino government, and Olalia was killed one week *before* another military coup attempt against the Aquino government.

Speculation at the time was that RAM had embarked on a cunning strategy: eliminate prominent left-wing agitators; fan the perception of national instability; and trigger calls for greater military powers to clamp down on dissidents. But RAM had problems of its own. Its politization and its destabilisation tactics against the Aquino government had caused dissention in its own ranks, tarnished its worsening public image, and had turned previous supporters into critics. Six failed military coups in the year after Aquino took power shattered any semblance of national stability at a decisively crucial time. Instead of an orderly transfer of power, military malcontents set the country on a course of political brinkmanship. This image of instability and uncertainty, exploited by Aquino's political opponents, sapped public confidence in the fledgling Aquino government and robbed it of the rock-solid authority necessary to bring in the myriad reforms the nation so badly needed, post Marcos.

THIRTEEN

Gloria's life in a box.

Apparently, sometime in the '70s, some big motor car manufacturer used to ship cars to the Philippines in massive, almost impenetrable cardboard boxes. One car per box.

Once off-loaded, these boxes took on a whole new life that the port authorities pretended not to know about, provided they were given 'tong' (a bribe) at the port gates. Far from being destroyed, as they should have been, these boxes had a new life awaiting them in the seething slums of Manila.

For those who had nothing, a box was something. It was a step up from the ramshackle, higgledy-piggledy shanties that for decades had housed generation after generation of Manila's most destitute, most downtrodden, most forgotten people. Hundreds of thousands of them.

The poorest beggars lived in cemeteries. They built hovels of scrap material on top of raised gravestones, which kept their feet dry. Inside these crude structures they sheltered from the sun and the rain, slept, ate, played, nursed children, and carried on living their lives among the dead. The lucky ones lived inside mausoleums among the crypts where it was dry but dark, and insects thrived, and rats bred. Generations lived their entire lives surrounded by death, and children clambered over the graves and played hide and seek among the tombstones.

It was a world with no basic services, no sanitation, and no water. A world where illegally tapped electricity was supplied by a tangle of low-slung electricity wires and cables that sprouted from power poles beyond the cemetery gate. A world where the poor had dug their own open-air pits to use as toilets, unseen between the rows of gravestones, and where the tops of gravestones were used to prepare and cook meals, often on little kerosene stoves. Even squatters ranked graveyard living as the worst.

In contrast, a flimsy shanty on unused land was pretty good, and a sturdy cardboard box was probably best of all. A weather-proof car-size cardboard box was much better than a teetering shanty, fashioned from scrounged materials and held together by rusty nails, wire, ropes, and old car tyres. Nothing was permanent. Every typhoon or torrential downpour proved destructive. So, too, the fires that regularly erased entire slum districts. Begging was existing, not living.

Owning one of these boxes had become an obsession for some, the object of envy. This fierce desire had not gone unnoticed by some underworld characters and dubious street merchants. It was they who stood outside the dockyard gates with bribe money for 'box drivers' and told them where they could unload their prized cargo. It was a lucrative, shady, and illegal trade.

Gloria lived in a box. It was perched halfway up a dusty hill that became a squishy muddy mess the moment it rained, which was often. There were open drains of stagnant sewage-like sludge, mixed with scraps of muck and floating plastic bottles. Unrecognisable slimy, oily goo overflowed, often into and through the shanties below. The whole place was criss-crossed by a shambolic network of commandeered electricity cables, some dangling dangerously low on teetering poles, and others looped ridiculously high to bring electricity to the few two-storey 'sari-sari' stores which provided the most basic and cheapest groceries and snacks.

Over the years, Gloria had become a resourceful scavenger, collecting sheets of rusted corrugated iron, rolls of used tarpaulin, and discarded plastic. She covered the roof of her box until the tell-tale cardboard beneath couldn't be seen. It made her box extra waterproof and blended in with the surrounding shanties.

Gloria was a single mother of two. Her husband died in a motorcycle accident several years ago. She earned a pittance cleaning the house of an uppity middle-class family that lived one suburb away. So how could Gloria afford a box? In this prying, nosey, no-secrets community, Gloria was viewed with envy. I met Gloria in a roundabout way.

Throughout the Marcos years, anti-unionism was rife. Physical violence against unionists, or ransacking of union offices was routinely initiated, encouraged, or tolerated by the government. And if the police weren't involved, it was the military. All methods were regularly used – harassment, raids on union offices, open discrimination against union workers, threats, intimidation, and particularly violent assaults, often death.

In most cases, employers flatly rejected any improvements to wages and conditions, and any effort to try to unionise the workforce was openly opposed, actively denied, or met with outright hostility or brutality. In a cautious counter move, the most committed union-trained workers were used to infiltrate worksites, to try to convince fellow workers to join the union. Mostly, their efforts failed. The union 'troublemakers', as they were called, were quickly identified and instantly sacked. Surveillance of union organisers was frequent and open, arrests were commonplace.

Within the union movement, Gloria was a hero. But the owners of the fish canning factory in suburban Manila where Gloria once worked saw her as nothing but a troublemaker. She had secured a much sought-after job in the factory, two bus rides away. It was a rare job offer which paid a barely liveable wage. Not good, but better than nothing.

The fish canning factory was contained in a vast corrugated iron shed. With concrete floors and few windows, the atmosphere was stifling, but individual fish quotas were expected to be met, and the conveyer belt never stopped. It certainly didn't stop for a toilet break. You were allowed to go to the toilet anytime – provided it coincided with your 20-minute lunch break, or your 10-minute afternoon break. At other times, if you had no control of your bladder, you had to squat and pee on the concrete floor. The pools of urine were hosed away at the end of each shift, along with the fish guts and fish heads which travelled down open drains under each gutting bench.

It didn't take long for Gloria's muttered complaints about conditions and pay to echo down the line. Others agreed. Over the next few weeks, annoyance turned to anger, and the muttering got louder. Quick to act, the factory manager called Gloria into his office and sacked her. The 'revolt' had been nipped in the bud, and to ensure no bad feelings or possible repercussions, the remaining workers were given a small pay rise. That did the trick. The factory workers, unused to the ways of union bargaining, fell into line and stopped complaining. They cherished their hard-to-get jobs in a dog-eat-dog world. Over the years, they had come to accept the painful reality: take the wages and put up with the conditions or lose your job.

Gloria had been a fish gutter, not an agitator. She was not a unionist, certainly not a union infiltrator, but what she had seen and suffered in the fish canning factory had awoken her union sympathies. Her only crime was to demand better pay and conditions. Even though Gloria's fellow workers had been too timid and too fearful to openly support her then, she was now their hero.

News of Gloria's confrontation with her factory boss, made her a much-admired worker's rights champion, and for a while she became a cause célèbre in the union movement. In fact, she joined the union after her sacking and her reputation spread among the squatter community. Several months after her sacking, a 'box truck' drove into the squatter settlement and unloaded Gloria's box. It was the union's gift to Gloria for being a worker's rights champion. Now that she was unemployed, it was the least they could do. Even though Gloria was no longer working, and no longer a unionist, she was the person the union suggested I talk to.

Directed to Gloria's box, I knocked on a large, heavy sheet of metal with rusty lopsided hinges. It was Gloria's door. She appeared and beckoned me inside. She had been told to expect me, the first non-Filipino to visit. I handed her a gift: a plastic bag of canned goods. It included a can of Spam – the salty processed pork was considered a luxury – plus a can of baked beans, a tin of sardines, and eggs. Gloria's box was such an object of desire and envy among squatters that I had expected more than just this oblong, human-size cardboard box in which I could barely stand and move about. But no amount of wall hangings and homely knickknacks could disguise the fact that it once contained a car, stored in a cargo ship's hold.

Oddly shaped pieces of foraged carpet samples covered the entire earth floor. The scavenged steel door had been made to fit a big hole in the cardboard wall, and another smaller hole next to the door was an open window which provided the only light and air in Gloria's box. Like a human-size doll's house, every effort had been made to make it homely. Plastic boxes of uniform size and without their lids had been placed on their sides to make a wobbly open chest of drawers. The boxes feature piece of furniture was a long and narrow open wooden box at least three metres long. A wire was strung from one end of the box to the other end along which a tiny handmade curtain was drawn. It was Gloria's treasured place for keepsakes.

On every available wall space were movie posters, magazine and newspaper clippings, several calendars of different years, a giant poster of swaying palms on a golden beach, dog-eared photos and, most curiously, a huge close-up photo of a steaming bowl of Sinigang, a favourite Filipino soup. It appeared every effort had been made to cover the entire inside of the box.

A floral plastic shower curtain, which hung limply from a piece of rope, cordoned off the tiniest sleeping space for Gloria and her two children. Each night, Gloria unrolled a tattered bamboo floor mat on which she and the girls slept among the strewn belongings. There was not enough space and no ventilation for inside cooking. That was done outside, under the cover of a large overhanging single sheet of tin. This 'squatters veranda' also provided some shade from the relentless sun. The prized cooking pots and pans were always kept inside for safe keeping.

With no husband and almost no work, Gloria's world was bleak. In halting English, Gloria recounted a life of relentless difficulties, hardship, and heartbreak. She was surprisingly sanguine about her life which had begun in miserable rural poverty in far-off Mindanao. It got even worse, when it should have got better, when she arrived in Manila. She did not regret her brief stint as a factory worker, she said. In fact, her fish canning days were a revelation: how can workers be so mistreated and exploited?

Gloria was not the poorest of the poor, even in this squatter village, but she recalled the time when life was so bad, she almost gave up. 'Rock bottom,' she said, referring to that period, almost two years ago. No work, she said. No money. No food. Living in the box was all very good, but having something to eat was better.

'What's been the most difficult thing?' I asked. In response, she turned her head and nodded to the picture above her bed space. 'I used to have four,' she said with tears in her eyes. The family photo I had barely noticed was in fact a photo of four smiling children.

Over the next few minutes, gentle prodding produced the answers I needed, but earnestly hoped I wouldn't hear. A sympathetic distant relative arrived at Gloria's door a few years ago after hearing that Gloria was slipping further into poverty and depression. Days went by when her four children only ate because of the generosity of neighbours, who could barely feed themselves.

A friendly childless couple was prepared to take two of the children, the relative told Gloria. They would look after Gloria's children as if they were theirs. The three-day deadline for an answer came and went, followed by another two days. Gloria delayed making the decision that she knew was the right one, her heart told her so: sacrifice her two younger children so she could keep the two older ones.

One Sunday morning, after mass, she said a harrowing goodbye to the two 'chosen' children, walked back inside the church and never saw them again. No money was exchanged, but the new parents did as they promised – a generous sum was deposited into a special account for Gloria's two remaining children.

The deposited money was more than Gloria had

ever imagined. She 'lost' two children, but the other two survived and they were doing well, she said. 'Things are much better now,' she assured me. 'I can feed my children, and I'm better too,' she added.

'Now let's eat,' she jumped up. I hadn't noticed the darkness closing in. A single light bulb sent a faint glow throughout Gloria's box. Gloria returned from outside with two pots and joined me, cross-legged, on a small mat.

Gloria crossed herself, as she did before every meal. 'Yes, I'm better,' she reassured me, and without another word, quickly scooped two large servings of rice onto our plates. Then, lifting the lid of the other pot, she placed on top of the rice equal servings of steamed grass.

FOURTEEN

Imelda's folly and the concrete tomb.

Picture this.

Picture a rubble-strewn, chaotic building site where the roof frame, unable to hold the weight of a massive amount of quick-setting concrete, has collapsed, sending a cascading wave of clammy concrete mix, wooden framework, and steel girders crashing onto workers below, burying them under tonnes of concrete and rubble, suffocating some, and impaling others.

It happened at about 3 a.m. 17 November 1981 during the rushed construction – on orders of Imelda Marcos – of Manila's Film Center.

Picture this several hours later.

Picture a barely discernible head of white, dust-encrusted matted hair sticking out of hard concrete. That's all. Just a head of hair, like a cleaner's mop, barely recognisable because it's so tousled. It's a labourer's head. I can see the dust caked hair, the tops of two ears, and his forehead. Nothing else. Somewhere, down there, is the rest of his face and his body, moulded in concrete. Entombed.

PICTURE ANOTHER SCENE.

Picture a man standing with his right foot encased in concrete. He is lean and tall, and except for his trapped foot, he appears uninjured. He has been trapped for so long that the quick-dry concrete has hardened and encased his foot, just above his ankle. Occasionally, he gulps from a plastic bottle of water. With his left hand, he holds onto a bent steel rod – a reinforcement bar – protruding from the concrete, while a rescuer uses a giant crowbar to try to free him. A companion of the rescuer squats, watching, a few metres away.

Thud… (three seconds). Thud… (three seconds). Thud… (three seconds). He strikes at the concrete near the man's trapped foot with a slow rhythmic effort. It's agonising to hear, agonising to watch. It's obvious there's a chain-gang rhythm in his head and he's keeping pace. Not once does his companion offer to help. He is content to squat and watch.

Even if they do manage to release his foot, I recall thinking, he will still be left with a concrete shoe. It's slow. Unbelievably slow. No jack hammers. Nothing. And it's quiet. I recall thinking how quiet it is for a disaster scene. Just these two rescuers, and only one of them actually doing something. Only later, hours after I left the scene, did I realised that these two men were not 'real' rescuers, they were on-site labourers in dust covered work clothes, who obviously had survived the disaster and had come to help free a fellow worker with the only thing they could find: the giant crowbar.

There were teams of rescuers outside the building when I arrived, and I passed many more when I clambered over rubble and eventually stumbled, literally, into the main theatre area where the roof collapsed. Now that I was there, where were the others? The rescuers, the firemen, policeman, the medics? I had arrived about two hours after it happened. Where was the rushing to and fro, the shouted orders, the frenzied hubbub of chaotic rescues? Was it all over? Was it possible that all the survivors had been rescued, and the victims retrieved before I arrived? Or was the opposite true? Bodies under concrete make no sound, don't need rescuing, just retrieval. No need to rush.

I had managed to get inside the very heart of the main hall, where the roof of wet concrete had collapsed, and yet I saw only a handful of rescuers around the sides of the destroyed hall.

The lasting image I have is of those two 'rescuers', a single crowbar, the agonisingly slow 'chain-gang' rhythm, and that dull steel on concrete sound. Thud… (three seconds). Thud… (three seconds). Thud… (three seconds). That's the lonely sound I remember, not sirens, not frantic yelling. Only, thud… (three seconds), thud… (three seconds), thud… (three seconds). I never did find out how that man managed to get his foot trapped in the concrete. Or if he survived.

Thinking back.

It was the sounds of sirens that woke me. Many, many, sirens. Different types. Police, ambulance, fire brigade. A cacophony of sound that no one could sleep through. I arrived just after daybreak, about 5 a.m.

I lived a five-minute drive away and arrived to find several ambulances, fire engines, police vehicles, and several dark-window official looking cars. A few survivors were being carried on stretchers to ambulances, several walking wounded were being assisted to ambulance transport vehicles. But that was it. Maybe the others had already been rescued or dug out, I remember thinking, because from the outside, the scope of the disaster wasn't apparent. I recall the ease I was able to sidle my way through an easily breached security cordon. It was 10 minutes before security agents found me inside the shattered structure and sternly marched me out. Inside, it was a scene of utter devastation, and strangely quiet. I recall seeing or hearing very few rescuers, other than the man with the crowbar, and he looked to be a worker not a rescuer.

After I left, I heard that a tight, armed, security cordon had been thrown up around the scene and a news blackout imposed. It lasted 15 hours, long enough for a rattled government to come up with its version of events and to claim three workers had died and more than 30 others had been injured.

My colleagues at UPI (United Press International) disagreed. By the end of the day, their conservative tally was 26 dead and at least 30 missing, feared dead. UPI also quoted hospital 'sources' as confirming a further 41 injured. The public, shocked but not surprised that such a rushed project collapsed so spectacularly, speculated that more than 100 workers died, based on the number of workers who went to work and never returned home.

THINKING FURTHER BACK TO THE BEGINNING.

As always, Imelda Marcos thought big. Manila, she believed, could become Asia's film capital. She had it all planned out, in her mind. First, build an extravagant Film Center in the style of the Parthenon on reclaimed land in Manila Bay. Next, launch the Manila International Film Festival. Be sure to make it the biggest film festival in Asia. Finally, model it on the famous French film festival in Cannes, and don't forget to import white sand from nearby Cavite for an instant beach.

Famous for having once said, 'What the first lady wants, the first lady gets', Imelda Marcos set a ridiculous deadline to get the job done. Construction began in August 1981 and Imelda Marcos had circled January 18, 1982, as the launch date for the Manila International Film Festival. To meet such a rigorous timetable, 1,500 workers were employed on the site. It was non-stop – eight-hour shifts, 24-hours a day, seven days a week. Shortcuts were taken. Mistakes were bound to happen. Accidents seemed inevitable, especially as the most important concrete pour of the entire project was set to occur at 3 a.m. But that was indicative of the pace Imelda Marcos demanded.

News of the building disaster was slow to get out,

hours went by, and when the government press office finally released details, they were sparse and confused and immediately ridiculed and rebutted by a shocked public which by then had already heard the survivors' eyewitness accounts, relayed mouth-to-mouth.

Days later, Imelda Marcos ordered that construction of the Film Center resume. The premature recommencement of work – before a full inquiry could be undertaken – only fuelled swirling rumours and gossip, most of which blamed Imelda Marcos for the disaster, and criticised her insensitivity. Some of the bereaved summoned their courage and denounced the culpability of Imelda Marcos, igniting the nation's hyperactive rumour mill.

One of the most gruesome rumours I heard – from all levels of society, the poor and the rich alike – was that Imelda Marcos had ordered that bodies already entombed in concrete be left where they were, and that any protruding limbs be cut off and the stumps plastered over.

Of all the rumours, this was the most outrageous; the fastest to emerge, the quickest to spread, and the one that most people believed. The palace denials were quick and emphatic, but the rumour's emergence was itself a story. Never, in all my years in the Philippines, did I witness such a dramatic re-casting of Imelda Marcos's public standing, at least in Manila. The people's trust in Imelda Marcos plummeted the moment the Film Center collapsed. The scuttlebutt imputed her character and honesty. For the families of those who died, Imelda Marcos bore most of the blame and they said so publicly. It was a rare moment.

Imelda Marcos was determined not to let a disaster jeopardise the Film Center's inauguration date. She ordered that work be accelerated. Up to the very last moment, tradesmen frantically worked to complete the Film Center on time. They did. News reports boasted that finishing touches were still being applied 15 minutes before the inauguration guests arrived.

Inevitably, the Film Center was dubbed 'Manila's Largest Tomb' by superstitious Filipinos, and many stayed away in droves when the 'cursed' building was opened. It was snubbed by ordinary Filipinos and boycotted by socialites. People claimed that in the center's corridors and rooms, they heard muffled cries and voices, strange sounds, sudden draughts, and eerie shadows.

FIFTEEN

To buy a life, you sacrifice three.

It was a seminal moment, the time I saw three people die in a luxury hotel fire in the mid-1980s.

I came across the fire by chance. My wife and I lived in a middle-class housing compound, immodestly called a village, just off Roxas Boulevard, that flanked Manila Bay. One morning, I was driving off to something I can't remember, when I saw distant smoke. Traffic had slowed to a stop-start crawl, the urgent alarms of fire engines and ambulances could be heard, and traffic cops were waving motorists on. They couldn't cordon off the onlookers, however, and scores gathered as close as they could around the hotel gates.

Normally, I'm not an ambulance chaser, nor a fire watcher. But this was different. I was close enough to see several hotel guests on their hotel room balconies, trapped by fire and smoke, waving and shouting, pleading to be rescued. As a foreigner, I had no trouble pushing my way through the crowd at the gates to join 30 or more hotel guests and bystanders gathered in the hotel forecourt, excitedly, frantically, yelling instructions and words of encouragement. Only one fire engine with an extension ladder was on the scene. There may have been others, but in the confusion, I saw only small fire-fighting units and a couple of ambulances.

Luckily, this hotel fire was half-way up the building's façade and reachable by the fire ladder which, when I arrived, had been extended out to maximum height. All eyes were on two figures – a father, and his daughter, probably. They were trapped by fire. Engulfed in smoke. Obviously terrified, they were waving their arms high above their heads and yelling. I couldn't hear their cries, but I could see their panic. They scurried frantically, hysterically, along the length of the balcony. Trapped. With no way out. Tongues of flames loomed behind them. Billowing black smoke coursed skywards. For a while, like cornered prey, they paced the small balcony, looking down, leaning over, before they eventually huddled defeated in a corner.

Next door, in an identical apartment on the same floor, was a woman, middle-aged, dark-haired. She was frantically waving what looked like a pillow. She, too, was distraught and shouting, sometimes doubling over in a coughing fit. There were no flames rising behind her, just clouds and clouds of the densest black smoke. I'm sure she couldn't see the man and young girl trapped in the room to her left. To the woman's right, three balconies away, I could see one other person, a man in white Arab robes, pacing back and forth, seeking rescue. There was some smoke, but no flames. He, too, looked agitated and desperate.

Rescue was close at hand, I thought. In the five minutes I had been there, the fire engine had slowly, ever so slowly, moved the extension ladder within what looked like a metre or two of the desperate father and daughter. They had priority. The fire had engulfed part of the bedroom behind them. The heat must have been intense, unbearable. I imagined the heat had melted the clothes on their backs. Suffocating smoke poured out in rolling dense black waves and tumbled skywards.

What was happening? Why had the ladder stopped moving? I wanted to shout. Instead, I looked on, totally bewildered. It's just a couple more metres. Move it! Move the ladder! It's almost within reach! Desperate, the father and daughter, reached out and frantically pawed the air, but the ladder was a metre away, maybe even less. It was out of reach. The rescue ladder didn't budge. Why? Like everyone else, I was flummoxed, angry, furious. I wanted to know what was going on. Why the delay? Surely there wasn't a mechanical problem.

Then, I saw something that chilled me. Instantly, I knew what was happening. Standing at the back of the fire engine, next to a man in uniform (probably the fire chief) was a civilian. He wore the same free-flowing Arab robes as the trapped hotel guest above, and he was in deep conversation with the uniformed fire brigade officer.

Almost immediately – 10 seconds at most – the ladder moved. Not towards the father and daughter, but away from them. It was agonizing to watch. Together, the two victims reached out so far, I'm surprised they didn't topple over the balcony. What must they be thinking? At that very moment, they must have known it was the end. The ladder, which had been only a metre away was now two metres away, three metres. It was gone. Forever.

With searing flames now roaring behind them, they had no choice. Suddenly. Inevitably. It happened. The father and daughter clambered onto the balcony ledge, immediately steadied, clasped hands, and jumped without a moment's hesitation, and without even exchanging a final look. Maybe the father said something. Who knows? They didn't propel themselves off the ledge with a mighty leap, they simply took one step forward and plummeted to their deaths.

Without stopping, the ladder moved on. Gradually, further and further to the left. Without stopping, it passed the balcony where the woman had been enveloped by billowing smoke. The pillow was gone. She hung limply over the balcony, lifeless.

By the time the ladder reached just below the balcony where the man in Arab clothing waited, a fireman had come to the rescue. He had climbed three-quarters up the ladder, even while it was moving, to make sure he could assist the hotel guest. In the end, it was a quick rescue. Both men descended the ladder backwards. The fireman first.

It was a moment of unspeakable immorality.

SIXTEEN

How did that body get there?

In genteel surroundings, like the luxury Manila Hotel, where the super-rich flaunt their wealth, politicians plan and plot, businessman huddle doing deals, and celebrities strut and preen, you expect the best in life. In fact, you demand it.

The Manila Hotel is the best place to be. The best place to be seen. When I lived in the Philippines, the Manila Hotel was the finest, most prestigious five-star hotel in the city, probably one of the best in Asia. It was the hotel of choice for so many world leaders, businessmen, international actors, singers, authors and 'look-at-me' celebrities.

It was historic too. Opened in 1912, the Manila Hotel was once the home and command centre of five-star American general, Douglas MacArthur. Destroyed in the Second World War, the hotel was rebuilt, refurbished, and relaunched.

Imelda Marcos, a regular guest, loved it. She would, I suppose! It probably reminded her of home: the royal entrance red carpet, the chandeliers, the marble columns, and the glitzy dripping ostentatiousness. The Manila Hotel was indeed the Philippines showcase hotel. Nothing was so pompous and so garishly swank, and nothing better personified the country's ever-widening chasm between the rich and the poor.

No building was better positioned, right on the edge of Rizal Park, one of the biggest in Asia, and the scene of inaugurations, Independence Day flag-raising ceremonies, and heads of state visits. The Manila Hotel was in the heart of the city, right next to Manila Bay. Many would probably say that the white-painted, Spanish inspired Manila Hotel stood on sacred ground. No hotel was more prominently positioned, or more prestigious.

So why was it, on this day, that a man lay dead, half his skull blown off, only about 100 metres from the polished doors of the Manila Hotel? The lifeless body was emblematic of the nation. Here was a country, and a leader, so determined to show to the world that he had delivered progress, stability, and normality to the Philippines, when in fact the evidence proved otherwise.

Minutes earlier, my wife and I had been passing nearby. We saw the small crowd and went to investigate. A man lay there, sprawled on his back, his legs tangled in a strangely twisted way, and his arms spread wide. A gunshot blast had demolished the right side of his head. Part of his skull – shaped eerily like half a coconut shell – and other pieces of his brain, lay on the ground, a short distance away.

On a roughly torn large piece of cardboard near his feet was scrawled one word: 'Thief'. My wife and I turned away. We had seen enough. But most of the onlookers didn't move, some children among them. In fact, the crowd had grown to a more than a dozen onlookers in just a few minutes.

This was midday. We were in Manila's biggest and most popular park – full of promenading couples, families, and playful children – and we were among people attracted not by a busker or an impromptu performer, but by the sight of a body. Instead of turning away in horror, they peered in curious, morbid silence. Had it come to this? Had a body, a gruesome body, displayed for all to see in a public park, become so normal, so commonplace, that it was little more than a sidewalk attraction?

I was shocked. Not just by the sight, but by the incongruity of it all – a body, left on public display, with a sign tagging him a thief! Who shot him? The police? The military? Why leave him there, in full view, abandoned so close to the steps of the nation's most prestigious hotel? To me, the death I saw that day burst the bubble of Manila's much vaunted big-city sophistication, the 'city of man', as Imelda Marcos called it. To others, Manila was a 'cowboy' town. But to me, this mangled corpse was brutally symbolic of what the Philippines had become under Marcos.

With no one around – no policeman or security guard – I approached a nattily dressed hotel doorman and told him of the body almost on the hotel's doorstep. Expressionless, and without a word, he turned and went inside. I suppose he went looking for help. I don't know if he found it because I left just as more and more hotel guests spilled out from the hotel lobby to investigate for themselves what was happening.

I never read anything about the killing on the hotel's doorstep. I wasn't surprised. The murder would have blemished the hotel's image of opulence and civility. This, after all, was where the rich and powerful elites gathered to exclude, for a time, the unpleasant reality of the world outside. In such a world, a news blackout was essential, inevitable, and sadly predictable. Afterall, the hotel's image was at stake. 'Image' was paramount, and death was brushed aside. Ignored.

Flanked by lavish furnishings, gaudy wall decorations, massive flower arrangements, and chandeliers galore, the lobby of the Manila Hotel was almost 40 metres long and about eight metres wide. It exuded wealth and it flaunted excess.

One man, in particular, loved it. Defence Minister Juan Ponce Enrile, the pretender to the Marcos crown, who never quite made it. I saw him on several occasions arrive at the hotel in a three- or four-vehicle convoy, at least two were gleaming white bullet-proof vehicles, with black tinted windows. Immediately behind was a military jeep or van.

Enrile was a civilian who loved the trappings and enjoyed all the privileges of a pretend general. He believed, unflinchingly, in his own self-importance. Many times, I saw his convoy speed through intersections, lights flashing, horns blaring. Often, he held 'casual' meetings at the Manila Hotel and several times I watched the show.

The moment Enrile's convoy stopped at the hotel's

entrance, bodyguards would fling open the passenger side doors. One or two bodyguards would secure the scene, their guns at the ready, while another bodyguard would usher aside the doorman so he could personally open the door for Enrile. It was a grand entrance, maybe not fit for a king, but certainly befitting a well-rewarded beneficiary of martial law. In a militarized country, nothing better personified the toppling of civilian pre-eminence than this man. Vaingloriously, he entered the hotel lobby as if he owned it. Every bodyguard was a soldier and every one of them was dressed in a Barong Tagalog, the formal long-sleeved shirt which was worn outside the pants, and which conveniently hid their pistols from view. Every time it was the same. An arrival performance to impress. At least two or three bodyguards flanked Enrile, shoulder to shoulder, as he imperiously strode the red carpet through the lobby. Hotel guests, instinctively, moved aside to let him pass. Several other bodyguards scampered ahead. It was their job to secure the premises, to make sure that no assassin, left-wing agitator, or protestor was among the mingling bourgeoise in the lobby of the hotel. Guests stared, ill at ease and disbelieving. Enrile's advance entourage cleared a path though the mingling guests. Doorways and adjoining rooms were checked.

Enrile, a smirk on permanent display, walked with a self-assured swagger. He looked as arrogant as he was. Here was a man who luxuriated in his unprecedented martial law powers. He oozed the pomposity of power. Next, he showed his utter rudeness. On this occasion, like others before it, I witnessed his bodyguards precede him to an open coffee lounge area, presumably Enrile's favourite, where they approached every seated person – no matter who they were – and asked, possibly ordered them to vacate their chairs. There was a surprise commotion as guests hastily retrieved glasses, food, and coffee cups from their tables and irritably searched for somewhere else to sit.

Enrile had arrived! Make way for Enrile! He settled into a chair, and miraculously the people Enrile had come to meet emerged from somewhere. They had been discretely waiting for the defence minister to arrive and they settled into the hastily vacated still warm seats. The ever-present, ever-ready bodyguards stood by at a discreet, respectful distance, behind miniature potted palm trees, doorways, and pieces of furniture, and shooed away everyone – hotel guests, tourists, and businesspeople – who dared to even get near Enrile's self-sanctified cordon sanitaire.

It was Enrile at his bombastic best. The Manila Hotel was his stage.

SEVENTEEN

I'M WATCHING YOU.

The three-year period, 1983 to 1986, was probably the most dramatically decisive political juncture in modern Philippine history.

This segment of history was bookended by two milestone events: the 1983 assassination of opposition leader, Benigno Aquino, and the 1986 toppling of Ferdinand Marcos. The choices, alliances, and decisions made in those in-between years decided the fate of the nation.

The Aquino assassination was the catalyst for change; it put the Philippines on an inexorable trajectory to revolution. Immensely popular, Aquino had ignited the hopes of millions of Filipinos downtrodden by years of grinding poverty, brutal police and military suppression, worsening health standards, and a growing chasm between the rich and the poor. With Aquino's death, nothing could stem the anger and the consequential protests that grew bigger and angrier in the following three years.

The influential Catholic church had grown more belligerent in its opposition to Marcos; the faction riven ranks in the senior levels of the Armed Forces had intensified to the point that the military's loyalty to Marcos was questionable; and the swelling membership of a united opposition showed a greater commitment to Marcos's removal than ever before.

Anti-Marcos agitation which was growing on all fronts – urban and rural workers, unions, students, and increasingly, the business class – was buoyed by a growing belief that the mobilisation of anti-Marcos forces was not just possible, it was unstoppable. This common goal – the ousting of Marcos – underpinned the emergence of a loose alliance of the old established political parties, and the cause-oriented movements for land reform, human rights, and social justice. Overriding all else, they saw Marcos's declining health, acuity, and acumen as adding to the nation's economic and political volatility. For once, Marcos's opponents and critics saw vulnerability; the future of the two-decades-old Marcos regime was increasingly uncertain. Few people believed it would end peacefully.

For the more radical street protestors, the gnawing frustration was at bursting point. They were growing restless and impatient for change; violence seemed inevitable. The growing radicalism of the left-wing activists was matched in recent demonstrations by the greater forcefulness of the security forces. In the months before Marcos's ouster, one demonstration I attended was reminiscent of a bloody street battle.

It was an angry demonstration from the start. This

was a demonstration by seasoned activists, and the signs were obvious: students, young people, few 'ordinary' citizens, almost no families. Many of the protestors wore facemasks, carried banners that could easily become batons, and wore backpacks or haversacks, most likely filled with demonstration 'paraphernalia'.

From their gathering point in downtown Manila, the protestors intention was to march through Binondo, a thriving commercial centre and the heart of the Filipino-Chinese business community. Blocked by police and paramilitary units, the protestor's chants quickly turned to taunts. Rocks, bottles, Molotov cocktails, and flares were hurled at the police who, caught off guard, were ill-prepared for the students' charge that broke their ranks. It was a momentary rare victory for the protestors, and a humiliating experience for the police, who quickly reassembled and called in armed military reinforcements.

Heavy rain had earlier drenched the city. Now Binondo was in gridlock with protestors scattering through the traffic, pursued by armed soldiers and police. Shoppers scampered for safety, some fled down side streets, some sought refuge in shops, many of which were already shuttered. Tension in the streets had turned to terror. I heard gunfire. Shots in front of me, shots from behind. Three or four shots, no more.

From where the gunshots came, I couldn't tell. The soldiers were behind me, the protestors somewhere ahead. I stayed back and was told by one soldier to take cover. They're shooting from the tops of buildings, he yelled, pointing at several three- to four-storey buildings overlooking the narrow street. Several more shots rang out. The soldiers returned fire.

Ahead, on the footpath, face down in a bloody puddle, was a body, a man in a T-shirt and wearing jeans. I doubt he was a protestor as he was bald and looked middle aged. Probably a 'wrong place, wrong time' victim. The soldiers, ducking in and out of doorways in a well-practised defensive tactic, rushed past and deliberately, one after another, stepped in the centre of the man's back to avoid getting their boots wet. His body was their convenient stepping stone.

Moving closer, I knelt beside him. His back was saturated in blood. I couldn't see any bullet wound but I could see bubbles coming from his nose even though his face was fully submerged in bloody water. He's alive, I yelled and looked around for help. To my right, cowering terrified behind the glass door of a shop, were three or four young women. They were horrified, unable or unwilling to move. Wide-eyed, they simply stared.

I bent down next to the man, one knee in the bloody water, and looked again. Where were the bubbles? Why were there no bubbles? Was he dead? He must be dead! Then, suddenly, above me, a soldier's boot landed flat and heavy in the centre of the man's back, brutally expelling the last remaining air in the man's lungs and releasing the final bubbles to the surface. His body was of no consequence. His death, of no concern. To the soldiers, he was a convenient, lifeless, human stepping stone in a puddle, which they used to keep their boots dry. Shocked. Helpless. I moved on. There was nothing I could do. Just another victim. No one seemed to care. The soldiers had abused a dead body, almost certainly an innocent bystander, in full public view because they didn't care. They knew they would never be chastised or admonished for their callousness.

Tear gas, acrid smoke, and petrol fumes filled my lungs. It was better I stay behind the soldiers and troops to avoid any gunfire. It was an active war zone for about 100 metres, then nothing, just fleeing protestors in the distance. Several protestors lay ahead, wincing, crying out in pain, clutching their arms, legs, stomachs. They had been mercilessly bashed by shield-carrying riot police who stood menacingly above them, brandishing their batons, threatening to continue the assault. Several metres away, on the opposite side of the road, another protestor was screaming and writhing in pain. His lower leg was drenched in blood. A bullet had shredded his jeans beneath the knee and left a gaping hole of bone and sinew.

A commotion further up the road caught my attention. A protestor was sprawled motionless in the gutter. Dead or injured? I couldn't tell. Nearby, a soldier struggled violently with two protestors and held them by the back of their shirts in a single grip. In his free hand he held a handgun and waved it close to the protestors' heads gesturing as if to kill, snarling, and yelling angrily. Sagging and half-limp, the two demonstrators in their early 20s, were unresisting and silent, probably fearful of being shot if they yelled and tried to wriggle free. Perhaps that's what happened to the other demonstrator. He lay sprawled and lifeless in the gutter nearby. He was dead. His eyes were open. But he was dead.

The soldier, like many others, had removed his name

tag. Now, he could do whatever he wished, anonymously, without restraint, with impunity. He appeared wildly out of control. In panic. Uncertain what to do next. He had caught two unarmed protestors. He had probably shot that protestor who lay in the gutter nearby. What now? What to do? His movements were frenetic. He swivelled left and right, grunting, almost yanking the protestors off their feet, and all the time holding a gun at their heads. As I approached, slowly, directly, staring, I pulled my tape recorder with its large BBC sticker to the front of my body, so it was in full view and held the microphone out in front of me as if I was recording. I wasn't. 'I'm watching you,' I said.

He seemed startled, confused. The soldier stopped struggling with his two captives and stared, disbelieving at my intervention. I was close. The microphone, outstretched, could have touched his chest. He looked me up and down. A slight smile crossed his face. He seemed relieved. I was. Hesitantly, he lowered his gun and released his grip on the two demonstrators and instantly they scampered away in opposite directions.

EIGHTEEN

An apology to Butch Cassidy.

Butch Cassidy's dead!

One of his friends relayed the news. Butch, a union organiser, had been found dead. Not just dead. Mutilated. Horribly butchered. He had disappeared weeks earlier. He just didn't come home one night from the factory. His friends and others searched all the regular spots, and unlikely locations too, hotel hangouts and girly bars, but Butch would never go there anyway. Nothing.

My bearer of bad news had heard that Butch and I were friends. We met once, I corrected him, and that was months ago. But who could forget the name Butch Cassidy, even though my memory of his face was a little blurry. I never did know Butch's real name. He liked to be known simply as Butch. And if you did press him for his real name, he'd say 'Okay, Butch Cassidy.'

'Butch' was a childhood nickname. Not his real name. And 'Cassidy' wasn't his real name either. Cassidy came from the film. He loved that movie *Butch Cassidy and the Sundance Kid*. He saw himself as a Filipino version of Paul Newman. I told him there was no comparison, although I joked that I could see a resemblance with Newman's horse. His real name could have been Jose Lopez for all I knew. But he insisted on Butch Cassidy.

Butch had sought me out. Apparently, a friend had told him he knew a foreign journalist who would be interested in the story Butch wanted to tell. It was about workers' rights, and unions, and union busting, and how dangerous it was.

It was one of those out-of-the-blue phone calls. Briefly, hesitantly, Butch introduced himself and gave a brief rundown of what he wanted to tell me. It was enough for me to set up a meeting; I knew the area he talked about, not the factory in which he worked, but I knew somewhere close by where we could meet, without attracting much attention.

We met. I took notes. We parted. He was a gutsy guy I remember thinking at the time. That was the first, only and last time I saw him. He was a talker. A half-hour chat turned into a ninety-minute natter. He said he lived in a 'hovel', had a wife and, surprisingly for a Filipino, no kids. Rarely, have I used the expression 'He wore his heart on his sleeve' – it's a bit passé – but it really did apply to Butch. I liked him. We got on well. In the passing parade of interviewees, he left an impression.

I knew he couldn't afford it, but he offered to pay for lunch. And when I said I admired his union activities and his courage, his response was a modest shrug of the shoulders. But I recall something he said, just as we were about to part. He admitted to being scared every time he 'took on' the bosses. It was a scary fatalism that turned prophetic.

His workmates in a local sales and repair factory for motorcycles and cargo-carrying tricycles, regarded Butch as a good guy, too. Friendly, always helpful. Maybe he spoke a little too much about poor wages and conditions. That sort of talk could get him into trouble. Lately, apparently, he had been trying to convince his fellow workers to unionize. And that, they said, was 'a big no-no.'

They knew the factory boss was more than bad. Loose talk had him pegged as the neighbourhood crime boss with a long criminal history. Over the years, they'd heard reports of stand-over tactics, extortion, and warehousing of stolen goods. And behind the scenes, it was known that the boss had a 'top dog' in the police force, a relative, who looked out for him and kept him out of jail.

They knew these things and so they kept their heads down and their mouths shut. Butch was the factory's new guy, who asked too many questions and demanded too many things. When these workers spoke to me, anonymously and in confidence, Butch had been dead for several weeks, but I had just found out. I wanted to know more. A day or two later, two of the factory workers met me at a small footpath coffee shop, too shabby to be called a café, but excellent for a clandestine rendezvous.

Without hesitation, and without evidence, they blamed Butch's murder on the factory boss. At least, everything pointed to him being behind the murder. The boss didn't like union talk, they said. He didn't want any unrest in his factory. Butch should have stayed out of sight and kept his mouth shut, was the common opinion. Butch was singled out for 'special' treatment, they said. It began slowly, and then quickly worsened. Security guards at the factory gates would watch Butch a little bit more closely than the others when he walked through the gates each morning to begin his shift. Sometimes, without reason, the guards would walk slowly through the factory's repair shop where Butch worked, and if they saw him talking, they would yell for him to stop.

It was minor, intimidatory stuff. Worse was to come. About a week after it began, the factory gate guards singled out Butch for a body search on check-out, at the end of the day. A quick pat-down soon became a daily arms-out, feet-apart, rough, full body search. Butch didn't need to tell his fellow workers what was happening, they could see it for themselves. They saw him being singled out for nothing more than speaking up for workers' rights. Butch's factory mates learned another thing – keep quiet about what they saw, otherwise what was happening to Butch would happen to them.

The toilet was where snatched conversations could be had. Out of earshot, Butch told one worker he was worried, really worried. Twice in the past week he had been followed home by two men he didn't know. Not the security guards, but two men dressed in gym clothes, and they looked pretty fit. Bodyguards maybe. Two days later, Butch didn't turn up for work. His wife was not just worried, she was sick with fear. Butch had told her of his problems, only a few days earlier. Up until then, he had kept the harassment to himself. But it had got so bad, he confessed to his wife that he honestly feared for his life.

It was a week before someone reported his body in a filthy laneway kilometres away. Even by Manila's gangland standards, this was a body you would not want to look at. Headless. Sawed and professional, not hacked off in a frenzy.

The news of his murder came late to me via one of Butch's friends who thought I should know. He was right. But as a journalist, I needed to know more. I needed to see Butch's wife, to speak to her about her husband. Butch, I remember, had a nickname for his wife. It was a joke. He was proud of it, but only he used it. He called her Etta. You know, the Katherine Ross character in the *Butch Cassidy and the Sundance Kid* movie he so loved.

I think Butch was smitten. He said his favourite scene was Katherine Ross balancing on the handlebars of Paul Newman's bicycle. I met 'Etta', commonly known by her real name, Stella, a month or so after Butch's funeral, in the same coffee shop where Butch and I first met. She recalled how, weeks earlier, she had been summoned to the police station because everyone knew her husband was missing. Even the police were reluctant to reveal the headless body under the sheet, but they had to. Stella said she almost fainted. I'm surprised she didn't.

Confronted with a headless body, only a wife would know where to look for any identification marks. There, in his right armpit, was the apple shaped purple birthmark that Stella knew so well. That was enough. The sheet was pulled back over the corpse, officially identified as Butch.

Later, back home, Stella told me how chuffed Butch was to meet me, a foreign correspondent. She remembered how Butch had returned home excited and enthusiastic.

He had met a foreign journalist who had talked to him about trade unionists and workers' rights. He said this foreign journalist wanted to know what Butch was doing, too. Wasn't Butch afraid of getting hurt by speaking out?

Butch was happy, Stella said. If the foreign press wrote up the story, maybe the local press would do the same. Up to now, they rarely reported about unions being raided, or activists being harassed, and people being jailed, tortured, and killed for their beliefs. Butch thought that maybe things would be different if the world knew. That's what Butch longed for. Maybe, the world would get to know what was happening in the Philippines through the BBC?

Your meeting with Butch meant so much to him, Stella told me. I felt ashamed. Absolutely awful. Unworthy to be called a journalist. I had let Butch down. I had not written a single word about our meeting. I had planned to use it as background for a newspaper feature and a radio documentary. But fast-moving events got in the way, and it was still unwritten.

Butch had counted on me; he had pinned his hopes on that story. He had died for his beliefs. I didn't say anything to Stella. I think she believed I had written about the conversation I had with her husband. It comforted her to think that. It left me deeply remorseful to know otherwise.

As it turned out, I worked a decade in the Philippines and often I reported about workplace suppression, unions, and union activists. But, up to now I've never talked about Butch Cassidy. I should have. I regret it.

I apologise Butch. You were the workers' hero. My hero.

EPILOGUE

Like frozen moments in time, I remember the decapitated union activist Butch Cassidy; the eight-year-old, Marela Yanai who survived a massacre of 45 civilians; and Gloria, the slum dweller who lived in a cardboard box and gave away two of her children; as well as Jose, who watched high up in a coconut tree the beheading of his father.

How could I not remember them and so many others. For decades they lingered, never forgotten at the back of my mind. This book brought them to front of mind. As silent victims of the Marcos regime, I could think of no better way to honour them than by telling their stories about how they survived, suffered, and for some, how they died during Marcos's autocratic rule. They earned their place in this book because their fate is so wretchedly symbolic of the sacrifices and the injustices suffered by countless others.

I have one dominant qualification to write this book. And one good reason. I was there, a foreign correspondent in the Philippines for half the time Marcos was in power, and it would have been a 'dereliction of duty' not to write about what I witnessed. I also had a duty to myself to write this book: to combat the 'alternative' social media history of Marcos that paints him to be a doer of good deeds. I knew him to be a ruthless and corrupt autocrat.

Social media has destroyed the long-held universal concept of the 'historic collective memory' of a nation – of popularly agreed national milestones; a consensus about the truthfulness of events, people, and incidents of the past. Ancient history is sacrosanct, it seems. Contemporary history is not. In the Philippines, events as recent as 50 years ago – events in the memories of people still living – are being questioned for their authenticity and credibility.

It seems to me that these history sceptics, or history deniers, also suffer from historical amnesia and only remember those things that may reinforce their biases or bolster their prejudices. To them, opinions are as good as facts. Social media disinformation is a weapon with no accountability – and therefore no responsibility – to say whatever you choose, with no regard for the truth. Inconvenient facts can be challenged, discarded, modified, cynically and criminally moulded to suit political ends.

Possibly, this book would not have been necessary for me to write if the importance of history had not been underplayed in the Philippines' education curriculum; underestimated in its importance to maintain an accurate historical narrative; and shackled by an internecine jockeying for influence among the nation's political powerbrokers.

For too long, history has been shunted aside, downplayed by successive governments. History needs to be elevated not diminished in Philippine schools. The ramifications are serious and inevitable when Philippine history is no longer taught as a stand-alone high school subject, but as a sub-topic in 'Asian Studies'.

History's neglectful ranking in the country's school syllabus is a shameful abrogation of the nation's responsibility to educate Filipinos. When questions aren't answered in the classroom, students and young adults find the answers – often questionable and controversial answers – on social media. Whether the answer is right or wrong, whether it is innocent misinformation or deliberate disinformation, does not matter. Truth does. Education should never be an intangible gamble for facts.

I wrote this book to set the record straight, to tell the truth, to refute the lies. I was there when Marcos ruled. An eyewitness to events, providing first-hand accounts. I recorded for radio and wrote for newspapers stories now regarded as history. But Philippine history requires vigilance. It is the reason I wrote this book.

'Reinventing Marcos' proves the fragility of history when it can be hijacked by social media.

REFLECTIONS

Almost every night for more than four decades, I have done the same thing: I have swapped my 'day' watch with my 'night' watch before going to bed. With its unusually bright luminous hands, my 'night' watch lets me know the exact time I awake, if it is time to listen to the 3 a.m. or 4 a.m. BBC news, or how long before dawn

It is the habit of a lifetime (I will probably check the time just before I die). My watch is a link to the present and a nightly reminder of my past. Back then – in the mid-1970s and 1980s – I was a foreign correspondent for 10 radio stations and three newspapers on four continents: every one of them working in different time zones, with clashing deadlines, and competing demands.

Being media companies, they worked a 24-hour clock, which meant I had to do the same. There was no curfew for telephone calls. Unthinkingly, these media companies would expect me to be awake and responsive no matter what the time. Luckily, I have always had a curious ability to sound fully awake and alert the instant I awake.

I've never been a good sleeper. Even as a kid, I would

tell myself what time to wake in the morning. And I did. Never have I used an alarm clock because my mind wakes me, five minutes either side of the designated wake-up time.

I was a self-aware 10-year-old who wanted to be a foreign correspondent when other kids had ambitions to become a fireman or a policeman or a racing car driver. Over the years, that dream became a vow, a promise, and then a pledge to leave Australia.

It was a dream that didn't fade. In fact, it transformed into play-acting in my late teens when I realised that real life questioning – in a journalistic style – of unsuspecting party goers was an interesting test of skills. Strange, but interesting. What other explanation is there for me – a teenager – to go to a party with a set goal: learn all I can about someone without revealing anything about myself. Ask them questions about themselves, their opinions, their activities, the sort of questions that you know will flatter them and elicit ready answers. Almost every time, the result was the same. They would be so engrossed in talking about themselves, they didn't ask me anything.

On getting home, I realised that I knew so-and-so's opinion about all sorts of things, some of them secret things I really shouldn't have been told. I believed then, as I do now, that the essence of a good reporter is to know as much as you can about your interviewee, and for them to know as little as possible about you. It was a game I played. Not for long, but long enough to realise the power of an interview, because that's what I was doing. I was practising. It was a signpost to my future career.

The power of observation fascinated me when I was

young. Perhaps influenced by TV cop shows, I challenged myself to remember the facial features and the clothing of a person, a rail passenger opposite me, or a fellow diner, perhaps. I would look and then look away. Then, in my mind, I would recall their hair colour, distinguishing facial features, and what they were wearing, from the top of their head to the shoes they were wearing. It was fun. It was another career signpost.

I was a bookish kid, but not a swot. I played few schoolyard games, disliked sports, and most importantly – considering my future – disliked teams. I have never been a team member of any sort, of any association, at any time in my life. I grew up thinking a foreign correspondent was a peripatetic lone operator. Perhaps that was the attraction.

It was not impetuosity that convinced me to leave Australia. I had been planning to become a journalist, and then a foreign correspondent, all my life. I was 25. Time to leave. I resigned, flew to Southeast Asia, and got off the plane, unemployed and clueless. I knew no one, and no one knew me. Except… I knew me. I was brimming with self-belief and large dollops of ambition, optimism, and enthusiasm. All of it, I would need in the years to come.

When planning my all-important trip to Southeast Asia, I never considered a travel companion. And once there, I eschewed tourist buses, or tourist 'hot spots'. Nothing could be worse. From my first day in the region, I was on my own and for 18 months I travelled through six countries by myself, taking the backroads, looking for places not mentioned in brochures, or highlighted in maps. Finally, I reached the Philippines and stayed for

10 years. It was a place of endless stories. It was the most politically volatile period in modern Philippine history.

Occasionally, after years abroad, I would return to Australia and confront a conundrum the moment I landed. Everything looked familiar, but I felt different, like I was tottering between two worlds – an observer in both, quietly aloof, unreasonably judgemental, but most of all disconnected. Subconsciously, I was observing my homeland through alien eyes. The same disconnection, but in reverse, occurred when I returned to Manila and found myself observing the Philippines through Australia-centric eyes.

Some things – random, even trifling things – inexplicably became symbolic of the differences between First and Third World countries. Often, they were things I had grown up with, took for granted, never gave them a second thought, but in fact they were points of difference, not similarity. And sometimes they were inconsequential, even humorous things. Pedestrian crossings, for example. In Australia, step onto a pedestrian crossing and cars stop. In the Philippines, cars whiz by in front and behind you. In the 1980s, as a guest on Philippine Airline's inaugural flight to Britain, I awoke in London to witness from my bedroom window a scene of merriment, normally typical of children, not men. In the street below, three Filipinos who had been on the same flight, were laughing uproariously. They could stop traffic simply by stepping off the footpath and onto the pedestrian crossing. I watched them take one step, stop the traffic, and hastily step back. The cars drove on. Then, one by one, in intervals of a minute or so, they each took a turn. Never once did they cross the road.

The joyous delight to stop traffic was enough, and they wallowed in pedestrian power, inconceivable in Manila.

Instinctively, I found myself comparing Manila to Sydney, and vice versa, and realising how surprisingly similar or jarringly different they were. Things I would never see in Australia were commonplace in the Philippines and sights familiar in the Philippines were nowhere to be seen in Australia. It was a reality check and often I felt uneasy when I looked around and saw the glaring differences. A common sight in the Philippines, for instance – a four- or five-year-old barrio girl carrying her infant brother or sister on her hip – was unheard of in Australia, where a girl of that age would carry a doll or push a toy pram.

In the Philippines, there were differences to be seen and experiences to be had. It was a world of contrasts, a world of 'haves' and 'have-nots'. It was a world I never got used to because I never wanted to. I never wanted to feel comfortable in a world of ingrained inequality and tolerated poverty. The social stratum in the Philippines was clearly split between the 'rich and powerful' few, the 'just making do' many, and the 'barely surviving' majority.

Not once in Australia had I seen a battlefield body or a slain demonstrator. In the Philippines I saw many, in street riots, in jungle battle zones. Possibly – and I make no boast – I saw more bodies than some soldiers. Scores of bodies. Poverty was everywhere in Manila. Until I became a familiar face in the streets near my home, I was hassled by scruffy children begging for food. In slum districts, entire families lived in hovels and rummaged for food scraps or for plastic bottles, or aluminium cans to sell. By contrast, in Australia, homeless shelters provided somewhere to sleep and food for the largely unseen down-at-heel. The dole was available, and a universal health scheme. The Philippines had neither.

In Australia, I could enter a shop – any shop – without an armed guard watching my every move. I will never forget the first time I saw a seated armed guard, cradling a double-barrel shotgun, in front of a drug store, or the sign 'Please leave all guns at the door'. Guns in Australia were rarely seen. In the Philippines, they were always seen. Several armed soldiers walking down the street was nothing unusual in Manila, but in Sydney such a sight would trigger alarm. Soldiers were never seen in Australian cities, but the Philippines biggest military camps were in the capital, Manila, and their ominous presence added to the unease.

One time, on a rare journey home, I arrived in the middle of a raging debate about noisy leaf blowers shattering the Sunday morning calm of suburban Sydney. I didn't feel sympathy, only headshaking bewilderment that such a trivial matter could evoke controversy. I had just arrived from Manila, where rich people hired poor people to be 'leaf gatherers', and where the only sounds I heard some mornings were gunshots in the lane behind my home where bodies were dumped. The juxtaposition of the two events was bizarre. Street bashings in Sydney were described as a 'crime wave', but in the Philippines many murders and other serious crimes went unreported and mostly unsolved. Other tell-tale societal differences were apparent, often in subtle ways. Television news was one example where bloodied bodies – battle casualties, murder, or accident victims – were seen on news bulletins in gruesome close-up, unlike in Australia where bodies were blurred or shown from a distance, making death palatable to a general audience.

I spent 10 years in the Philippines. The first nine years were a prelude to the milestone tenth year when I witnessed the People Power revolution. The germinating seeds of revolt – the poverty, the militarisation, the abuses, the corruption, and violence – were everywhere. They sprung out from all corners of the nation and the despairing victims cried out for action, for some reprieve, for some resolution. And then there were the people – oppressed, repressed, suppressed – every adjective sadly true. But powerless, they were not. The Filipino people in 1986 rose up, rebelled, and reclaimed their rights, and nothing in all my reporting years felt so exhilarating and so satisfying to watch. I was a privileged and troubled witness to the events that unfolded.

I was 35. I had spent more than a third of my life as a foreign correspondent and, before that, another six years learning and practicing the craft of journalism so that I could be what I had always wanted to be – not a writer, a journalist, or a reporter, but a foreign correspondent.

Meandering to Manila

A JOURNALIST'S SLOW JOURNEY TO
BECOME A FOREIGN CORRESPONDENT.

AN EXCERPT

Meandering to Manila is the author's companion book to *Reinventing Marcos*. It is an illuminating account of a lone traveller, with a typewriter in his backpack, on a quest to become a self-made foreign correspondent. Southeast Asia was his testing ground.

THE INTRODUCTION

When I left Australia, I did not have a return air ticket, an itinerary, or any bookings of any sort in any country because I was not sure where in Southeast Asia I would go. I told my family I wanted to be a foreign correspondent, probably in the Philippines, but I didn't know how I would get there, or how long it would take.

I set off from Melbourne on a rambling journey –

with Manila my destination – and happily left it to fate, luck, and intuition to fill the 'in-between' parts of my travels. That's the reason I titled this book 'Meandering to Manila' because that is what happens when you shun airplanes and choose to travel by land and sea. You get to travel on roads and rail tracks that travel up, down, and around mountains; cross farmlands and plains; negotiate swamplands, barren lands, and plateaus; pass through jungles; skirt lakes; span rivers; bypass towns; and criss-cross cities.

Topography determines where the roads and the rail lines go, and it is the depth of rivers and the ocean that determines where it's possible for ships and boats to traverse. I like that! I like to travel on the ground, not in the air. I like to be surprised and delighted by the view from a railway carriage window, or a bus, or a truck, or from the deck of a boat, or from a tiny seat on a river canoe. I like the unexpected, not the predictable.

If you travel overland, you expect to divert, detour, and change directions. I am not a 'straight-ahead' traveller. If you want to go straight to your destination, take a plane. It's predictable, often boring, and fast. And at 35,000 feet there is not much to see. I could have boarded a plane in Melbourne and disembarked in Manila in 12 hours. But if I had done that – flown from 'A' to 'B' – everything beneath would have gone unseen. Why travel from 'A' to 'B' in the air when you have the entire alphabet to choose from on the ground? And why hurry?

I am an impetuous, impulsive, and curious traveller. For me, the destination is important, but sometimes it is how you get there and who you see and what you do along the way that's more fun, and more satisfying. Let's face it. Travel has its own momentum, a certain predictability, a reassuring familiarity and routine. Usually, but not always, I awoke most mornings knowing – or believing – where I would be at the end of the day. Most times I was right. Sometimes I was not even close, yet it didn't matter. Beyond a destination is another destination, and another, and on it goes. This 'one-day-at-a-time' travel suited me because I didn't have a travel plan. Instead, I had a map which marked where I had been, not where was going. That made me an impromptu 'spur-of-the-moment' traveller. That's why it took me 18 months to travel a most circuitous route to the Philippines. I now realise why. Back then, in 1976, I was about to undertake the most momentous life-changing event of my life, to fulfil my vow to leave Australia, travel to the Philippines, and become a self-made foreign correspondent. It was a commitment I made to myself, way back as a 10-year-old. Now, it was up to me to turn that childhood dream into reality.

It was a prescient moment, years earlier, when I decided my journalistic future lay in the Philippines. It was a considered choice – not a dart thrown at a wall map – because I knew the Philippines was awash with stories. In some countries, a foreign correspondent can wake up and ask: is there a story today? In the Philippines, a foreign correspondent wakes up and asks: what story will I cover today?

Intuitively, as a journalist, I felt some sort of affinity with the Philippines because of its newsworthiness. I envisaged I would be there many years. But there was no rush. There was plenty to see. Things to do. I could hone my journalism along the way. And that's what I did. I travelled and I wrote. I set out to prove to myself, and to the news bosses, that I had the journalistic acuity to transition from journalist to foreign correspondent.

I made Southeast Asia my hunting ground for newspaper and magazine feature articles which I posted from remote places, and which took a couple of weeks to reach Hong Kong, Sydney, or London. I was on the lookout for stories. I took my time. Inquisitiveness and a 'nose for the newsworthy' guided me through Singapore, Malaysia, Thailand, Burma, Indonesia, and Borneo because I wanted to experience the region up-close. I travelled by bus, truck, plane, train, boat, cargo ship, ferry, and canoe. Everywhere I went, I travelled alone.

I may have looked like a tourist, but what I carried in my backpack made me a traveller. A unique one, too! Squashed on top of the clothes was a typewriter; a spare pack of typewriter ribbons; a small cassette recorder; two radios (AM and shortwave); two dictionaries; spare batteries; a handful of pens; and a spiral notepad. In Southeast Asia, I learned 'on-the-spot' journalism. It was my foreign correspondent baptism.

What happened in the year-and-a-half before I reached Manila is the subject of this book. It is about the sights I saw, the things I did, and the people I met. I didn't keep a diary. But I did write lots and lots of letters to my parents back home in Australia, and they wrote lots and lots of letters to me.

For almost 50 years, those letters in a shoebox – passed on to me by my parents when I eventually returned home after 13 years – remained unread, virtually forgotten, until I retrieved them from the back of a cupboard in the hope that they would bring back memories that would help me write this book. They certainly did.

About the Author

Keith Dalton was for 20 years a journalist and a foreign correspondent. Then, for another 20 years he was a speechwriter, a press secretary, and a communications manager. At 25, he left Australia and spent the next 12 years in Southeast Asia, principally in the Philippines where he reported on the 1986 People Power revolution that overthrew former president Ferdinand E. Marcos. He broadcast for 10 radio stations and wrote for three newspapers.

Radio Stations

BBC – British Broadcasting Corp.	ABC – Australian Broadcasting Corp.
ABC – American Broadcasting Co.	CBC – Canadian Broadcasting Corp.
MBS – Mutual Broadcasting System	NPR – National Public Radio
Radio Australia	Radio New Zealand
Radio Netherlands	Radio Television Hong Kong

Newspapers

The Times	The Sydney Morning Herald	The Australian

On returning to Australia, he spent a further three years covering Australian and Pacific news for the BBC, Radio New Zealand, Radio Netherlands, and Radio Television Hong Kong.

For several years, Dalton was a press secretary and a speech writer for the New South Wales government, and speech writer for the NSW premier. He also was the speech writer and corporate communications manager at Westpac bank for three years. He spent 11 years as the Corporate Communications Manager for the Special Broadcasting Service (SBS), Australia's multilingual and multicultural national broadcaster.

www.ingramcontent.com/pod-product-compliance
Lightning Source LLC
Chambersburg PA
CBHW010824070526
44583CB00022B/2922